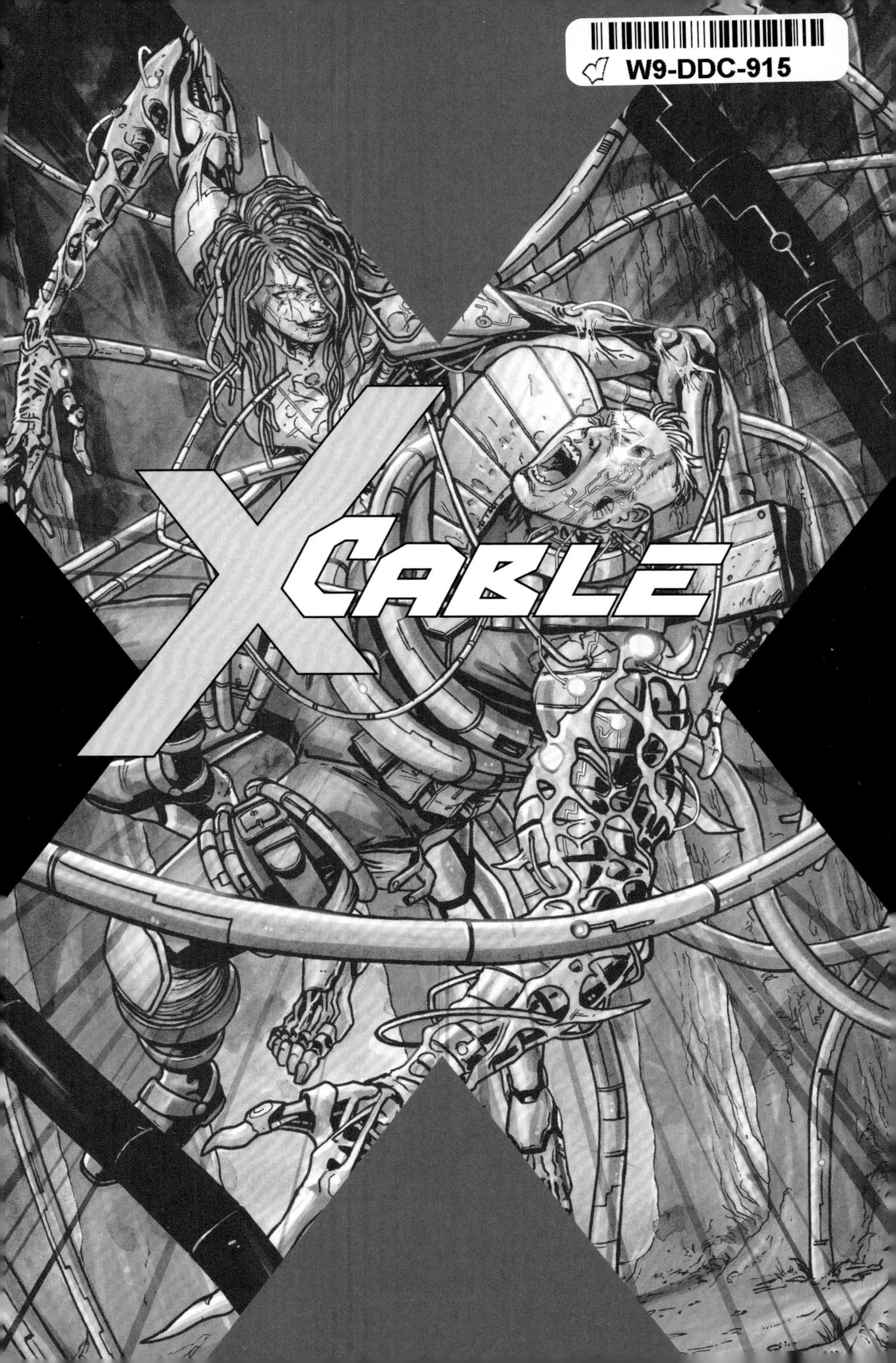
X
CABLE

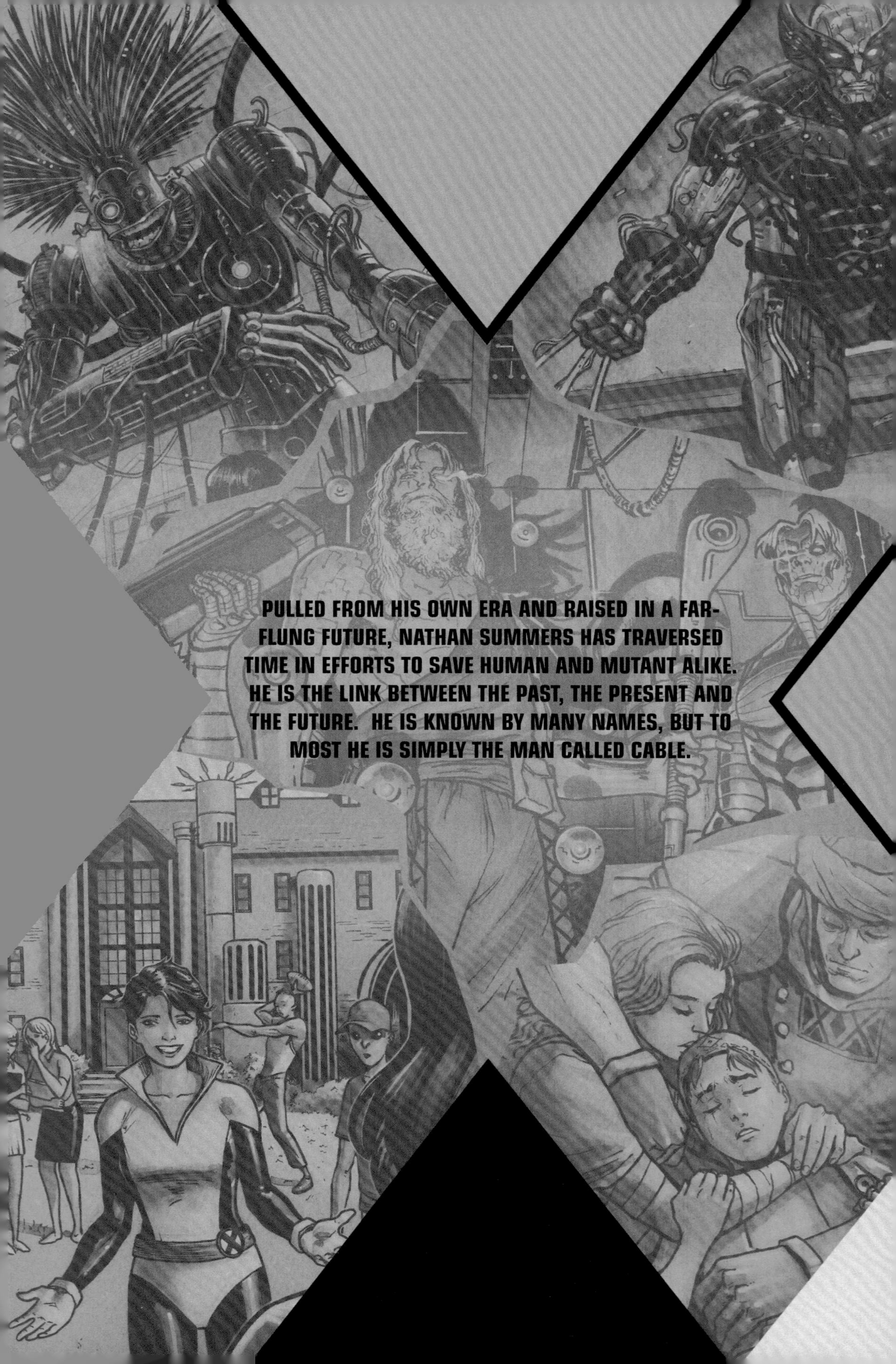
PULLED FROM HIS OWN ERA AND RAISED IN A FAR-FLUNG FUTURE, NATHAN SUMMERS HAS TRAVERSED TIME IN EFFORTS TO SAVE HUMAN AND MUTANT ALIKE. HE IS THE LINK BETWEEN THE PAST, THE PRESENT AND THE FUTURE. HE IS KNOWN BY MANY NAMES, BUT TO MOST HE IS SIMPLY THE MAN CALLED CABLE.

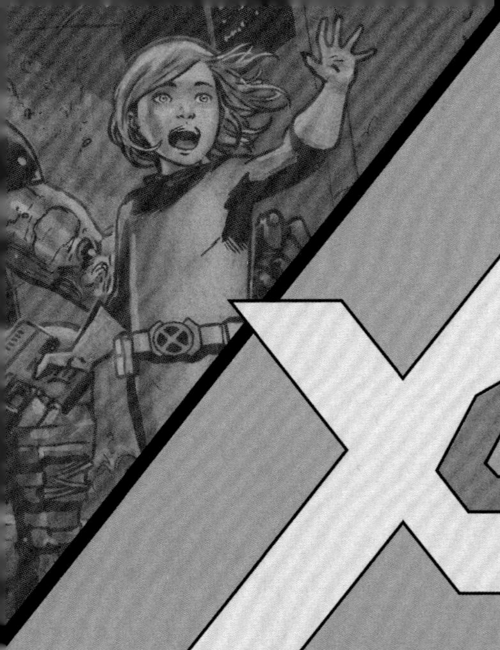

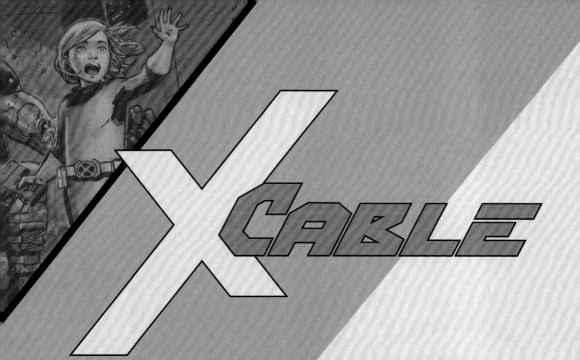

X-CABLE

PAST FEARS

Writers/**ZAC THOMPSON** & **LONNIE NADLER**

Artist/**GERMÁN PERALTA**
Color Artist/**JESUS ABURTOV**

Letterer/**VC's TRAVIS LANHAM**
Cover Art/**DANIEL WARREN JOHNSON** & **MIKE SPICER**

Assistant Editor/**CHRIS ROBINSON**
Editor/**DARREN SHAN**
X-Men Group Editors/**MARK PANICCIA** & **JORDAN D. WHITE**

Collection Editor/**JENNIFER GRÜNWALD** • Assistant Editor/**CAITLIN O'CONNELL**
Associate Managing Editor/**KATERI WOODY** • Editor, Special Projects/**MARK D. BEAZLEY**
VP Production & Special Projects/**JEFF YOUNGQUIST** • SVP Print, Sales & Marketing/**DAVID GABRIEL**
Book Designer/**SALENA MAHINA**

Editor in Chief/**C.B. CEBULSKI** • Chief Creative Officer/**JOE QUESADA**
President/**DAN BUCKLEY** • Executive Producer/**ALAN FINE**

CABLE VOL. 3: PAST FEARS. Contains material originally published in magazine form as CABLE #155-159. First printing 2018. ISBN 978-1-302-91196-6. Published by MARVEL WORLDWIDE, INC., a subsidiary of MARVEL ENTERTAINMENT, LLC. OFFICE OF PUBLICATION: 135 West 50th Street, New York, NY 10020. **Printed in Canada.** DAN BUCKLEY, President, Marvel Entertainment; JOHN NEE, Publisher; JOE QUESADA, Chief Creative Officer; TOM BREVOORT, SVP of Publishing; DAVID BOGART, SVP of Business Affairs & Operations, Publishing & Partnership; DAVID GABRIEL, SVP of Sales & Marketing, Publishing; JEFF YOUNGQUIST, VP of Production & Special Projects; DAN CARR, Executive Director of Publishing Technology; ALEX MORALES, Director of Publishing Operations; DAN EDINGTON, Managing Editor; SUSAN CRESPI, Production Manager; STAN LEE, Chairman Emeritus. For information regarding advertising in Marvel Comics or on Marvel.com, please contact Vit DeBellis, Custom Solutions & Integrated Advertising Manager, at vdebellis@marvel.com. For Marvel subscription inquiries, please call 888-511-5480. **Manufactured between 7/27/2018 and 8/28/2018 by SOLISCO PRINTERS, SCOTT, QC, CANADA.**

10 9 8 7 6 5 4 3 2 1

155

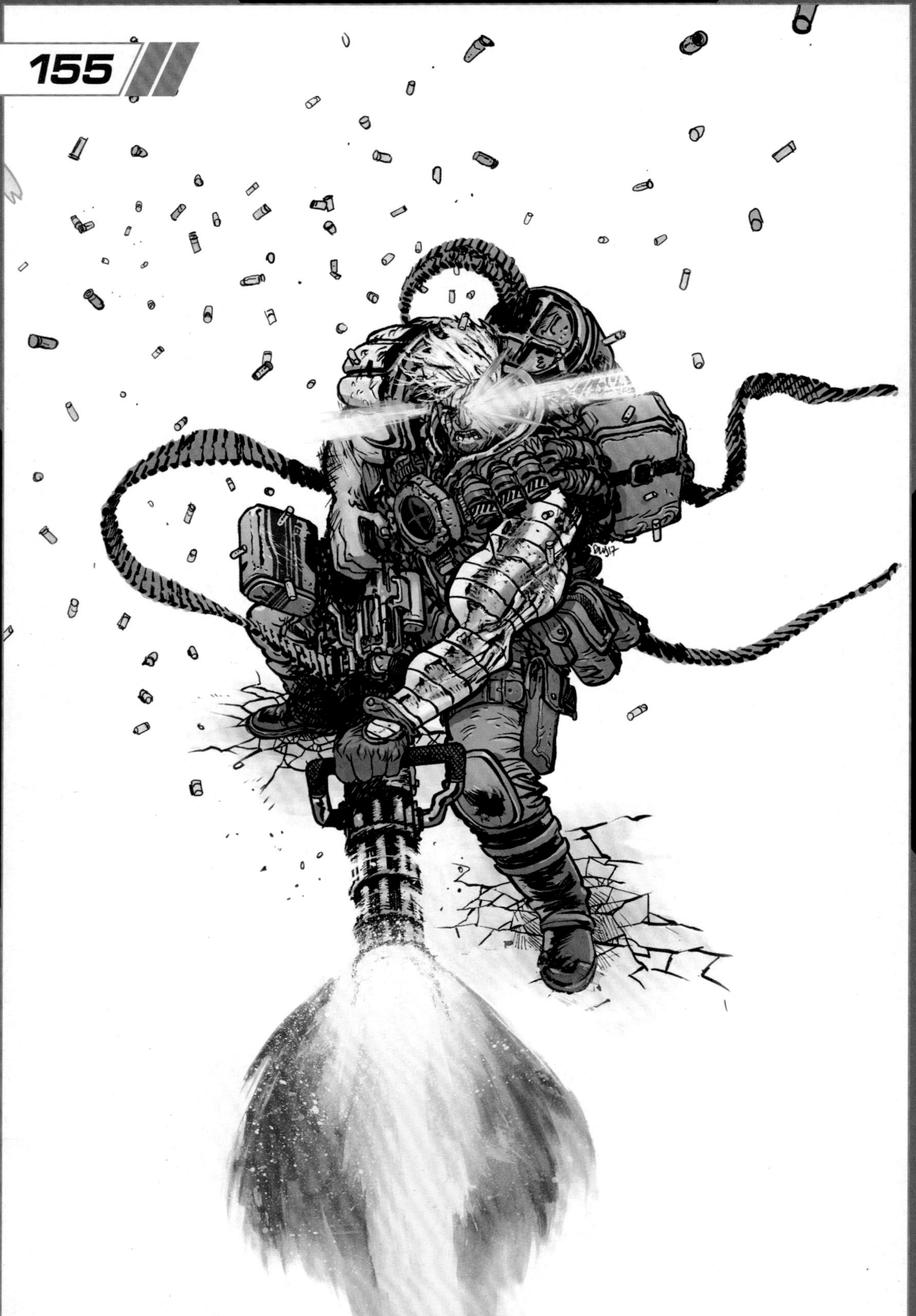

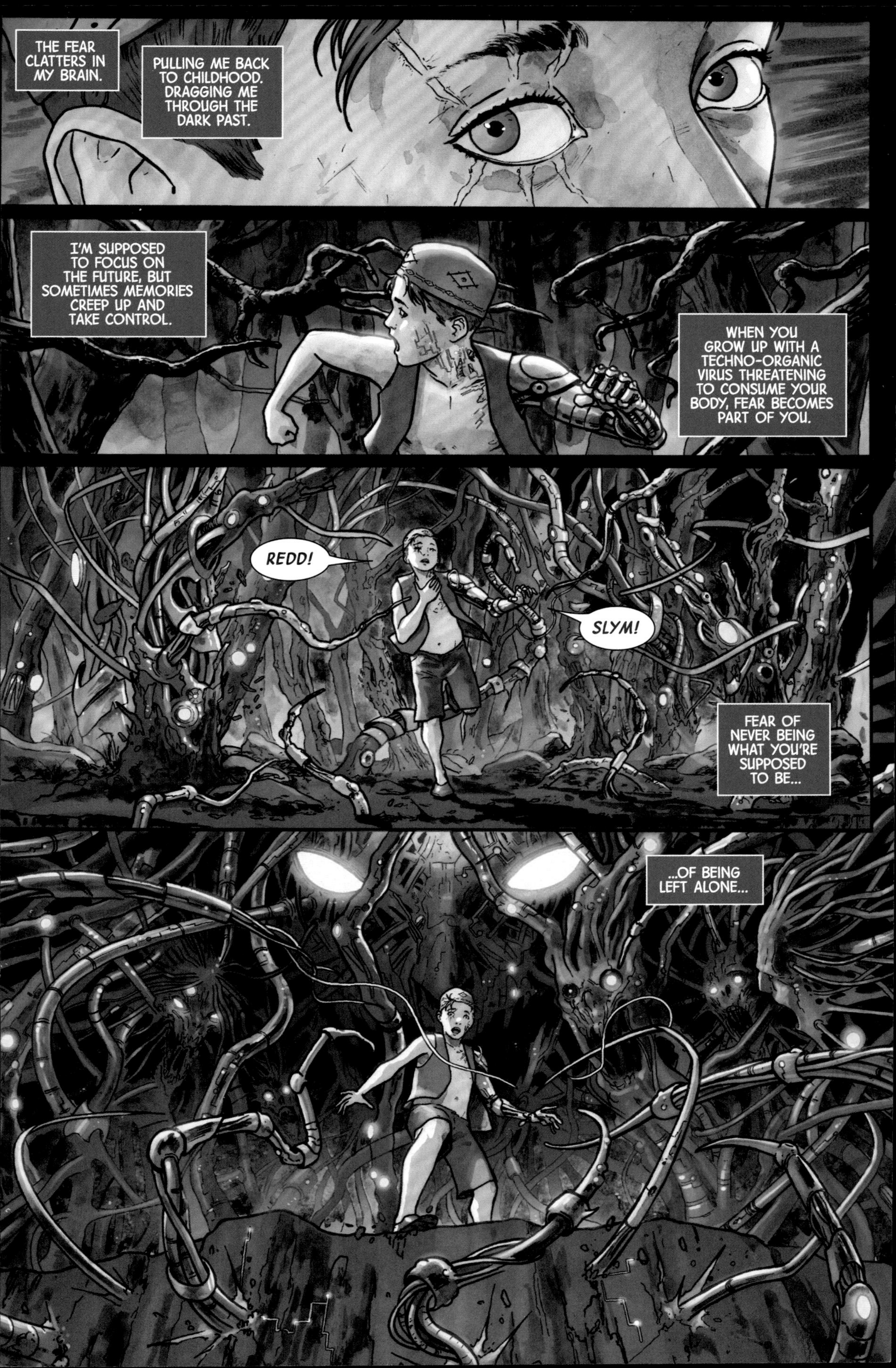
THE FEAR CLATTERS IN MY BRAIN.
PULLING ME BACK TO CHILDHOOD. DRAGGING ME THROUGH THE DARK PAST.
I'M SUPPOSED TO FOCUS ON THE FUTURE, BUT SOMETIMES MEMORIES CREEP UP AND TAKE CONTROL.
WHEN YOU GROW UP WITH A TECHNO-ORGANIC VIRUS THREATENING TO CONSUME YOUR BODY, FEAR BECOMES PART OF YOU.
REDD!
SLYM!
FEAR OF NEVER BEING WHAT YOU'RE SUPPOSED TO BE...
...OF BEING LEFT ALONE...

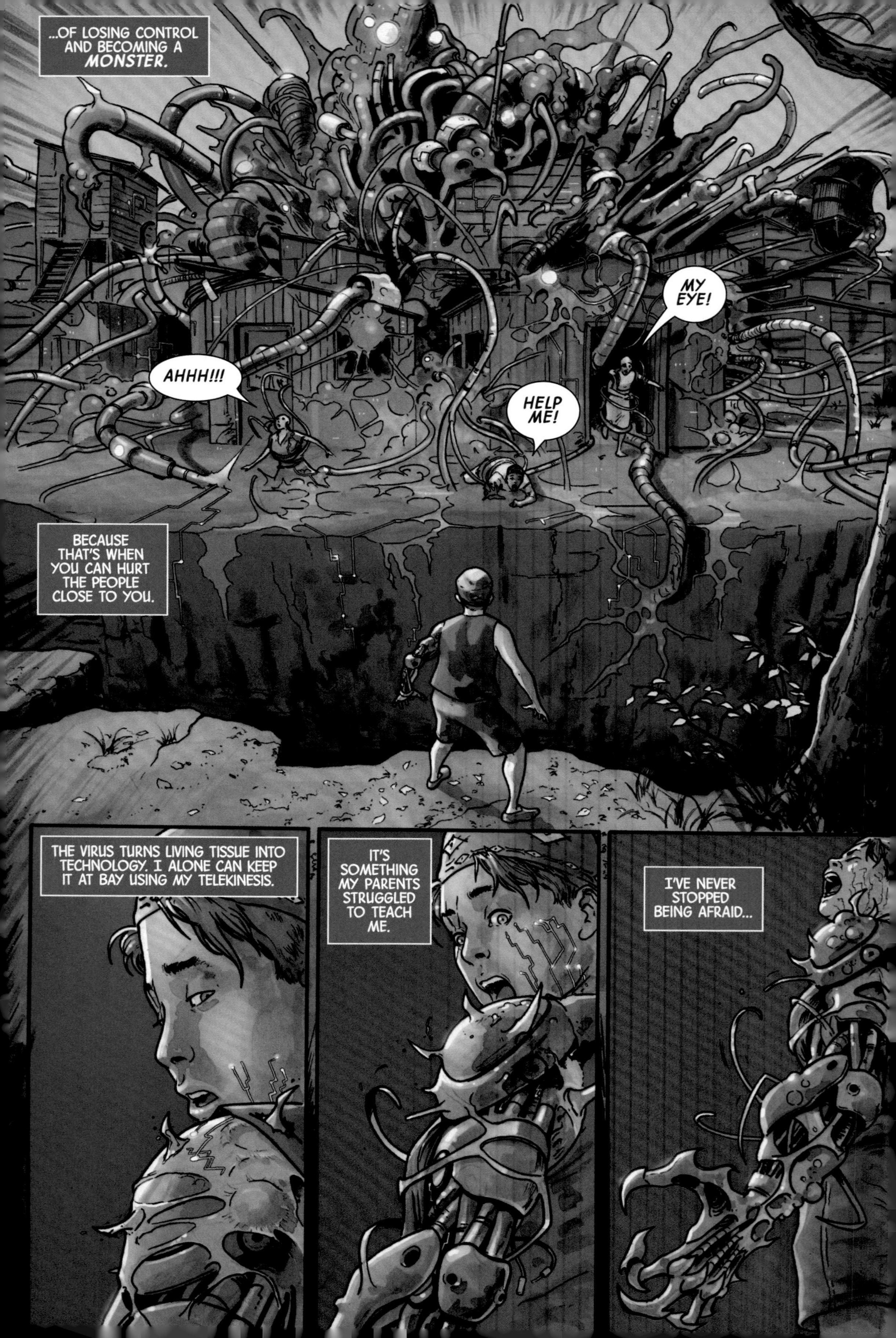
...OF LOSING CONTROL AND BECOMING A MONSTER.
AHHH!!!
HELP ME!
MY EYE!
BECAUSE THAT'S WHEN YOU CAN HURT THE PEOPLE CLOSE TO YOU.
THE VIRUS TURNS LIVING TISSUE INTO TECHNOLOGY. I ALONE CAN KEEP IT AT BAY USING MY TELEKINESIS.
IT'S SOMETHING MY PARENTS STRUGGLED TO TEACH ME.
I'VE NEVER STOPPED BEING AFRAID...

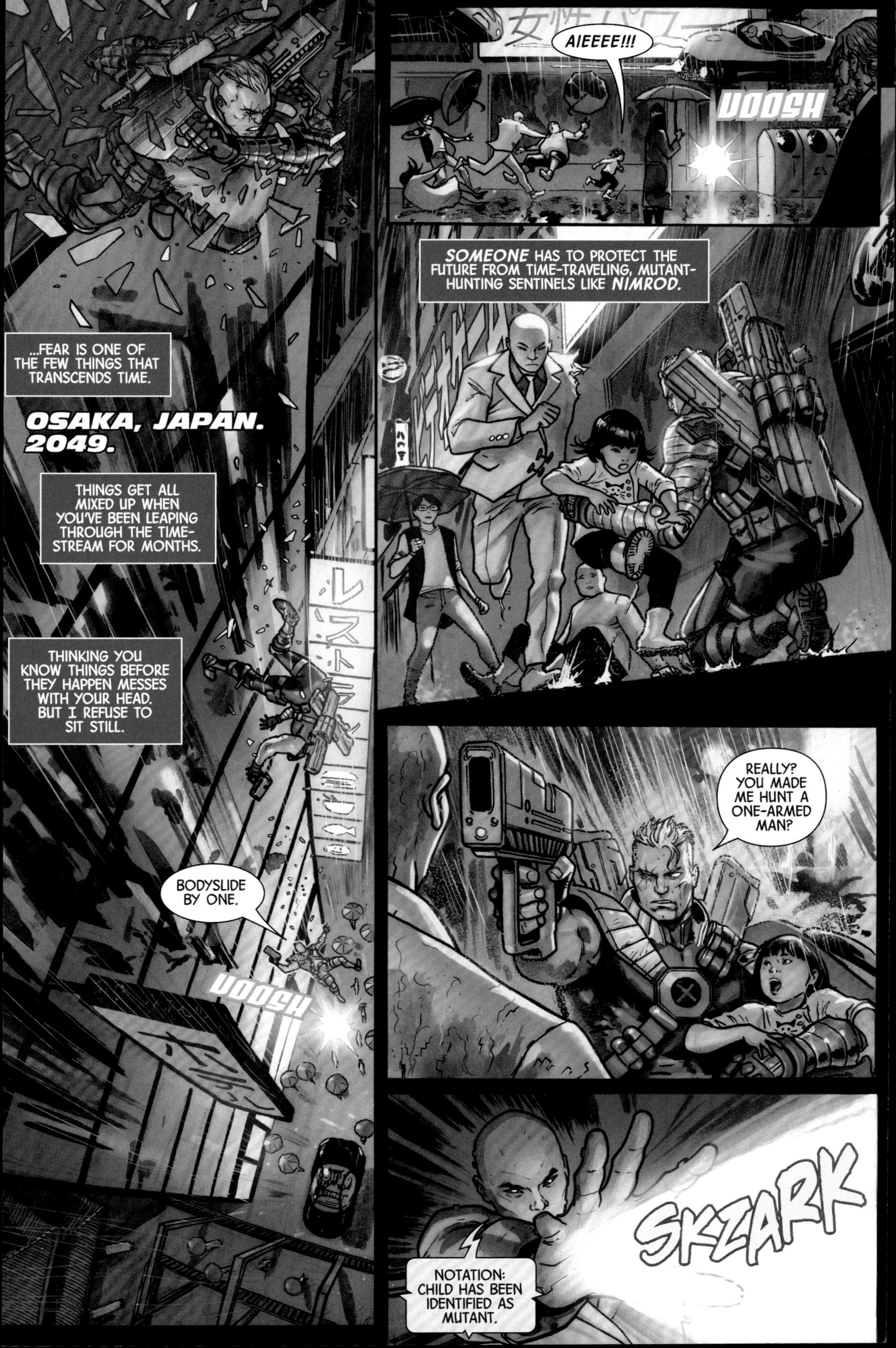
...FEAR IS ONE OF THE FEW THINGS THAT TRANSCENDS TIME.
OSAKA, JAPAN. 2049.
THINGS GET ALL MIXED UP WHEN YOU'VE BEEN LEAPING THROUGH THE TIME-STREAM FOR MONTHS.
THINKING YOU KNOW THINGS BEFORE THEY HAPPEN MESSES WITH YOUR HEAD. BUT I REFUSE TO SIT STILL.
BODYSLIDE BY ONE.
VOOSH
AIEEEE!!!
VOOSH
SOMEONE HAS TO PROTECT THE FUTURE FROM TIME-TRAVELING, MUTANT-HUNTING SENTINELS LIKE NIMROD.
REALLY? YOU MADE ME HUNT A ONE-ARMED MAN?
SKZARK
NOTATION: CHILD HAS BEEN IDENTIFIED AS MUTANT.

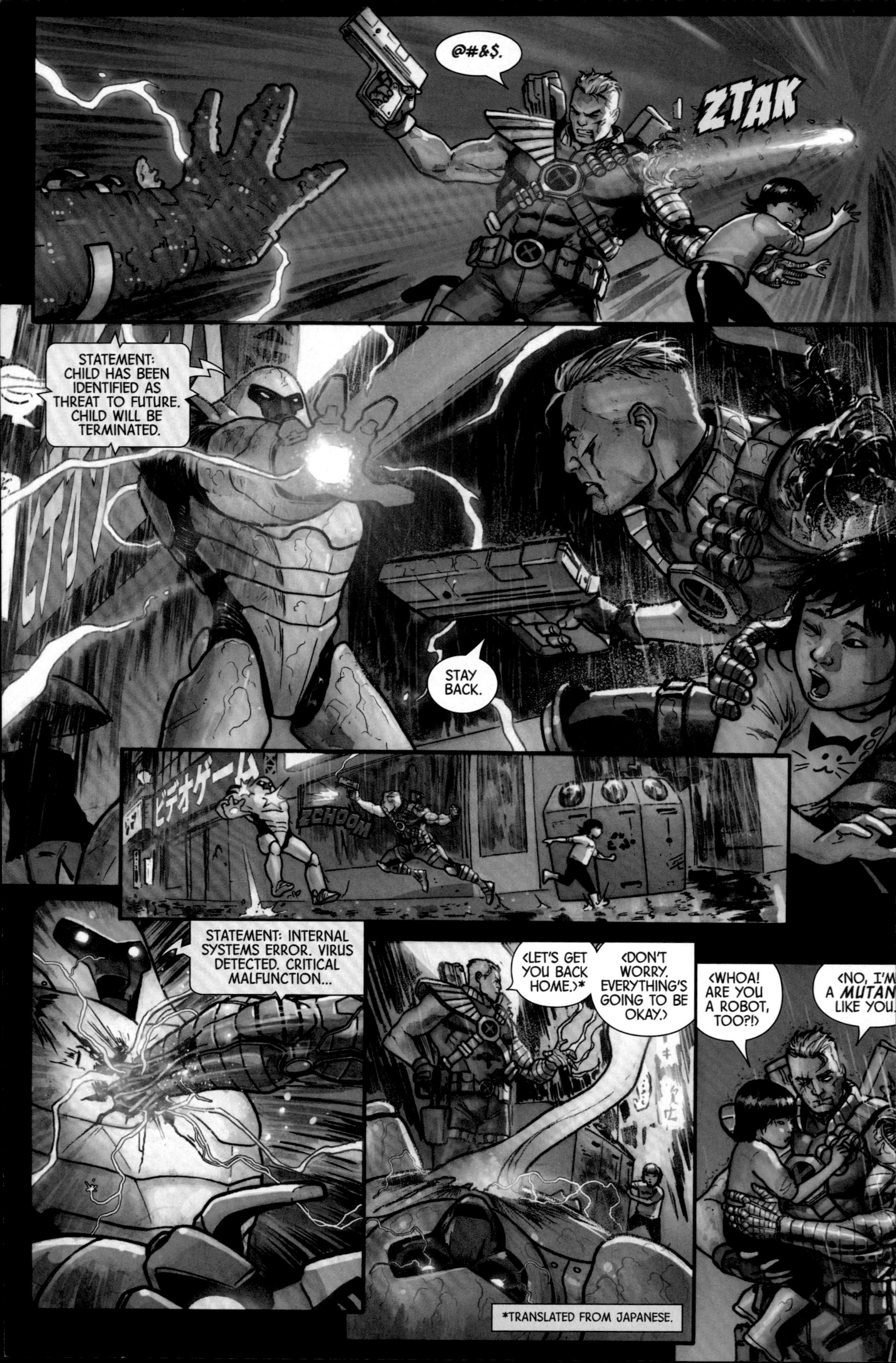
@#&$.
ZTAK
STATEMENT: CHILD HAS BEEN IDENTIFIED AS THREAT TO FUTURE. CHILD WILL BE TERMINATED.
STAY BACK.
ビデオゲーム
ZCHOOM
STATEMENT: INTERNAL SYSTEMS ERROR. VIRUS DETECTED. CRITICAL MALFUNCTION...
‹LET'S GET YOU BACK HOME.›*
‹DON'T WORRY. EVERYTHING'S GOING TO BE OKAY.›
‹WHOA! ARE YOU A ROBOT, TOO?!›
‹NO, I'M A MUTAN LIKE YOU.
*TRANSLATED FROM JAPANESE.

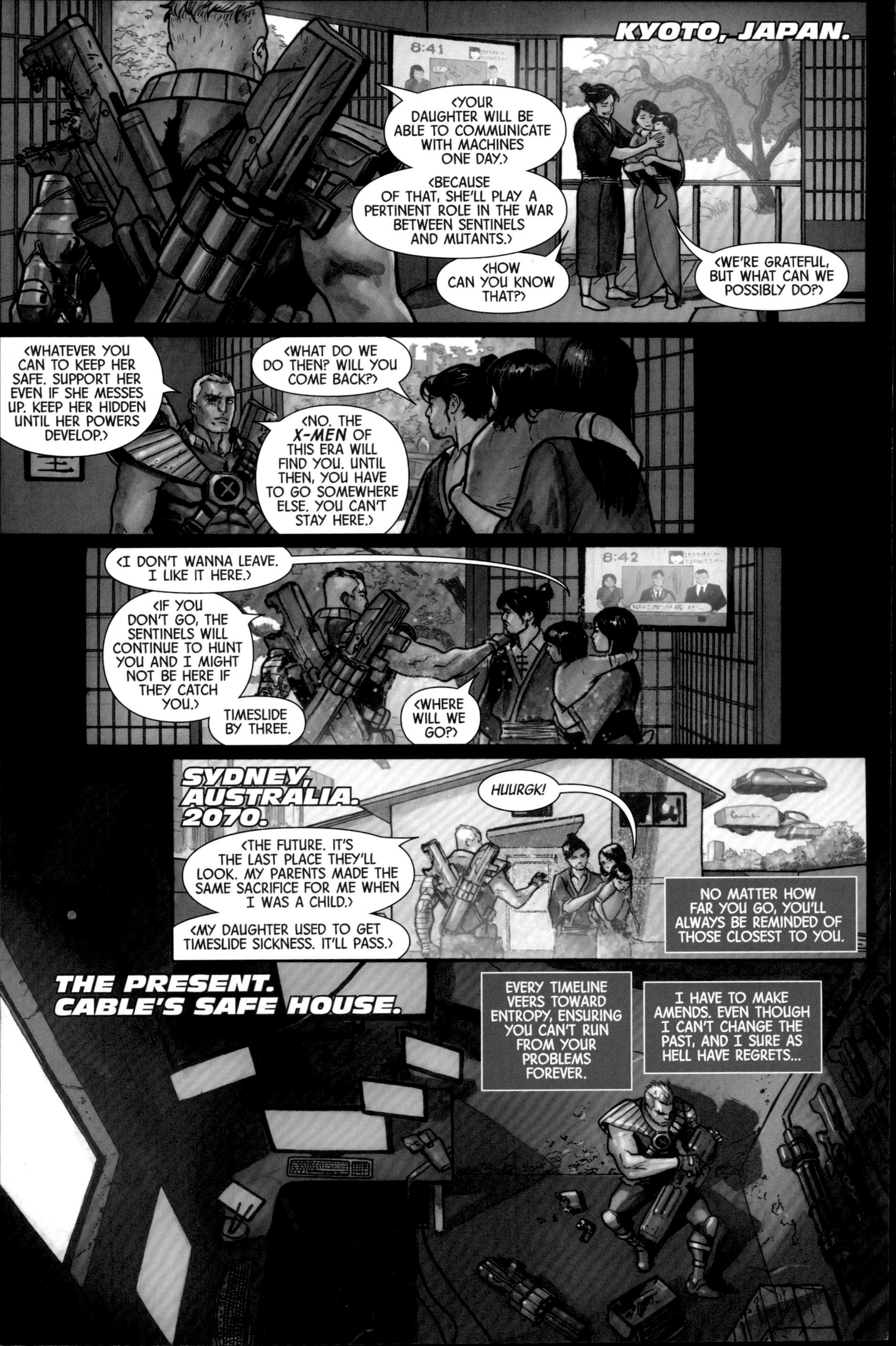
KYOTO, JAPAN.
8:41
<YOUR DAUGHTER WILL BE ABLE TO COMMUNICATE WITH MACHINES ONE DAY.>
<BECAUSE OF THAT, SHE'LL PLAY A PERTINENT ROLE IN THE WAR BETWEEN SENTINELS AND MUTANTS.>
<HOW CAN YOU KNOW THAT?>
<WE'RE GRATEFUL, BUT WHAT CAN WE POSSIBLY DO?>
<WHATEVER YOU CAN TO KEEP HER SAFE. SUPPORT HER EVEN IF SHE MESSES UP. KEEP HER HIDDEN UNTIL HER POWERS DEVELOP.>
<WHAT DO WE DO THEN? WILL YOU COME BACK?>
<NO. THE X-MEN OF THIS ERA WILL FIND YOU. UNTIL THEN, YOU HAVE TO GO SOMEWHERE ELSE. YOU CAN'T STAY HERE.>
<I DON'T WANNA LEAVE. I LIKE IT HERE.>
8:42
<IF YOU DON'T GO, THE SENTINELS WILL CONTINUE TO HUNT YOU AND I MIGHT NOT BE HERE IF THEY CATCH YOU.>
TIMESLIDE BY THREE.
<WHERE WILL WE GO?>
SYDNEY, AUSTRALIA. 2070.
HUURGK!
<THE FUTURE. IT'S THE LAST PLACE THEY'LL LOOK. MY PARENTS MADE THE SAME SACRIFICE FOR ME WHEN I WAS A CHILD.>
<MY DAUGHTER USED TO GET TIMESLIDE SICKNESS. IT'LL PASS.>
NO MATTER HOW FAR YOU GO, YOU'LL ALWAYS BE REMINDED OF THOSE CLOSEST TO YOU.
THE PRESENT. CABLE'S SAFE HOUSE.
EVERY TIMELINE VEERS TOWARD ENTROPY, ENSURING YOU CAN'T RUN FROM YOUR PROBLEMS FOREVER.
I HAVE TO MAKE AMENDS. EVEN THOUGH I CAN'T CHANGE THE PAST, AND I SURE AS HELL HAVE REGRETS...

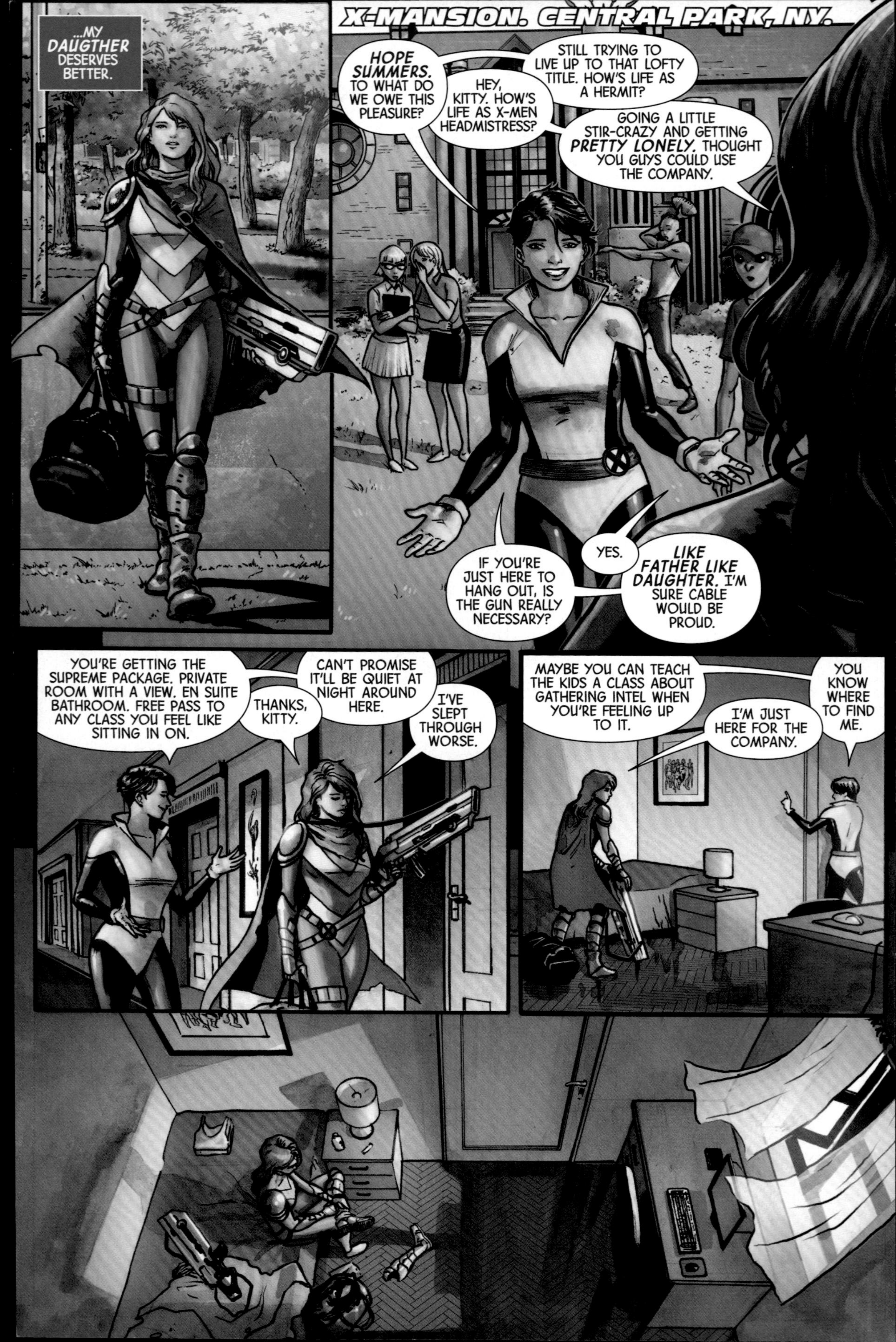
...MY DAUGHTER DESERVES BETTER.
X-MANSION. CENTRAL PARK, NY.
HOPE SUMMERS. TO WHAT DO WE OWE THIS PLEASURE?
HEY, KITTY. HOW'S LIFE AS X-MEN HEADMISTRESS?
STILL TRYING TO LIVE UP TO THAT LOFTY TITLE. HOW'S LIFE AS A HERMIT?
GOING A LITTLE STIR-CRAZY AND GETTING PRETTY LONELY. THOUGHT YOU GUYS COULD USE THE COMPANY.
IF YOU'RE JUST HERE TO HANG OUT, IS THE GUN REALLY NECESSARY?
YES.
LIKE FATHER LIKE DAUGHTER. I'M SURE CABLE WOULD BE PROUD.
YOU'RE GETTING THE SUPREME PACKAGE. PRIVATE ROOM WITH A VIEW. EN SUITE BATHROOM. FREE PASS TO ANY CLASS YOU FEEL LIKE SITTING IN ON.
THANKS, KITTY.
CAN'T PROMISE IT'LL BE QUIET AT NIGHT AROUND HERE.
I'VE SLEPT THROUGH WORSE.
MAYBE YOU CAN TEACH THE KIDS A CLASS ABOUT GATHERING INTEL WHEN YOU'RE FEELING UP TO IT.
I'M JUST HERE FOR THE COMPANY.
YOU KNOW WHERE TO FIND ME.

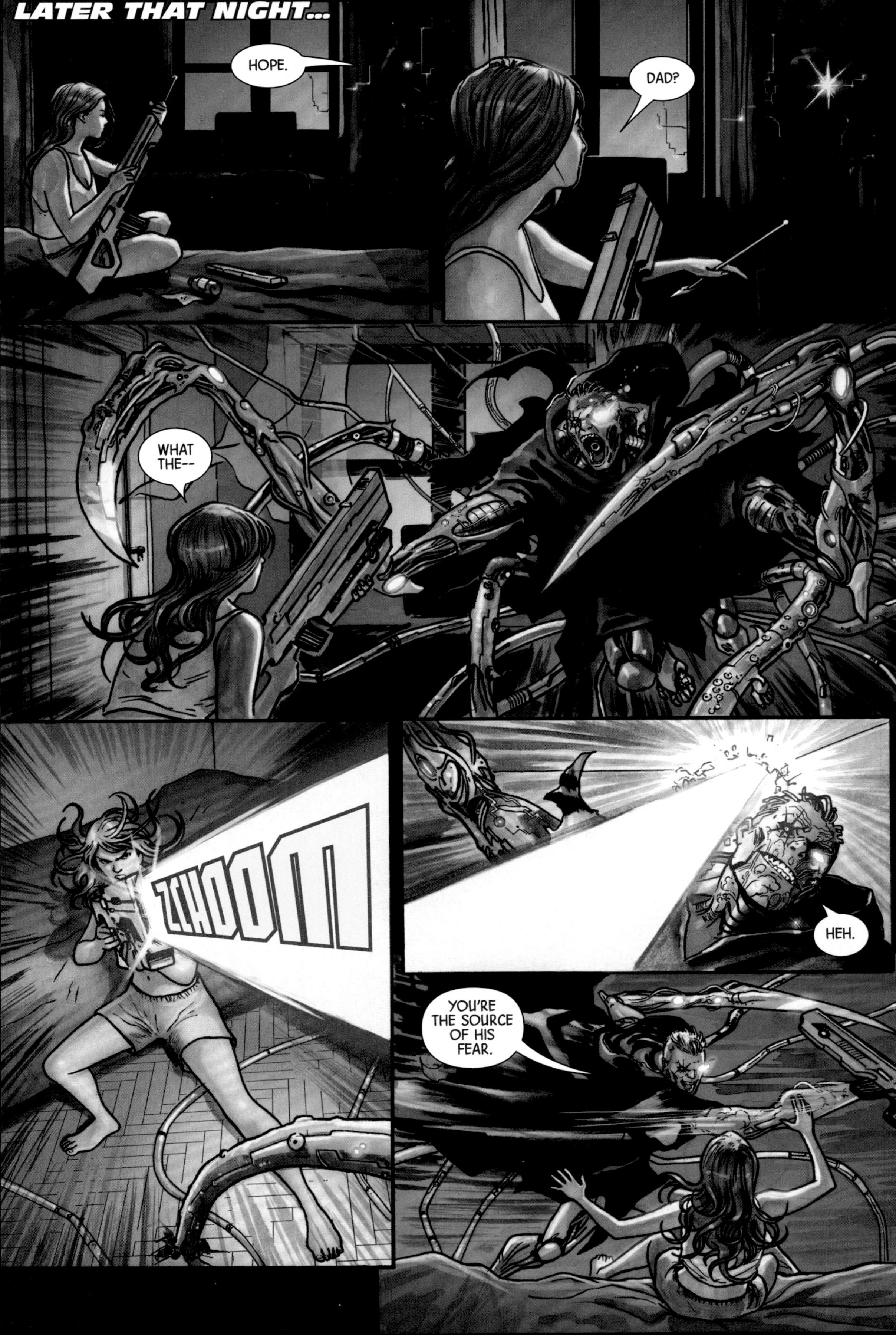
LATER THAT NIGHT...
HOPE.
DAD?
WHAT THE--
ZCHOOM
HEH.
YOU'RE THE SOURCE OF HIS FEAR.

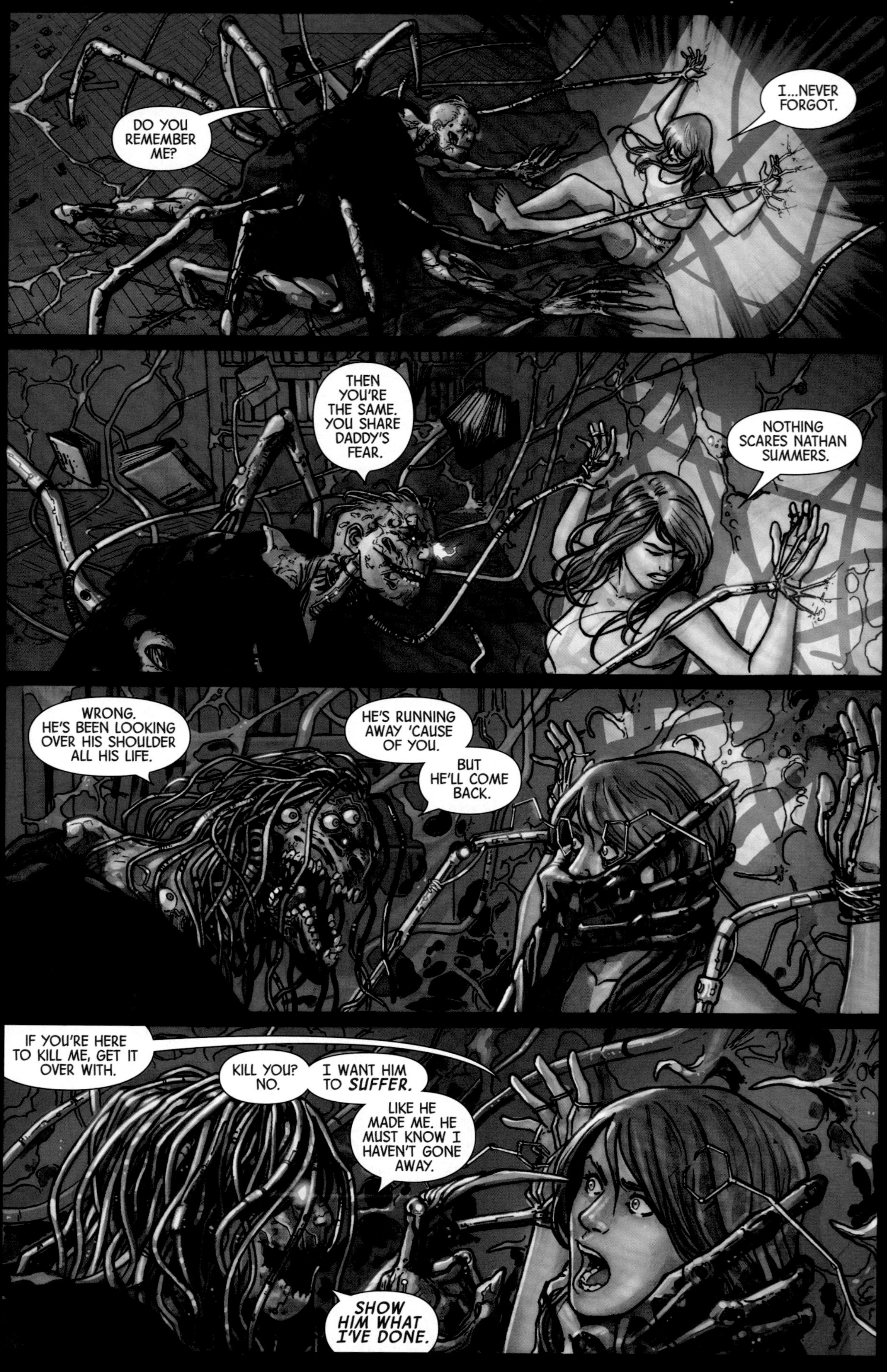
DO YOU REMEMBER ME?
I...NEVER FORGOT.
THEN YOU'RE THE SAME. YOU SHARE DADDY'S FEAR.
NOTHING SCARES NATHAN SUMMERS.
WRONG. HE'S BEEN LOOKING OVER HIS SHOULDER ALL HIS LIFE.
HE'S RUNNING AWAY 'CAUSE OF YOU.
BUT HE'LL COME BACK.
IF YOU'RE HERE TO KILL ME, GET IT OVER WITH.
KILL YOU? NO.
I WANT HIM TO *SUFFER.*
LIKE HE MADE ME. HE MUST KNOW I HAVEN'T GONE AWAY.
SHOW HIM WHAT I'VE DONE.

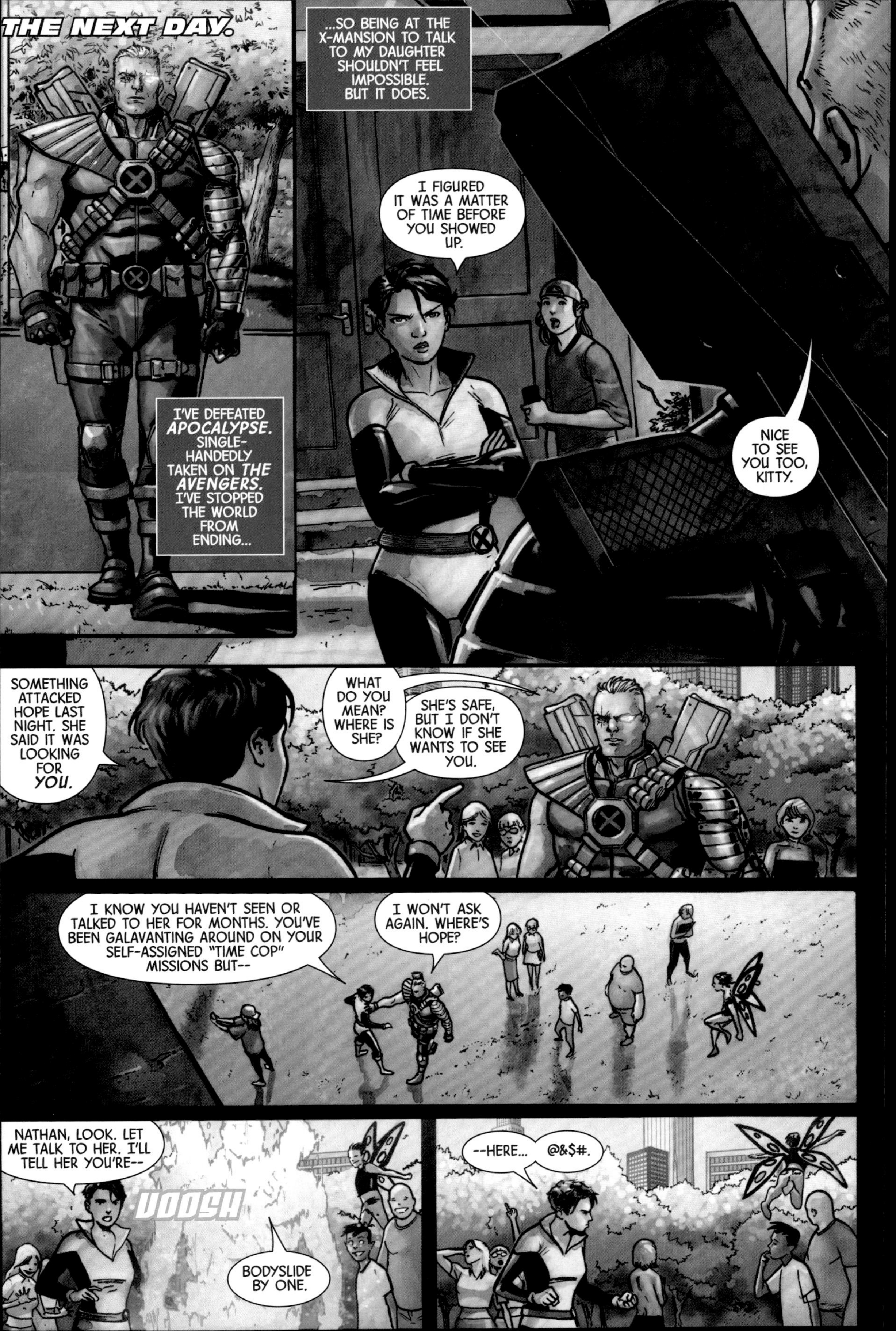
THE NEXT DAY.
...SO BEING AT THE X-MANSION TO TALK TO MY DAUGHTER SHOULDN'T FEEL IMPOSSIBLE. BUT IT DOES.
I'VE DEFEATED APOCALYPSE. SINGLE-HANDEDLY TAKEN ON THE AVENGERS. I'VE STOPPED THE WORLD FROM ENDING...
I FIGURED IT WAS A MATTER OF TIME BEFORE YOU SHOWED UP.
NICE TO SEE YOU TOO, KITTY.
SOMETHING ATTACKED HOPE LAST NIGHT. SHE SAID IT WAS LOOKING FOR YOU.
WHAT DO YOU MEAN? WHERE IS SHE?
SHE'S SAFE, BUT I DON'T KNOW IF SHE WANTS TO SEE YOU.
I KNOW YOU HAVEN'T SEEN OR TALKED TO HER FOR MONTHS. YOU'VE BEEN GALAVANTING AROUND ON YOUR SELF-ASSIGNED "TIME COP" MISSIONS BUT--
I WON'T ASK AGAIN. WHERE'S HOPE?
NATHAN, LOOK. LET ME TALK TO HER. I'LL TELL HER YOU'RE--
VOOSH
BODYSLIDE BY ONE.
--HERE...
@&$#.

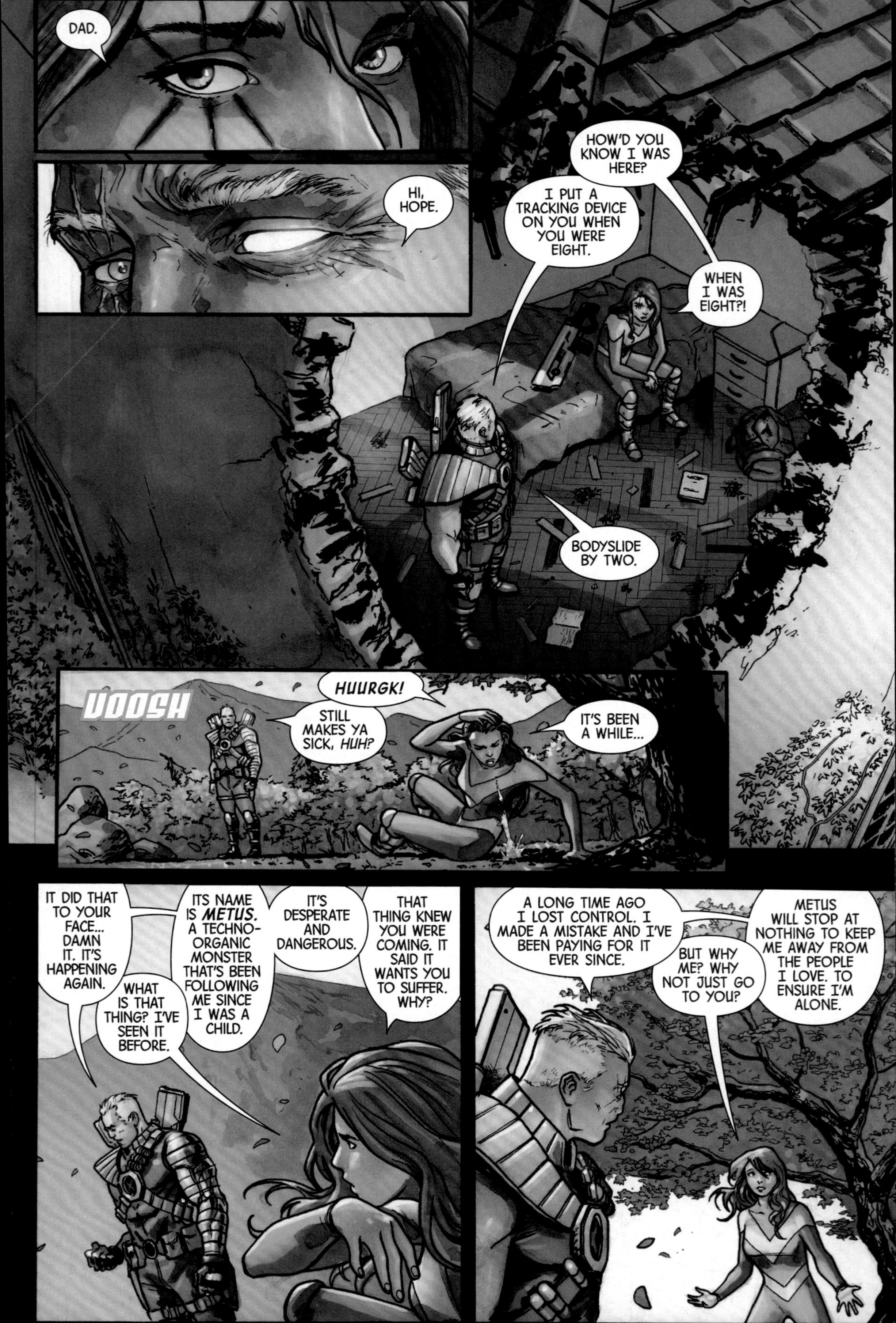

DAD.
HI, HOPE.
HOW'D YOU KNOW I WAS HERE?
I PUT A TRACKING DEVICE ON YOU WHEN YOU WERE EIGHT.
WHEN I WAS EIGHT?!
BODYSLIDE BY TWO.
VOOSH
HUURGK!
STILL MAKES YA SICK, HUH?
IT'S BEEN A WHILE...
IT DID THAT TO YOUR FACE... DAMN IT. IT'S HAPPENING AGAIN.
WHAT IS THAT THING? I'VE SEEN IT BEFORE.
ITS NAME IS METUS. A TECHNO-ORGANIC MONSTER THAT'S BEEN FOLLOWING ME SINCE I WAS A CHILD.
IT'S DESPERATE AND DANGEROUS.
THAT THING KNEW YOU WERE COMING. IT SAID IT WANTS YOU TO SUFFER. WHY?
A LONG TIME AGO I LOST CONTROL. I MADE A MISTAKE AND I'VE BEEN PAYING FOR IT EVER SINCE.
BUT WHY ME? WHY NOT JUST GO TO YOU?
METUS WILL STOP AT NOTHING TO KEEP ME AWAY FROM THE PEOPLE I LOVE. TO ENSURE I'M ALONE.

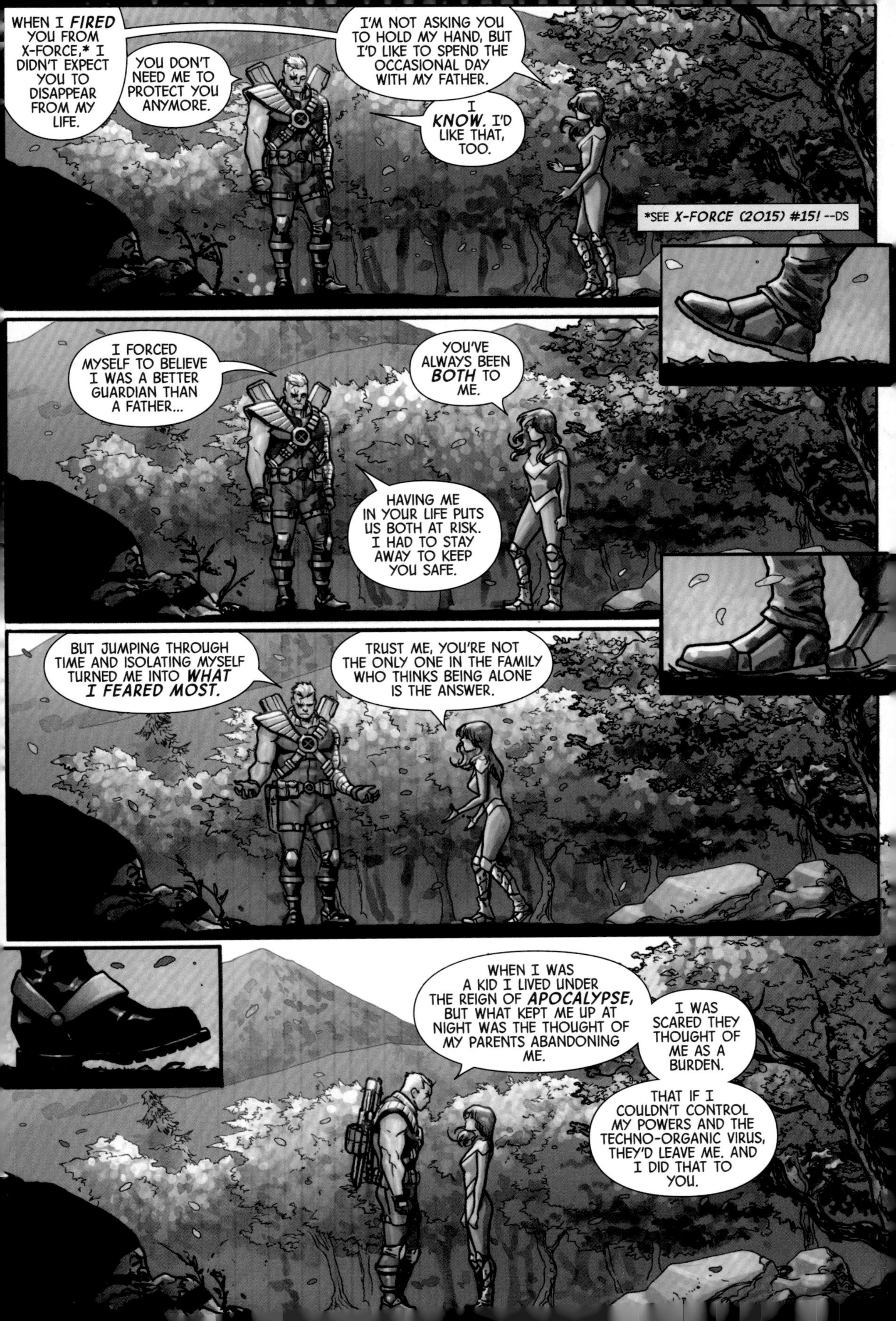
WHEN I FIRED YOU FROM X-FORCE,* I DIDN'T EXPECT YOU TO DISAPPEAR FROM MY LIFE.
YOU DON'T NEED ME TO PROTECT YOU ANYMORE.
I'M NOT ASKING YOU TO HOLD MY HAND, BUT I'D LIKE TO SPEND THE OCCASIONAL DAY WITH MY FATHER.
I KNOW. I'D LIKE THAT, TOO.
*SEE X-FORCE (2015) #15! --DS
I FORCED MYSELF TO BELIEVE I WAS A BETTER GUARDIAN THAN A FATHER...
YOU'VE ALWAYS BEEN BOTH TO ME.
HAVING ME IN YOUR LIFE PUTS US BOTH AT RISK. I HAD TO STAY AWAY TO KEEP YOU SAFE.
BUT JUMPING THROUGH TIME AND ISOLATING MYSELF TURNED ME INTO WHAT I FEARED MOST.
TRUST ME, YOU'RE NOT THE ONLY ONE IN THE FAMILY WHO THINKS BEING ALONE IS THE ANSWER.
WHEN I WAS A KID I LIVED UNDER THE REIGN OF APOCALYPSE, BUT WHAT KEPT ME UP AT NIGHT WAS THE THOUGHT OF MY PARENTS ABANDONING ME.
I WAS SCARED THEY THOUGHT OF ME AS A BURDEN.
THAT IF I COULDN'T CONTROL MY POWERS AND THE TECHNO-ORGANIC VIRUS, THEY'D LEAVE ME. AND I DID THAT TO YOU.

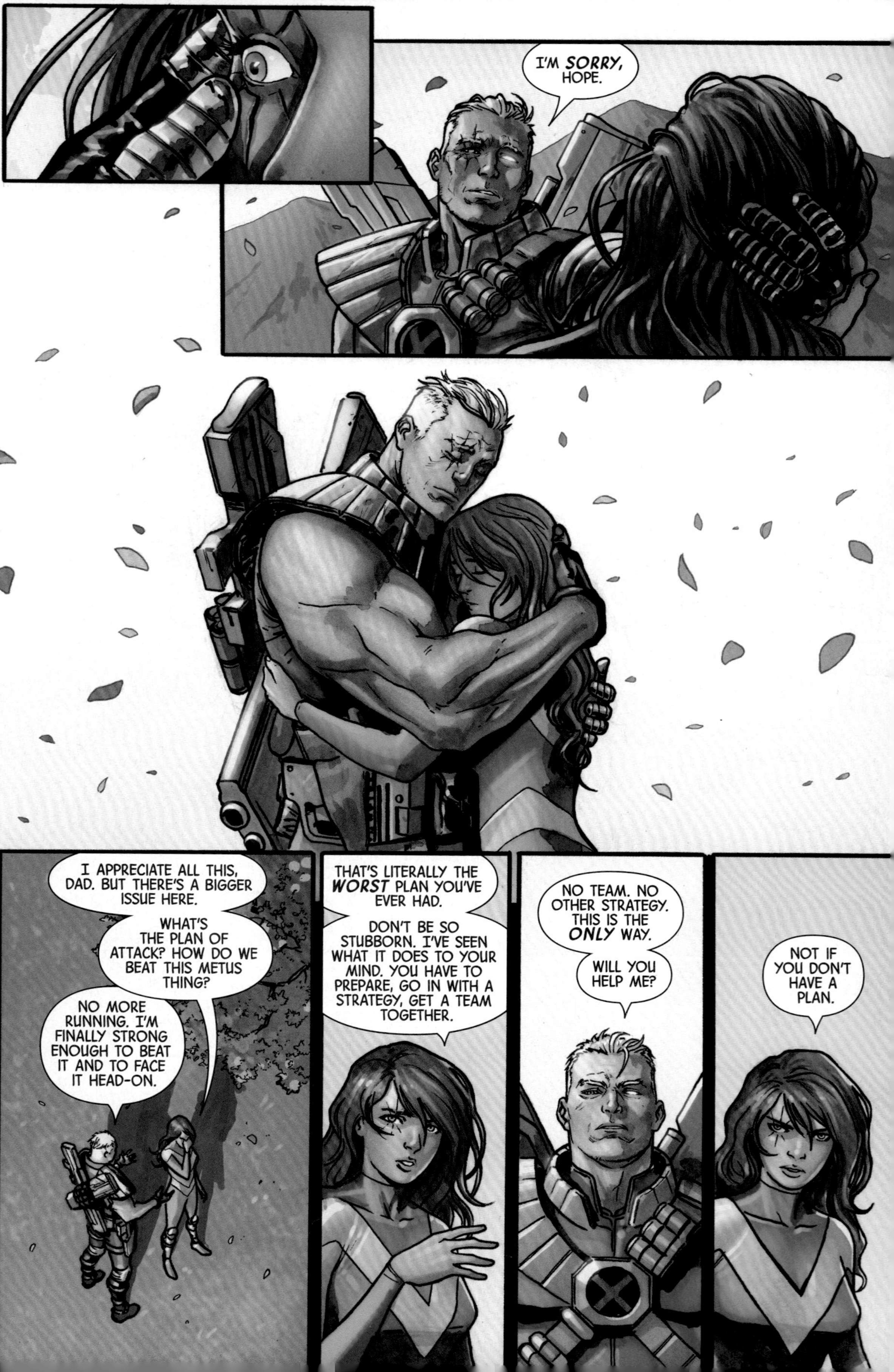
I'M SORRY, HOPE.
I APPRECIATE ALL THIS, DAD. BUT THERE'S A BIGGER ISSUE HERE.
WHAT'S THE PLAN OF ATTACK? HOW DO WE BEAT THIS METUS THING?
NO MORE RUNNING. I'M FINALLY STRONG ENOUGH TO BEAT IT AND TO FACE IT HEAD-ON.
THAT'S LITERALLY THE WORST PLAN YOU'VE EVER HAD.
DON'T BE SO STUBBORN. I'VE SEEN WHAT IT DOES TO YOUR MIND. YOU HAVE TO PREPARE, GO IN WITH A STRATEGY, GET A TEAM TOGETHER.
NO TEAM. NO OTHER STRATEGY. THIS IS THE ONLY WAY.
WILL YOU HELP ME?
NOT IF YOU DON'T HAVE A PLAN.

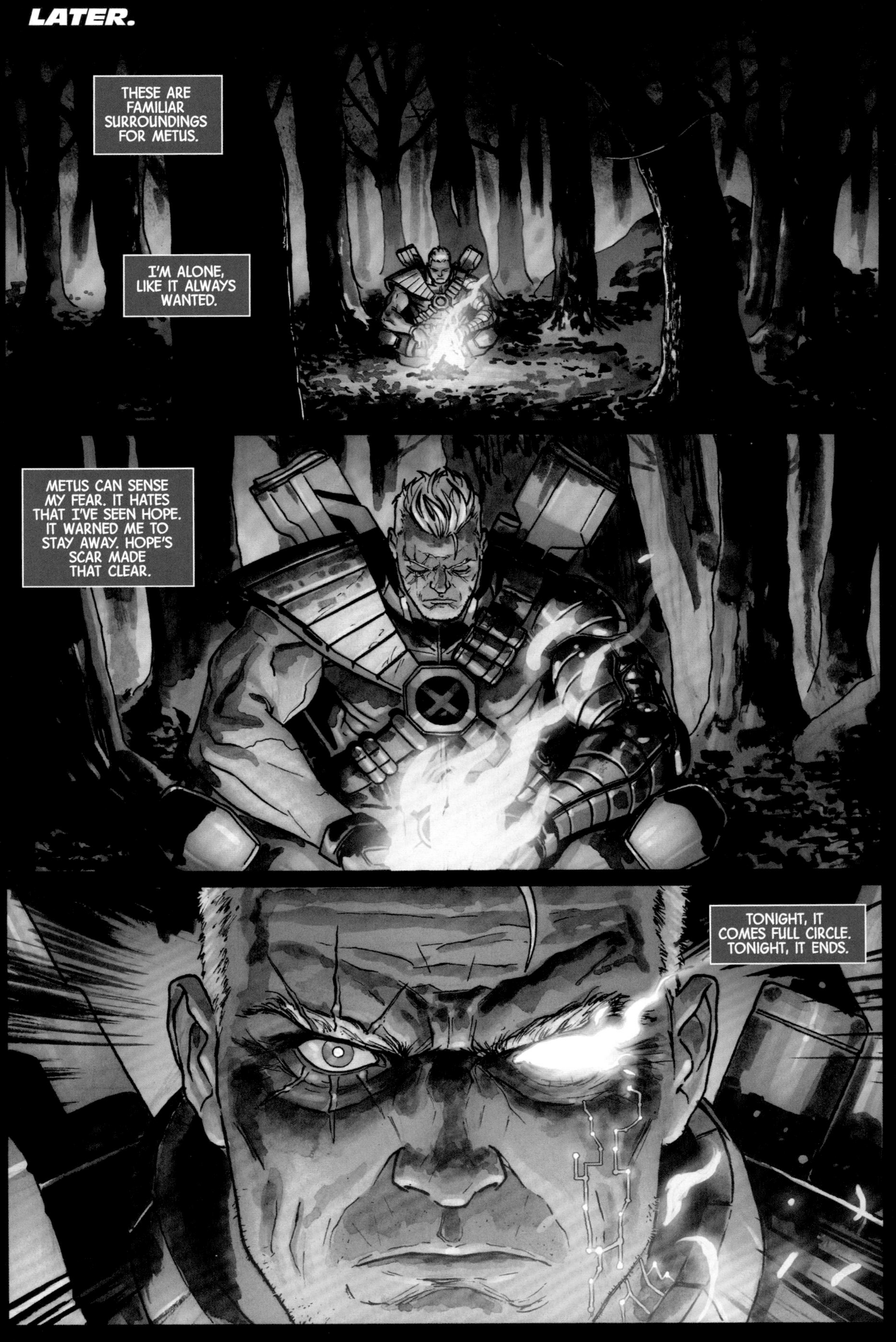
LATER.
THESE ARE FAMILIAR SURROUNDINGS FOR METUS.
I'M ALONE, LIKE IT ALWAYS WANTED.
METUS CAN SENSE MY FEAR. IT HATES THAT I'VE SEEN HOPE. IT WARNED ME TO STAY AWAY. HOPE'S SCAR MADE THAT CLEAR.
TONIGHT, IT COMES FULL CIRCLE. TONIGHT, IT ENDS.

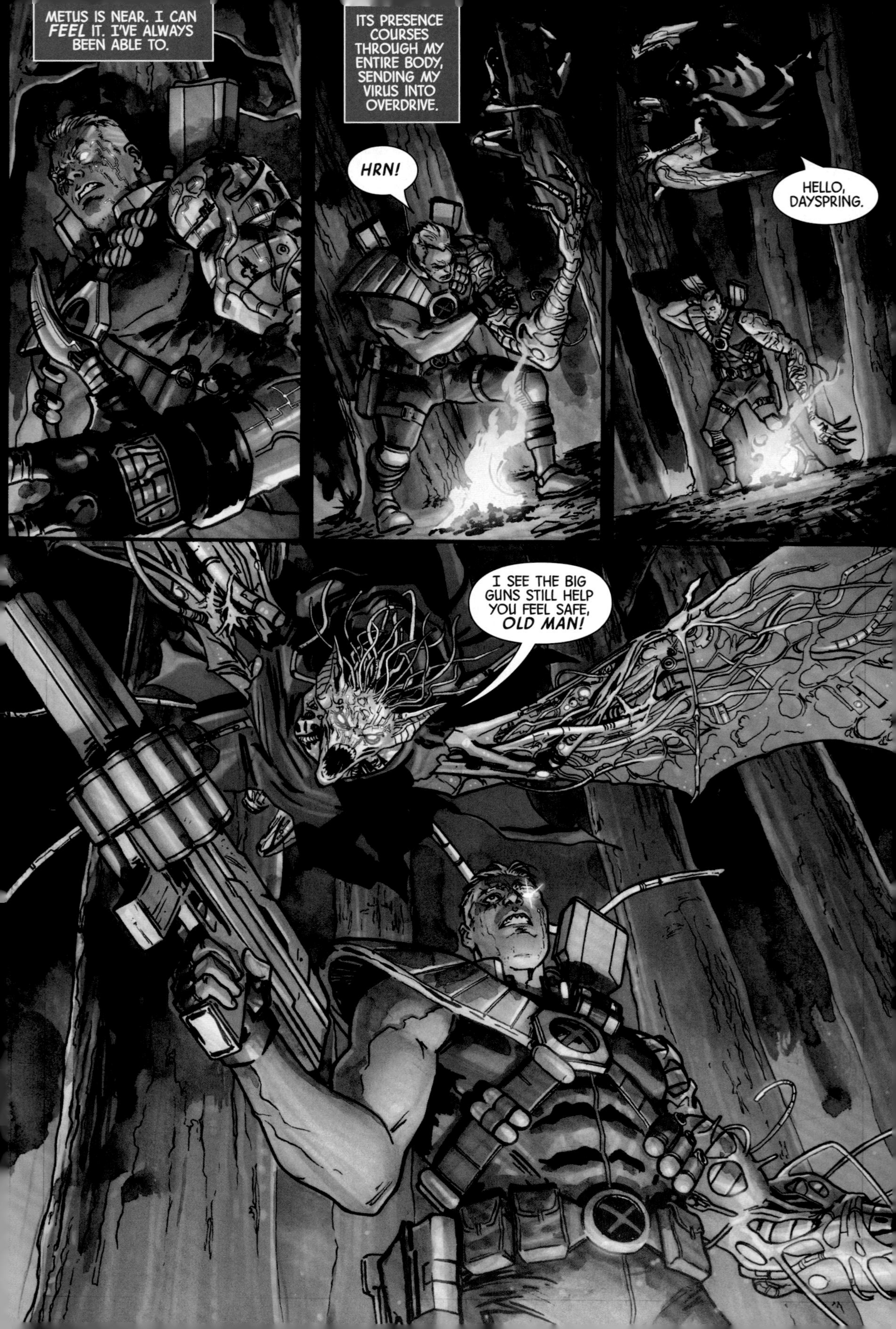
METUS IS NEAR. I CAN *FEEL* IT. I'VE ALWAYS BEEN ABLE TO.
ITS PRESENCE COURSES THROUGH MY ENTIRE BODY, SENDING MY VIRUS INTO OVERDRIVE.
HRN!
HELLO, DAYSPRING.
I SEE THE BIG GUNS STILL HELP YOU FEEL SAFE, ***OLD MAN!***

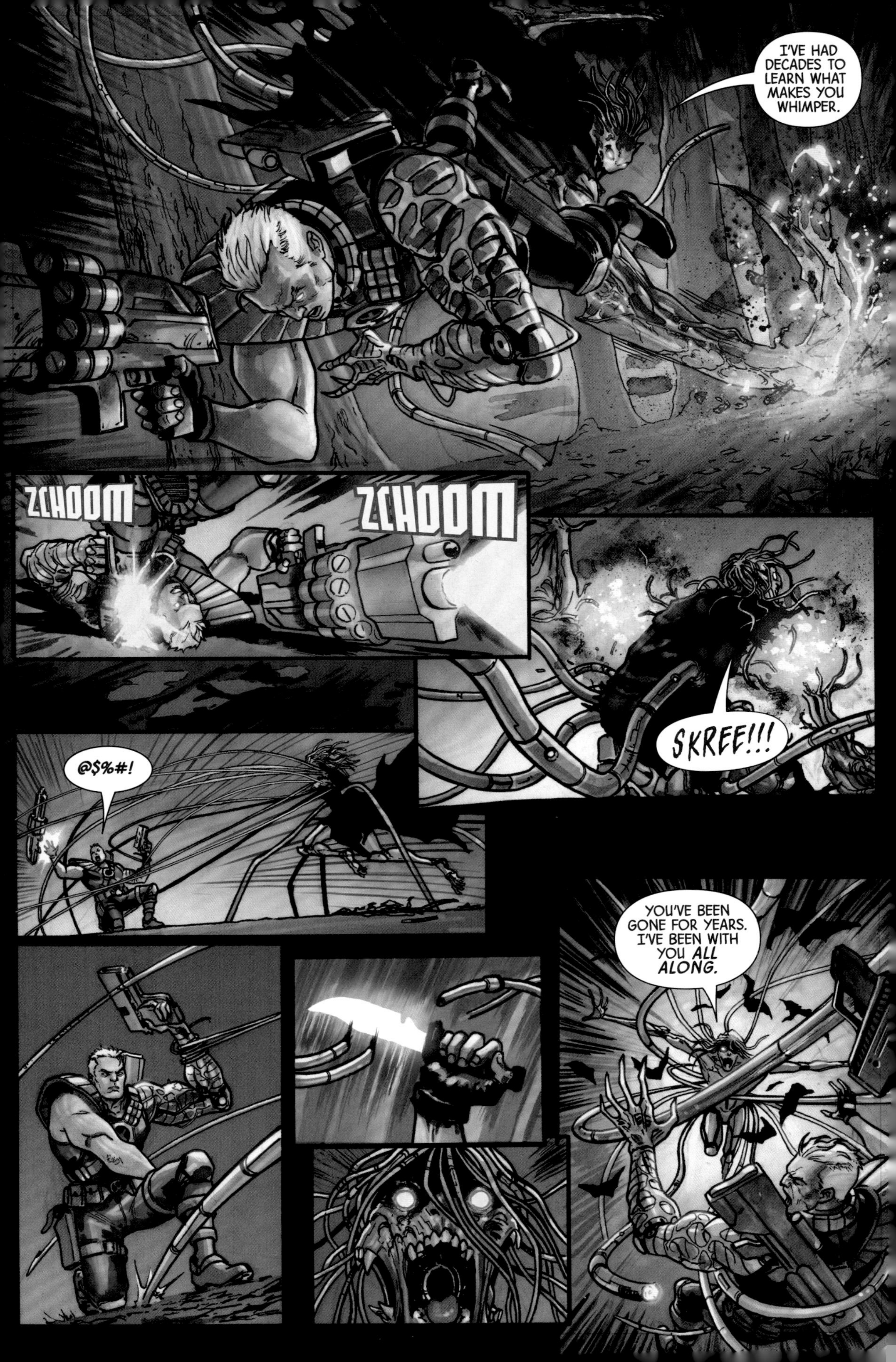
I'VE HAD DECADES TO LEARN WHAT MAKES YOU WHIMPER.
ZCHOOM
ZCHOOM
SKREE!!!
@$%#!
YOU'VE BEEN GONE FOR YEARS. I'VE BEEN WITH YOU ALL ALONG.

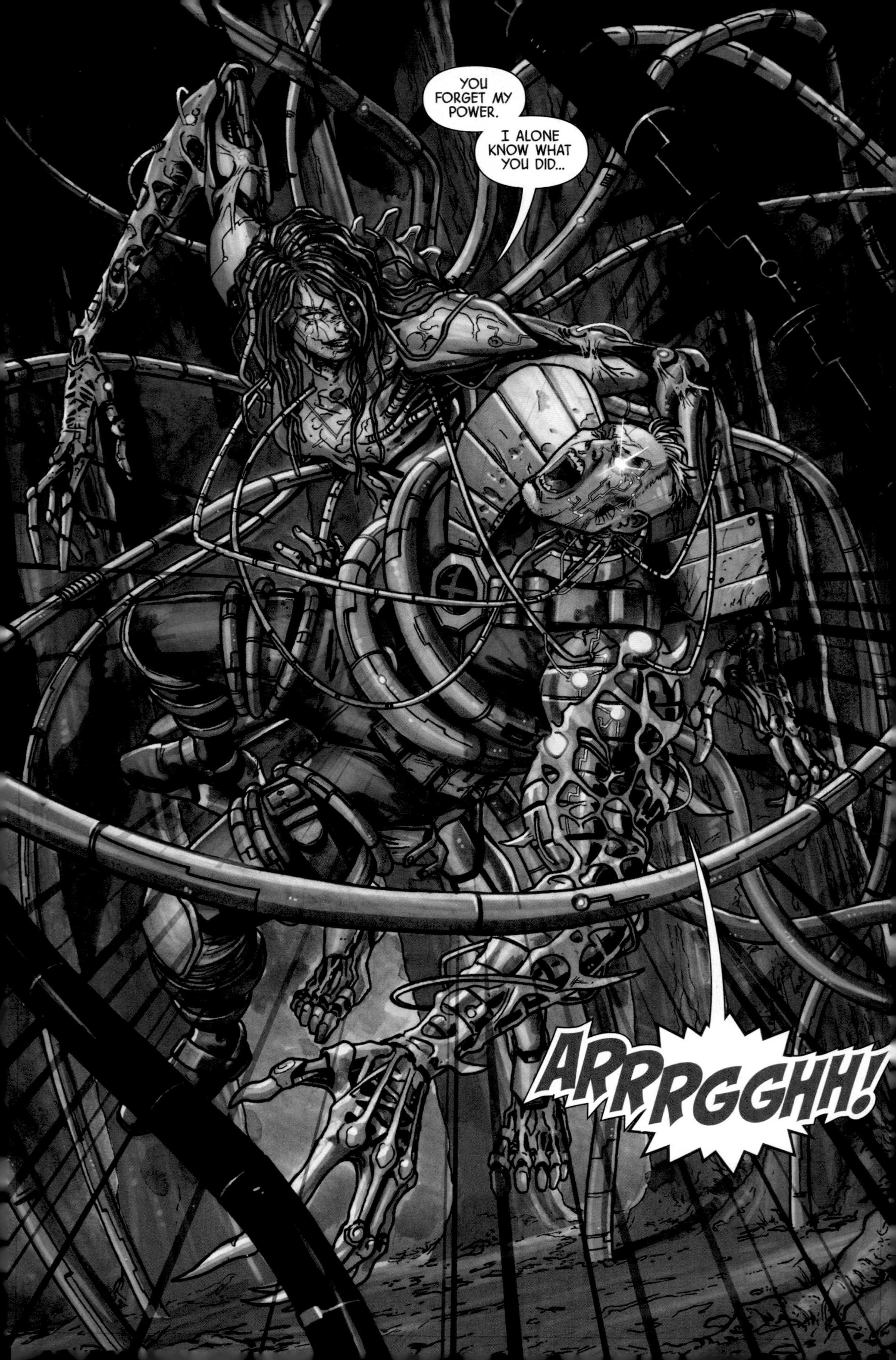
YOU FORGET MY POWER.
I ALONE KNOW WHAT YOU DID...
ARRRGGHH!

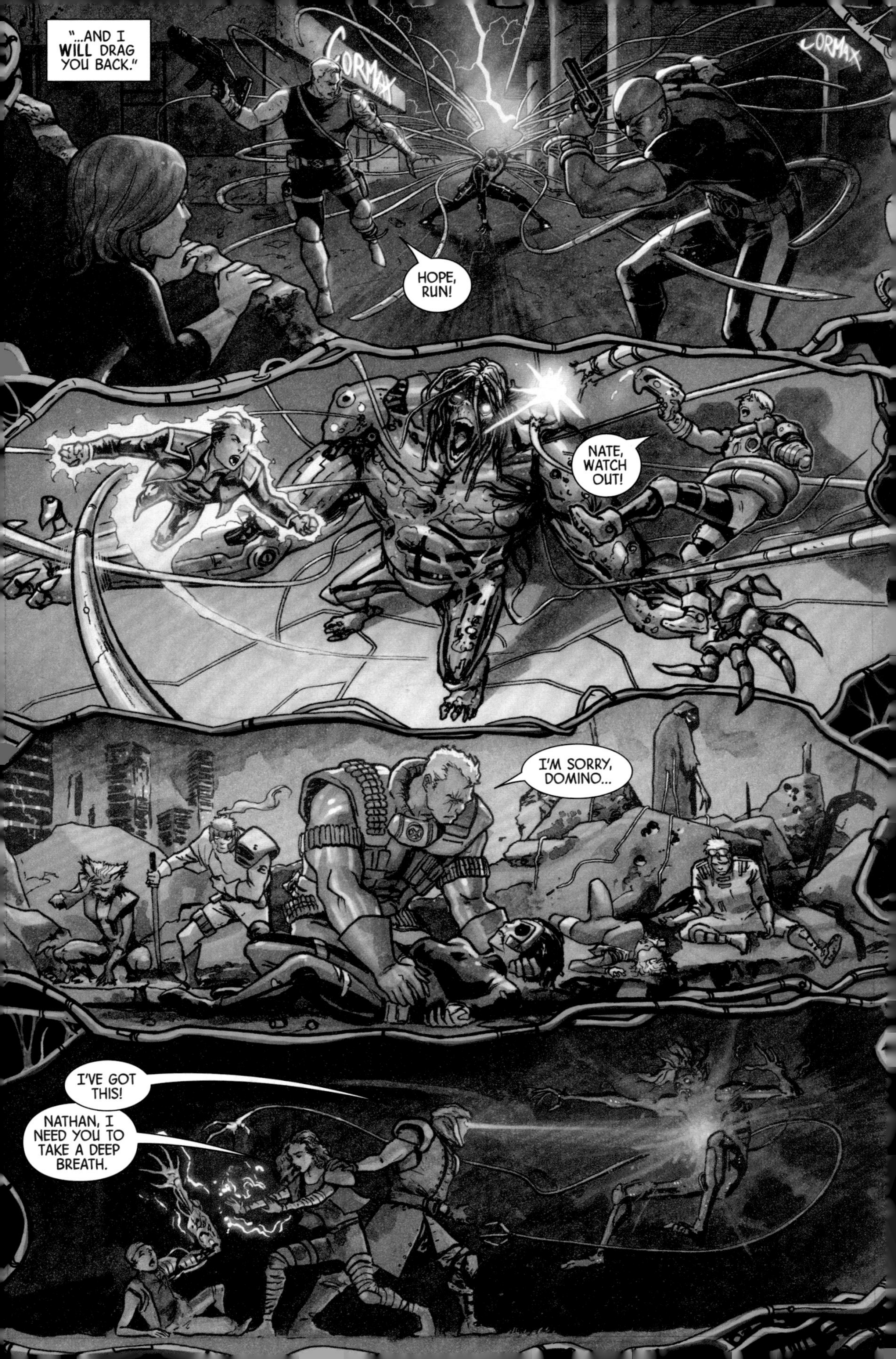
"...AND I WILL DRAG YOU BACK."
HOPE, RUN!
NATE, WATCH OUT!
I'M SORRY, DOMINO...
I'VE GOT THIS!
NATHAN, I NEED YOU TO TAKE A DEEP BREATH.

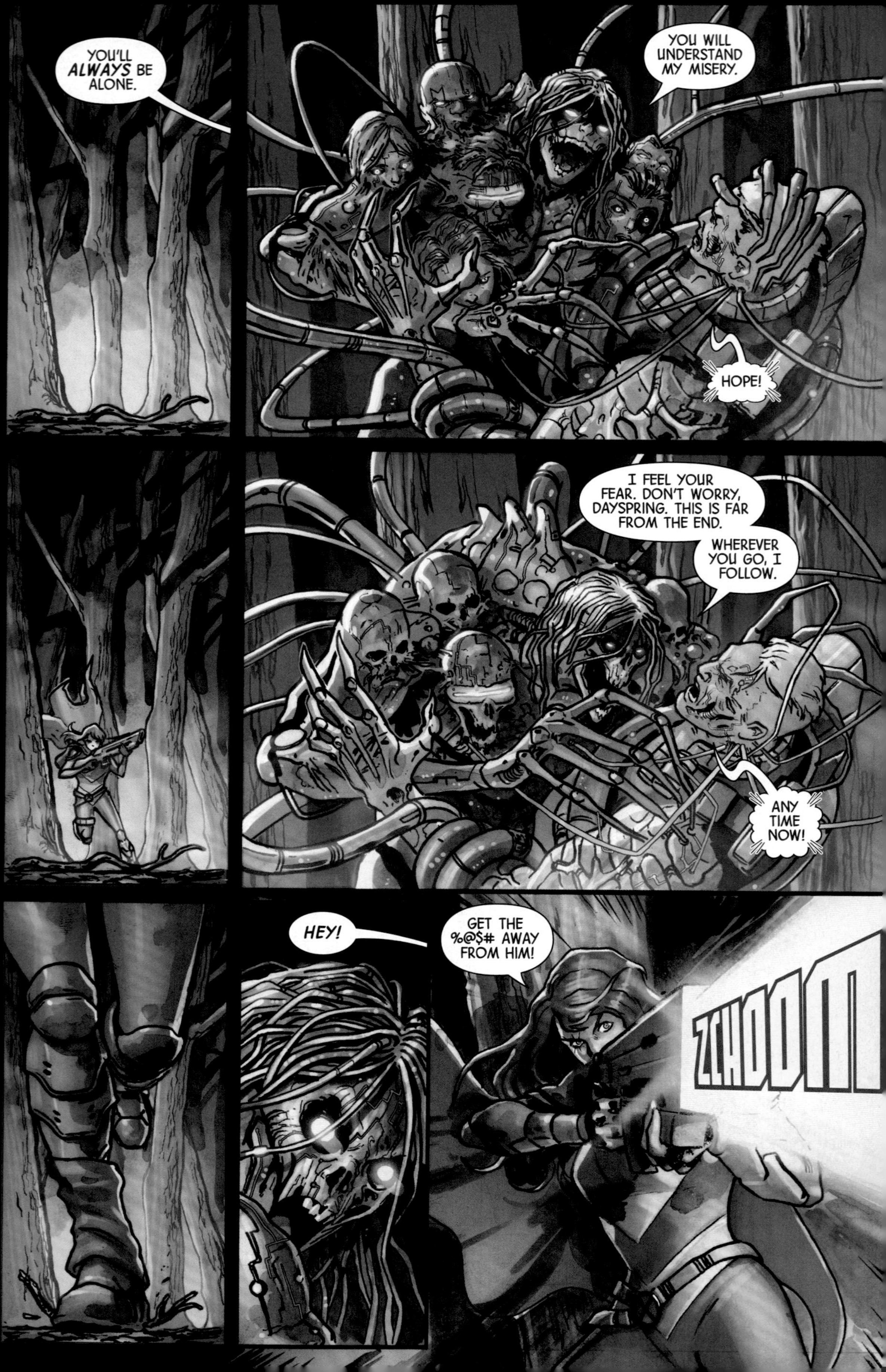

YOU'LL *ALWAYS* BE ALONE.
YOU WILL UNDERSTAND MY MISERY.
HOPE!
I FEEL YOUR FEAR. DON'T WORRY, DAYSPRING. THIS IS FAR FROM THE END.
WHEREVER YOU GO, I FOLLOW.
ANY TIME NOW!
HEY!
GET THE %@$# AWAY FROM HIM!
ZCHOOM

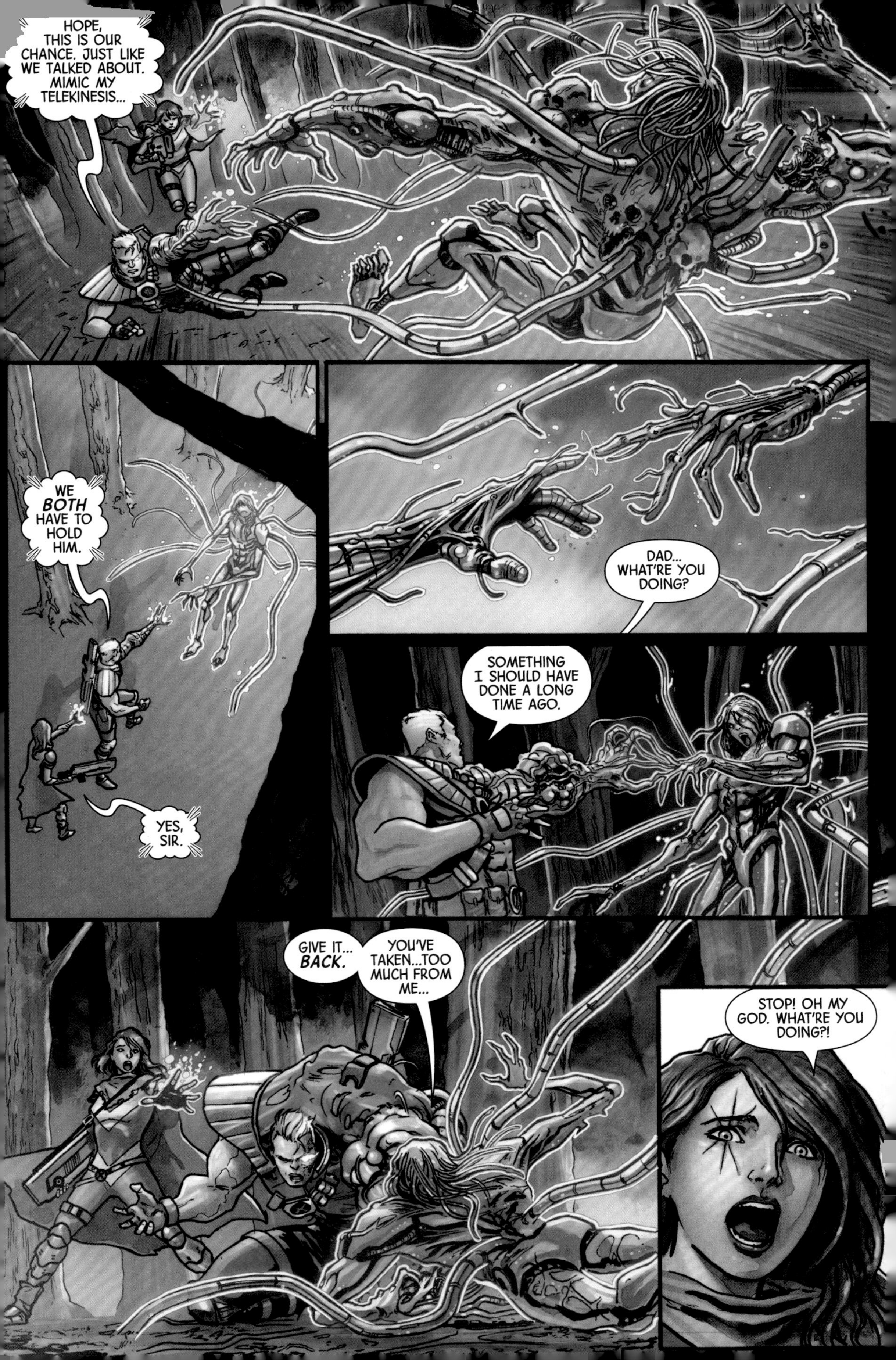
HOPE, THIS IS OUR CHANCE. JUST LIKE WE TALKED ABOUT. MIMIC MY TELEKINESIS...
WE *BOTH* HAVE TO HOLD HIM.
YES, SIR.
DAD... WHAT'RE YOU DOING?
SOMETHING I SHOULD HAVE DONE A LONG TIME AGO.
GIVE IT... *BACK.*
YOU'VE TAKEN...TOO MUCH FROM ME...
STOP! OH MY GOD. WHAT'RE YOU DOING?!

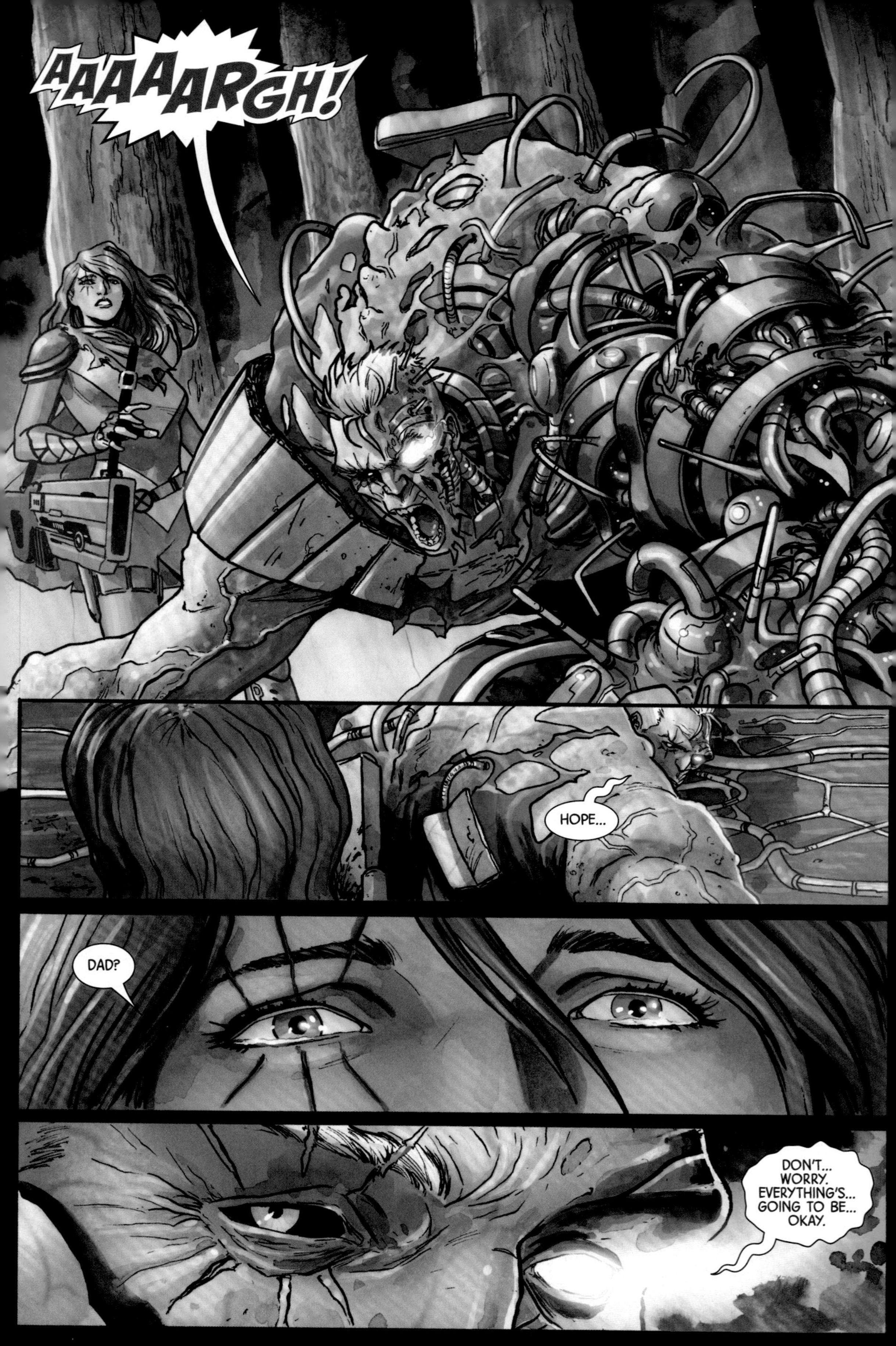
AAAAARGH!
HOPE...
DAD?
DON'T... WORRY. EVERYTHING'S... GOING TO BE... OKAY.

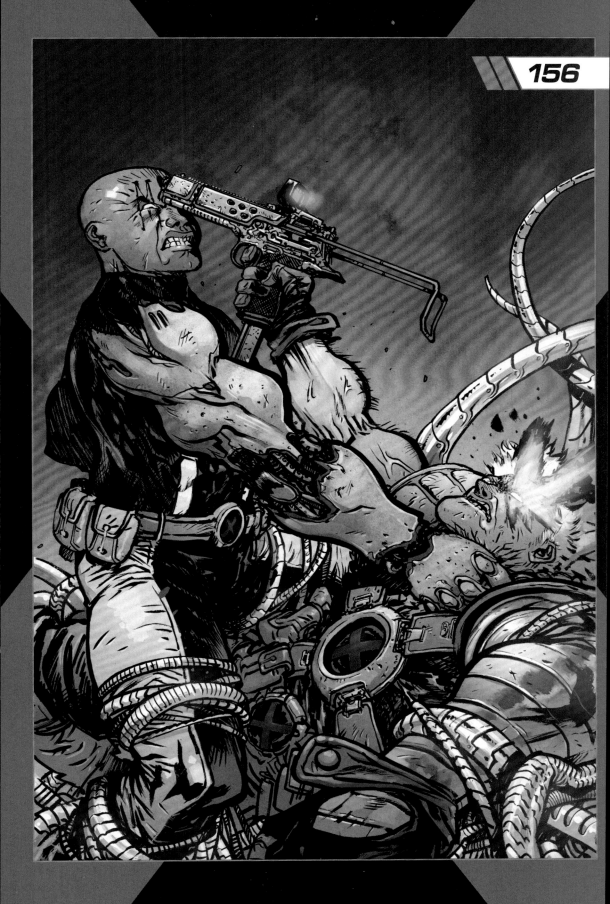

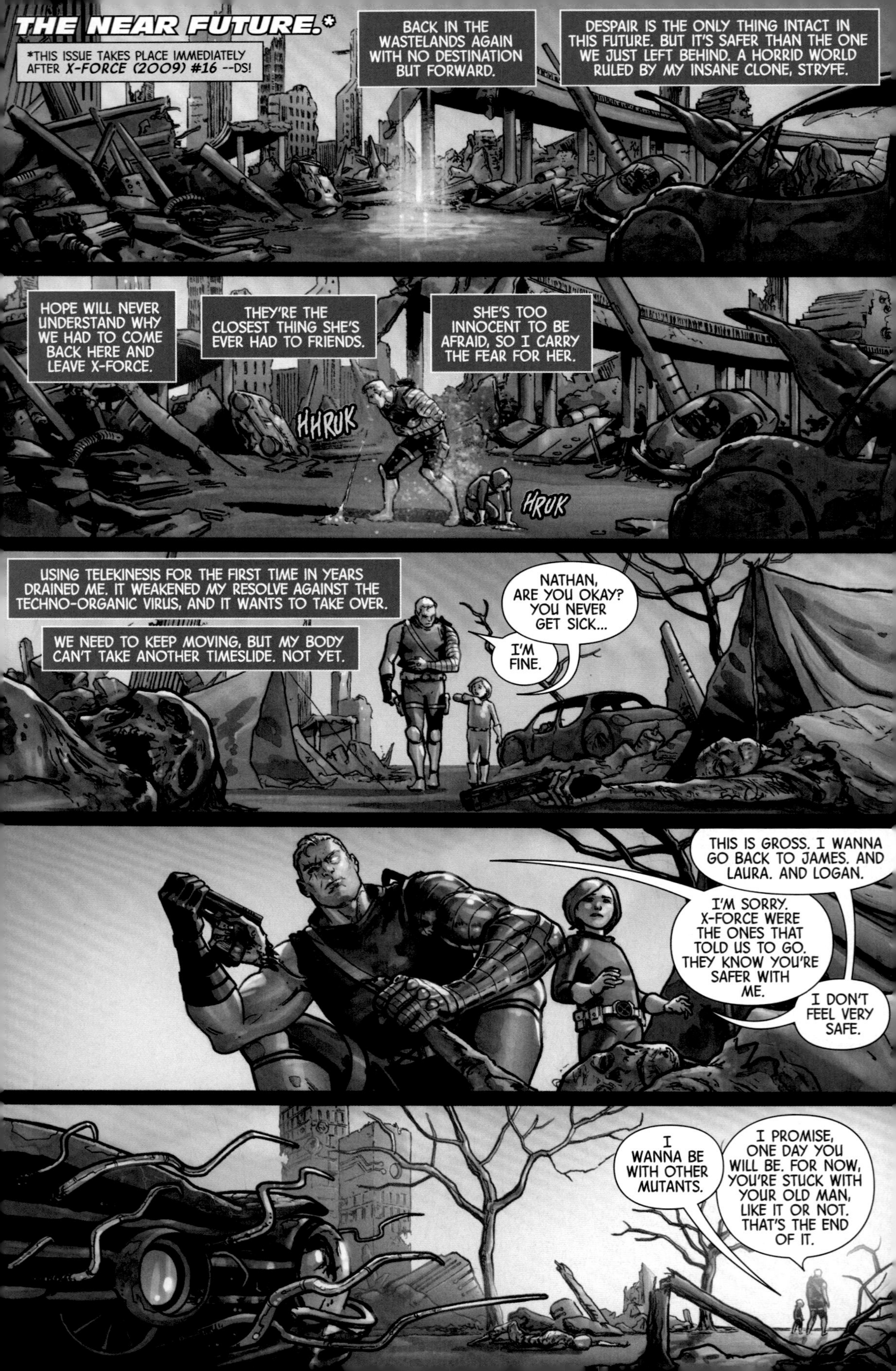

THE NEAR FUTURE.*
*THIS ISSUE TAKES PLACE IMMEDIATELY AFTER X-FORCE (2009) #16 --DS!
BACK IN THE WASTELANDS AGAIN WITH NO DESTINATION BUT FORWARD.
DESPAIR IS THE ONLY THING INTACT IN THIS FUTURE. BUT IT'S SAFER THAN THE ONE WE JUST LEFT BEHIND. A HORRID WORLD RULED BY MY INSANE CLONE, STRYFE.
HOPE WILL NEVER UNDERSTAND WHY WE HAD TO COME BACK HERE AND LEAVE X-FORCE.
THEY'RE THE CLOSEST THING SHE'S EVER HAD TO FRIENDS.
SHE'S TOO INNOCENT TO BE AFRAID, SO I CARRY THE FEAR FOR HER.
HHRUK
HRUK
USING TELEKINESIS FOR THE FIRST TIME IN YEARS DRAINED ME. IT WEAKENED MY RESOLVE AGAINST THE TECHNO-ORGANIC VIRUS, AND IT WANTS TO TAKE OVER.
WE NEED TO KEEP MOVING, BUT MY BODY CAN'T TAKE ANOTHER TIMESLIDE. NOT YET.
NATHAN, ARE YOU OKAY? YOU NEVER GET SICK...
I'M FINE.
THIS IS GROSS. I WANNA GO BACK TO JAMES. AND LAURA. AND LOGAN.
I'M SORRY. X-FORCE WERE THE ONES THAT TOLD US TO GO. THEY KNOW YOU'RE SAFER WITH ME.
I DON'T FEEL VERY SAFE.
I WANNA BE WITH OTHER MUTANTS.
I PROMISE, ONE DAY YOU WILL BE. FOR NOW, YOU'RE STUCK WITH YOUR OLD MAN, LIKE IT OR NOT. THAT'S THE END OF IT.

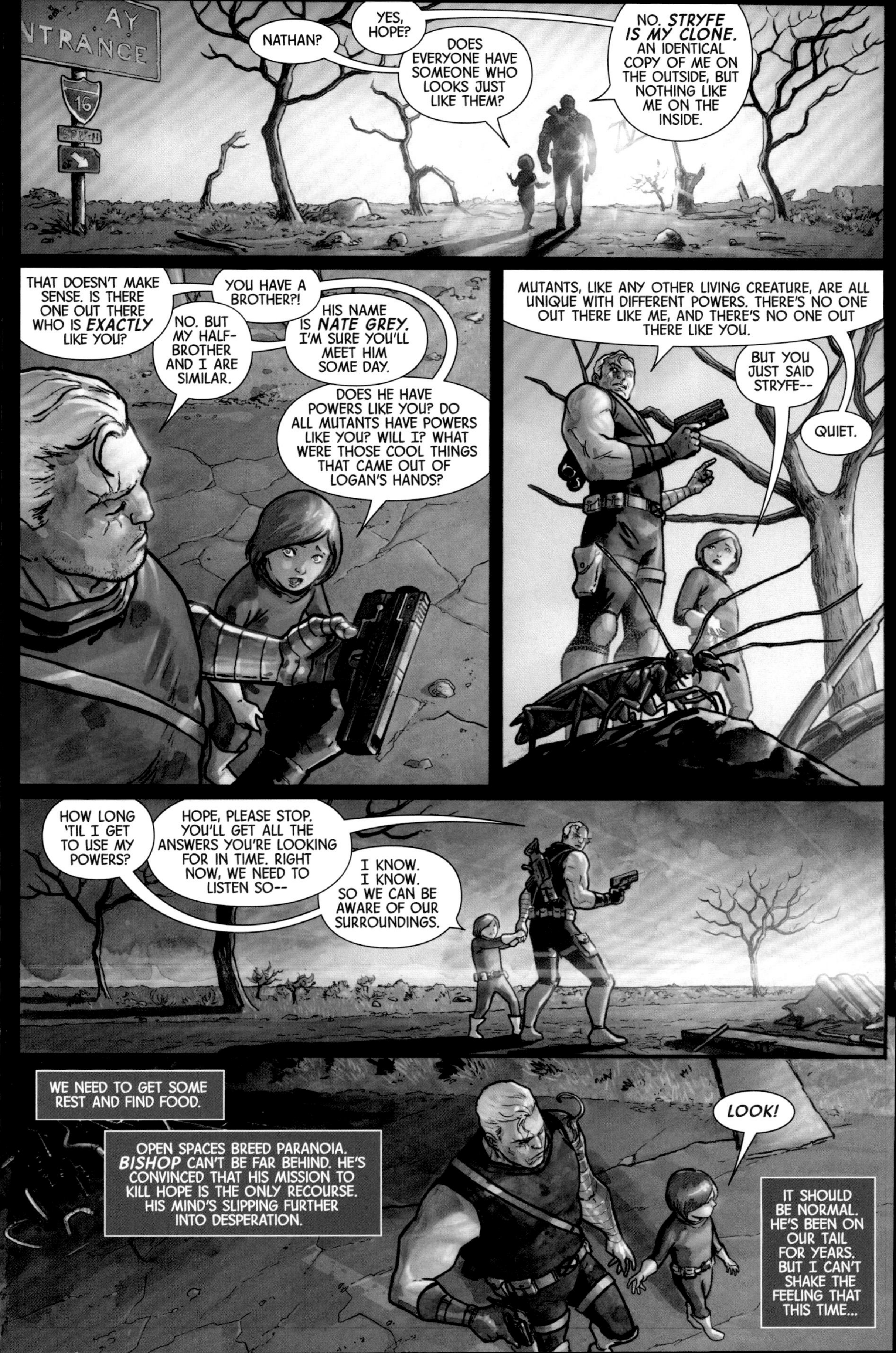
AY
NTRANCE
16
NATHAN?
YES, HOPE?
DOES EVERYONE HAVE SOMEONE WHO LOOKS JUST LIKE THEM?
NO. *STRYFE IS MY CLONE.* AN IDENTICAL COPY OF ME ON THE OUTSIDE, BUT NOTHING LIKE ME ON THE INSIDE.
THAT DOESN'T MAKE SENSE. IS THERE ONE OUT THERE WHO IS *EXACTLY* LIKE YOU?
NO. BUT MY HALF-BROTHER AND I ARE SIMILAR.
YOU HAVE A BROTHER?!
HIS NAME IS *NATE GREY.* I'M SURE YOU'LL MEET HIM SOME DAY.
DOES HE HAVE POWERS LIKE YOU? DO ALL MUTANTS HAVE POWERS LIKE YOU? WILL I? WHAT WERE THOSE COOL THINGS THAT CAME OUT OF LOGAN'S HANDS?
MUTANTS, LIKE ANY OTHER LIVING CREATURE, ARE ALL UNIQUE WITH DIFFERENT POWERS. THERE'S NO ONE OUT THERE LIKE ME, AND THERE'S NO ONE OUT THERE LIKE YOU.
BUT YOU JUST SAID STRYFE--
QUIET.
HOW LONG 'TIL I GET TO USE MY POWERS?
HOPE, PLEASE STOP. YOU'LL GET ALL THE ANSWERS YOU'RE LOOKING FOR IN TIME. RIGHT NOW, WE NEED TO LISTEN SO--
I KNOW. I KNOW. SO WE CAN BE AWARE OF OUR SURROUNDINGS.
WE NEED TO GET SOME REST AND FIND FOOD.
OPEN SPACES BREED PARANOIA. *BISHOP* CAN'T BE FAR BEHIND. HE'S CONVINCED THAT HIS MISSION TO KILL HOPE IS THE ONLY RECOURSE. HIS MIND'S SLIPPING FURTHER INTO DESPERATION.
LOOK!
IT SHOULD BE NORMAL. HE'S BEEN ON OUR TAIL FOR YEARS. BUT I CAN'T SHAKE THE FEELING THAT THIS TIME...

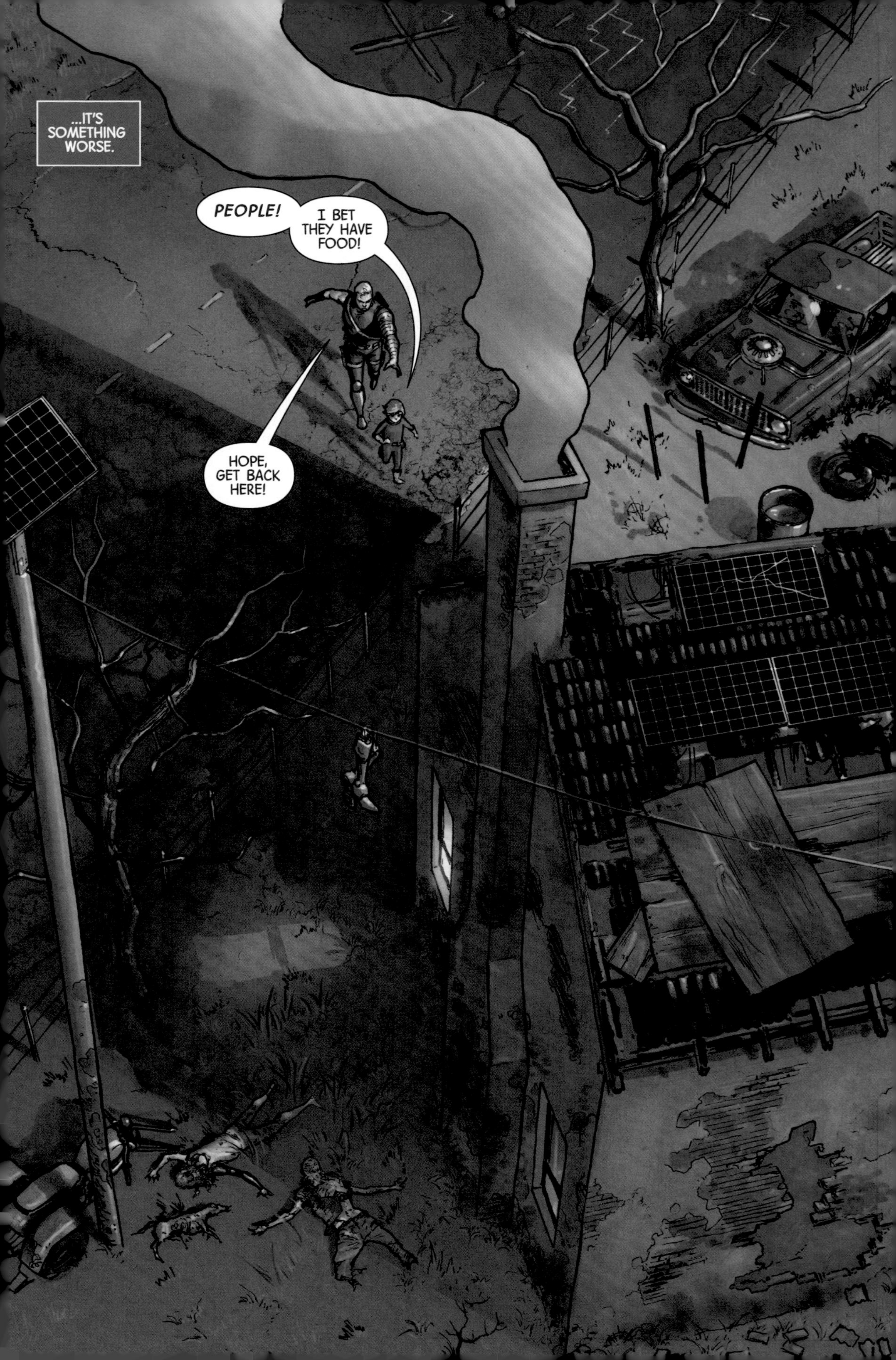
...IT'S SOMETHING WORSE.
PEOPLE!
I BET THEY HAVE FOOD!
HOPE, GET BACK HERE!

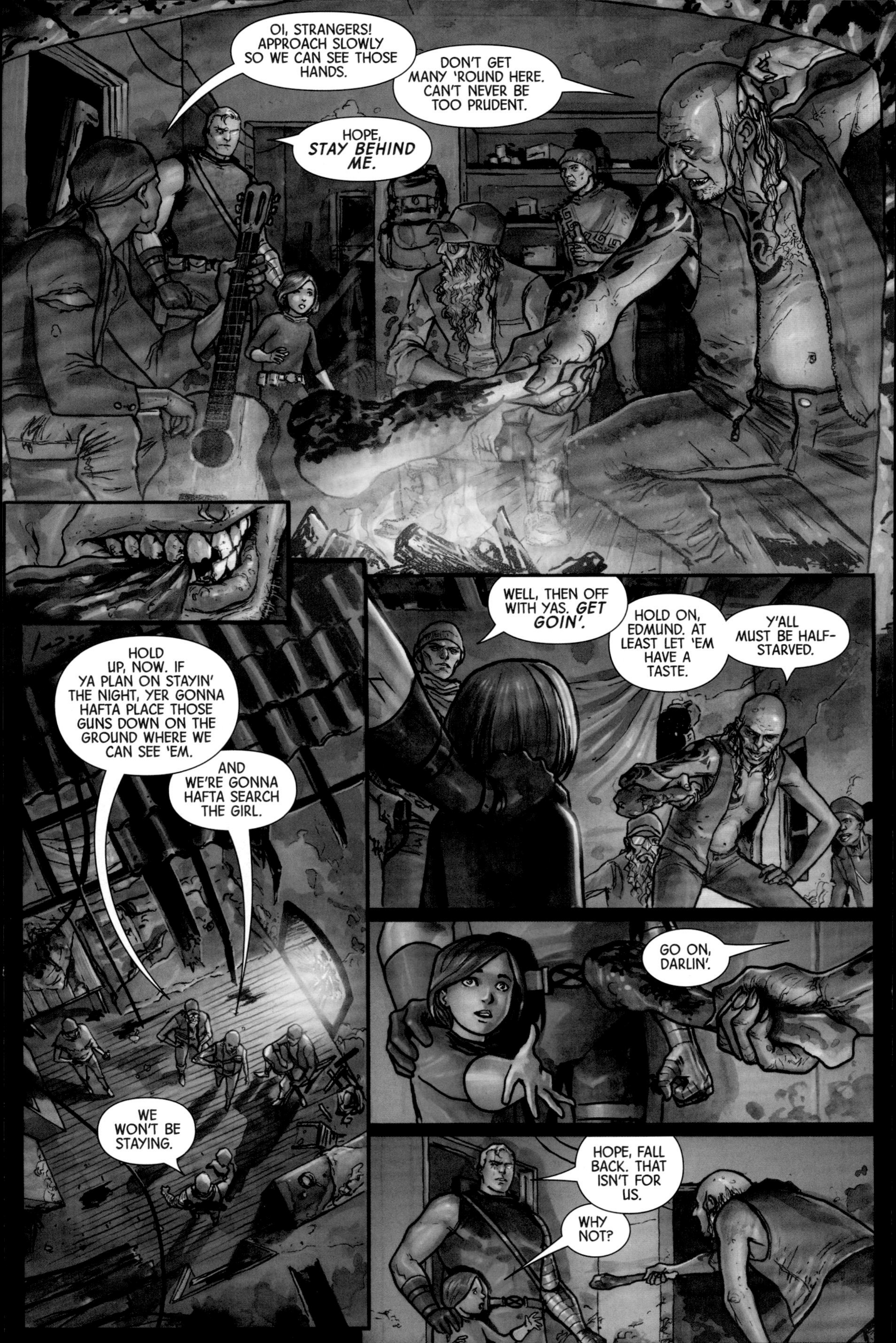
OI, STRANGERS! APPROACH SLOWLY SO WE CAN SEE THOSE HANDS.
DON'T GET MANY 'ROUND HERE. CAN'T NEVER BE TOO PRUDENT.
HOPE, STAY BEHIND ME.
HOLD UP, NOW. IF YA PLAN ON STAYIN' THE NIGHT, YER GONNA HAFTA PLACE THOSE GUNS DOWN ON THE GROUND WHERE WE CAN SEE 'EM.
AND WE'RE GONNA HAFTA SEARCH THE GIRL.
WE WON'T BE STAYING.
WELL, THEN OFF WITH YAS. GET GOIN'.
HOLD ON, EDMUND. AT LEAST LET 'EM HAVE A TASTE.
Y'ALL MUST BE HALF-STARVED.
GO ON, DARLIN'.
HOPE, FALL BACK. THAT ISN'T FOR US.
WHY NOT?

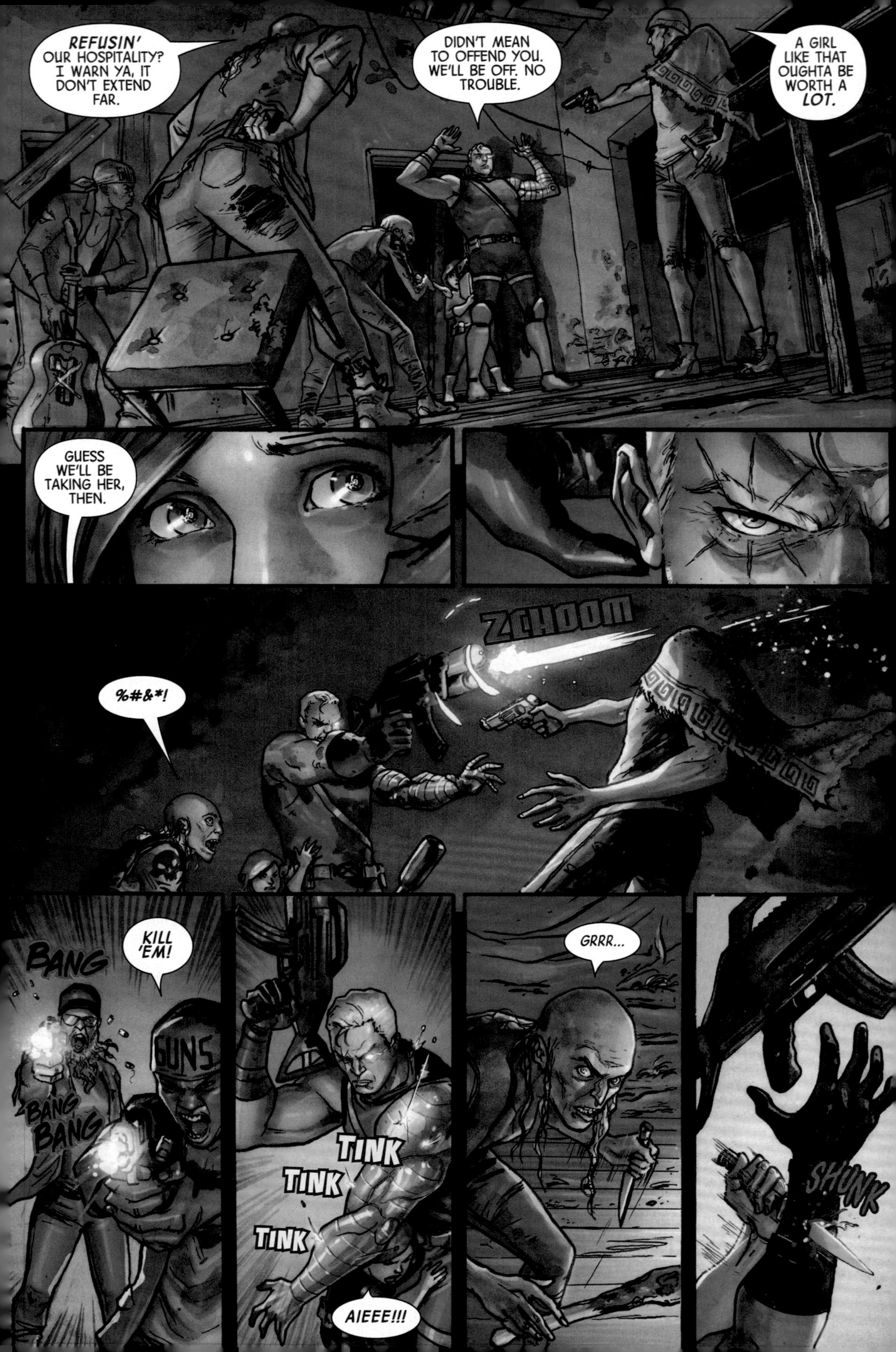
REFUSIN' OUR HOSPITALITY? I WARN YA, IT DON'T EXTEND FAR.
DIDN'T MEAN TO OFFEND YOU. WE'LL BE OFF. NO TROUBLE.
A GIRL LIKE THAT OUGHTA BE WORTH A LOT.
GUESS WE'LL BE TAKING HER, THEN.
ZCHOOM
%#&*!
BANG
KILL 'EM!
GUNS
BANG BANG
TINK
TINK
TINK
AIEEE!!!
GRRR...
SHUNK

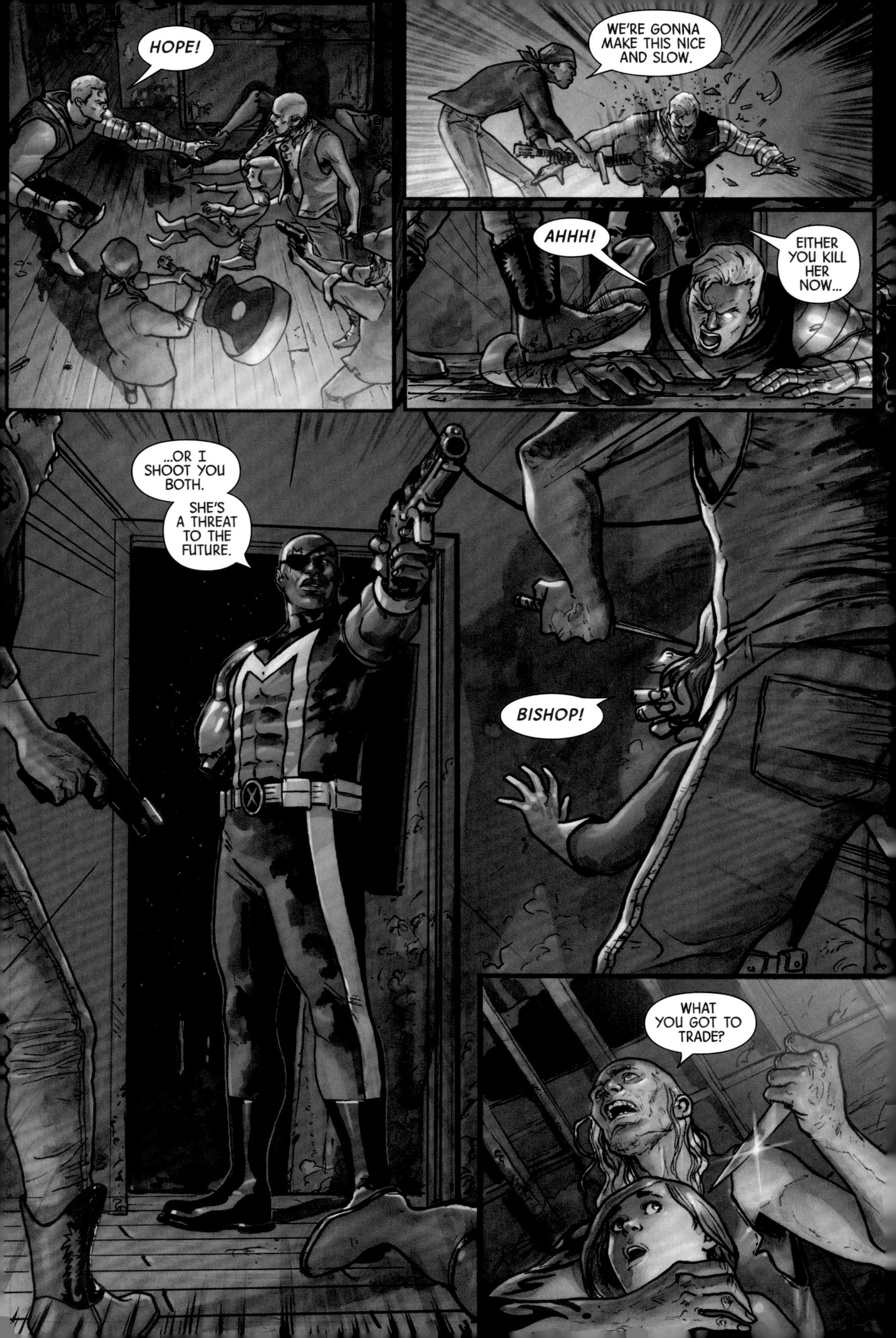
HOPE!
WE'RE GONNA MAKE THIS NICE AND SLOW.
AHHH!
EITHER YOU KILL HER NOW...
...OR I SHOOT YOU BOTH.
SHE'S A THREAT TO THE FUTURE.
BISHOP!
WHAT YOU GOT TO TRADE?

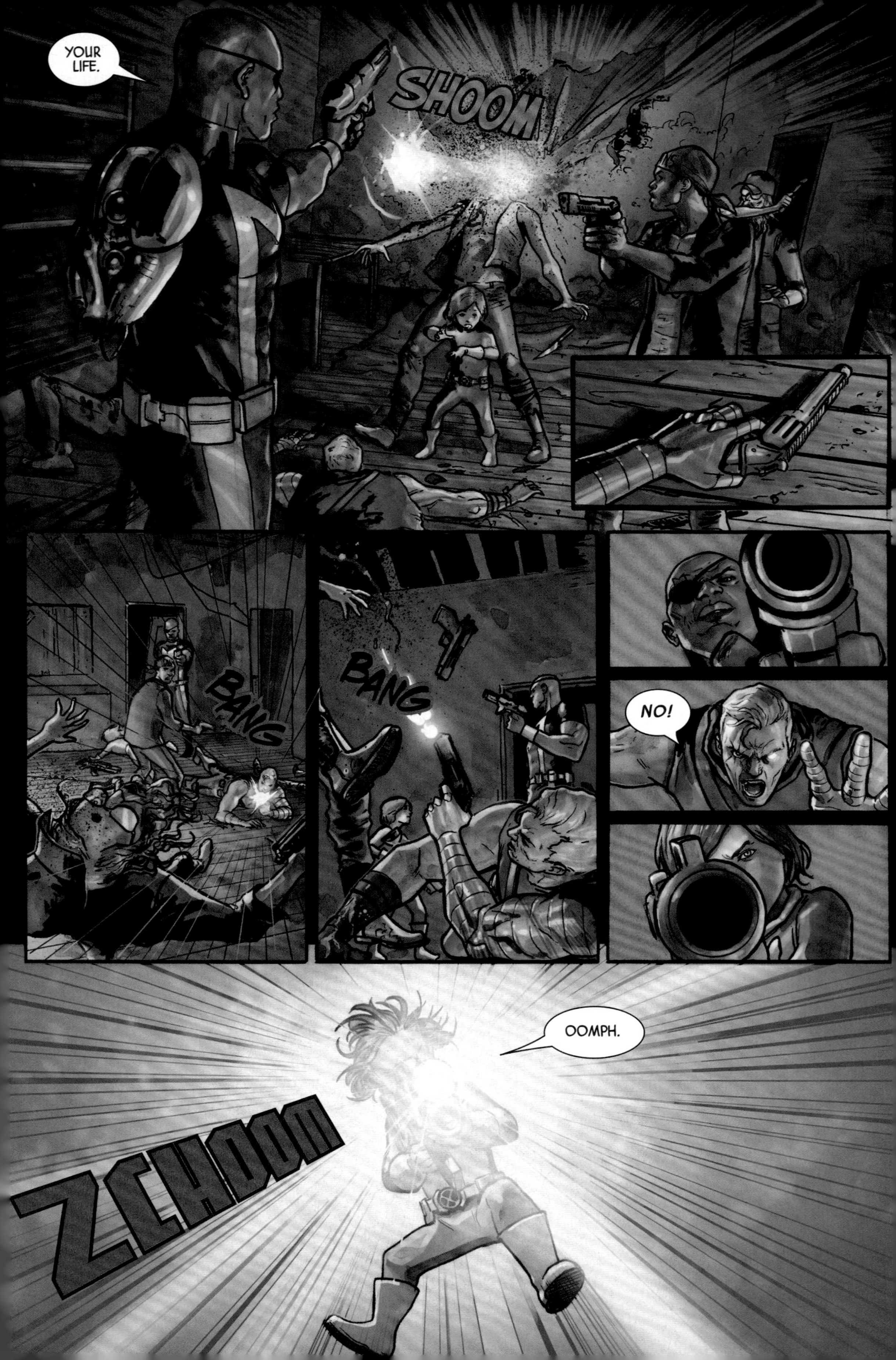
YOUR LIFE.
SHOOM
BANG
BANG
NO!
OOMPH.
ZCHOOM

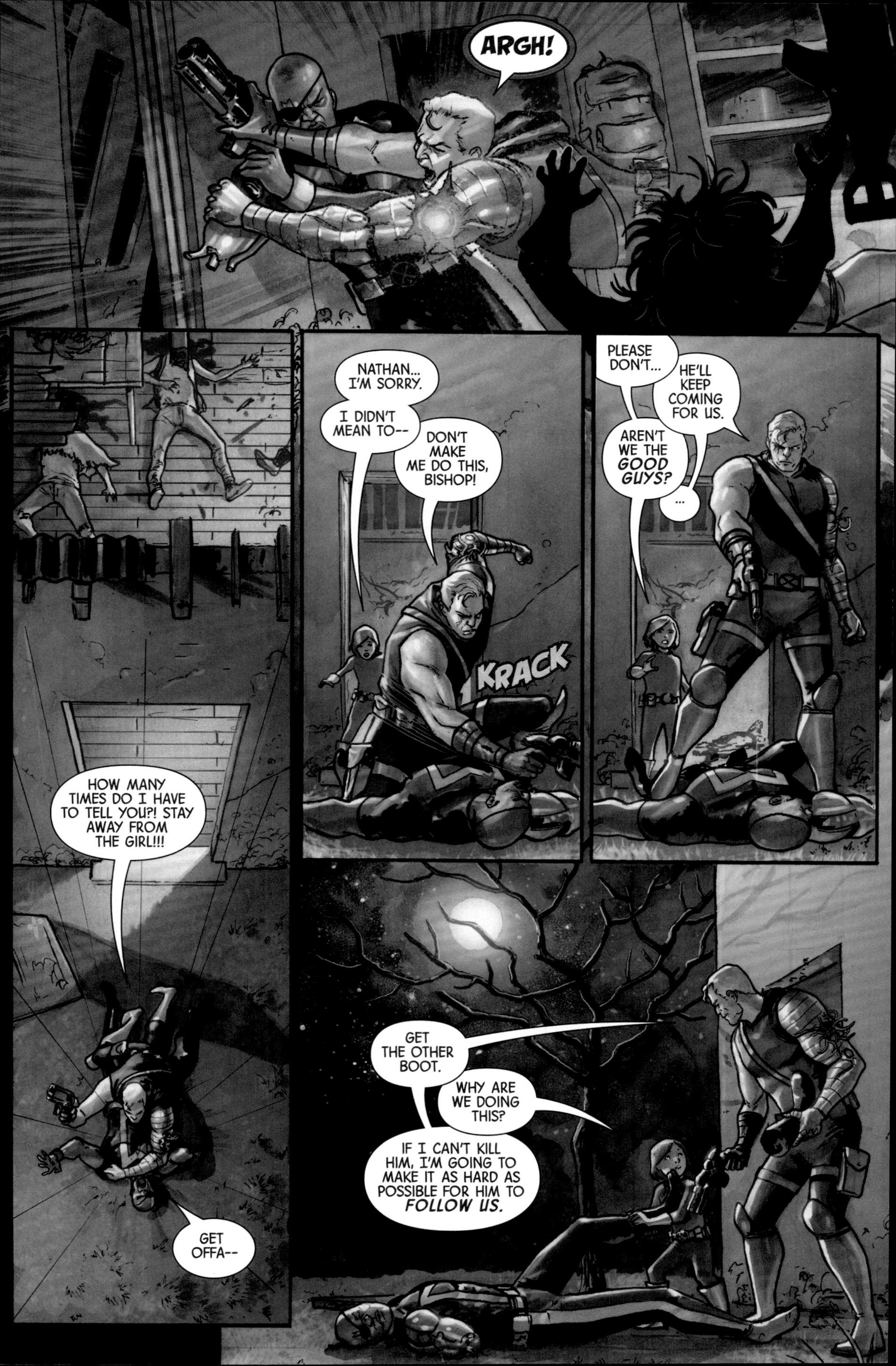
ARGH!
NATHAN... I'M SORRY.
I DIDN'T MEAN TO--
DON'T MAKE ME DO THIS, BISHOP!
KRACK
PLEASE DON'T...
AREN'T WE THE GOOD GUYS?
HE'LL KEEP COMING FOR US.
...
HOW MANY TIMES DO I HAVE TO TELL YOU?! STAY AWAY FROM THE GIRL!!!
GET OFFA--
GET THE OTHER BOOT.
WHY ARE WE DOING THIS?
IF I CAN'T KILL HIM, I'M GOING TO MAKE IT AS HARD AS POSSIBLE FOR HIM TO FOLLOW US.

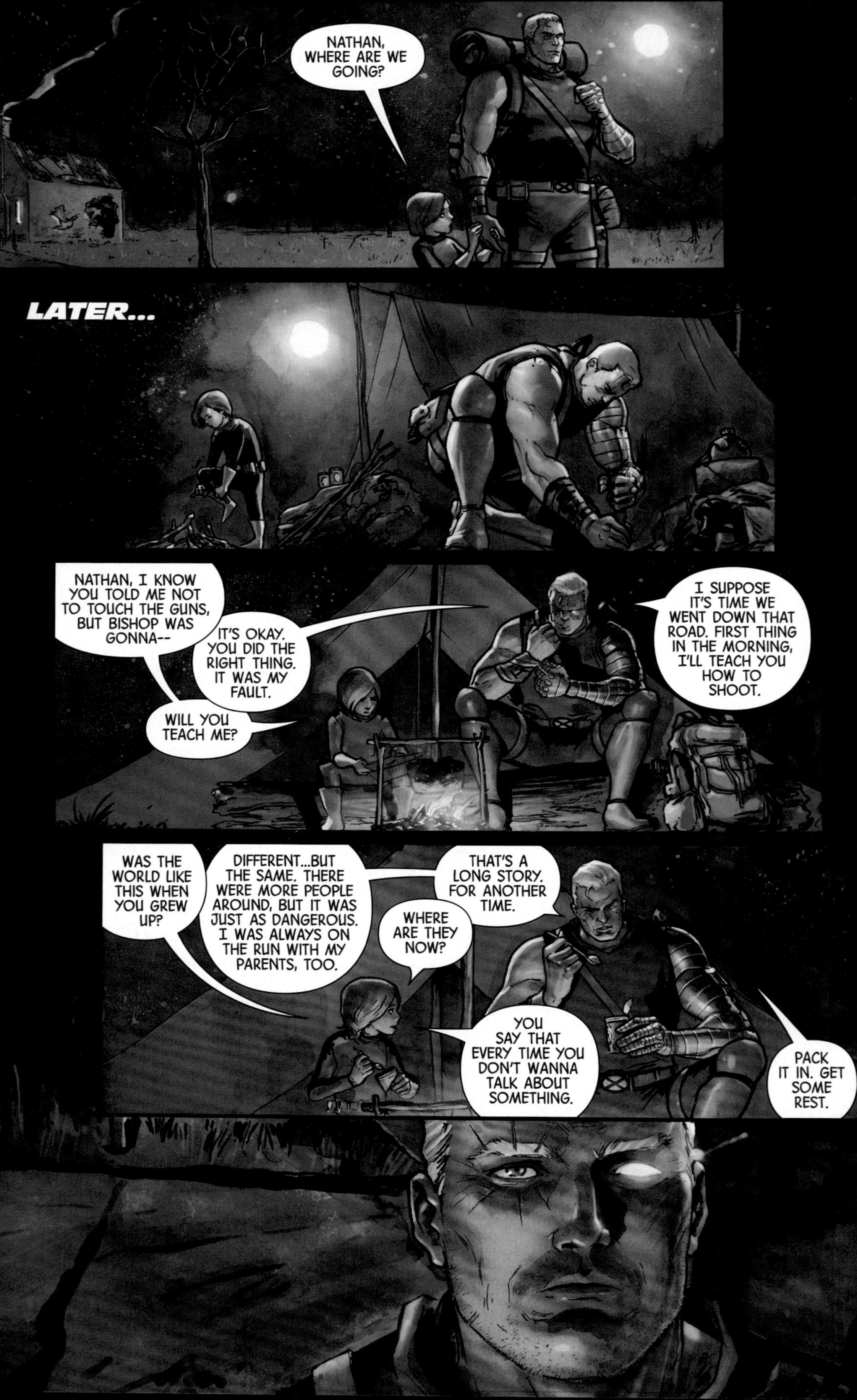
NATHAN, WHERE ARE WE GOING?
LATER...
NATHAN, I KNOW YOU TOLD ME NOT TO TOUCH THE GUNS, BUT BISHOP WAS GONNA--
IT'S OKAY. YOU DID THE RIGHT THING. IT WAS MY FAULT.
WILL YOU TEACH ME?
I SUPPOSE IT'S TIME WE WENT DOWN THAT ROAD. FIRST THING IN THE MORNING, I'LL TEACH YOU HOW TO SHOOT.
WAS THE WORLD LIKE THIS WHEN YOU GREW UP?
DIFFERENT...BUT THE SAME. THERE WERE MORE PEOPLE AROUND, BUT IT WAS JUST AS DANGEROUS. I WAS ALWAYS ON THE RUN WITH MY PARENTS, TOO.
WHERE ARE THEY NOW?
THAT'S A LONG STORY. FOR ANOTHER TIME.
YOU SAY THAT EVERY TIME YOU DON'T WANNA TALK ABOUT SOMETHING.
PACK IT IN. GET SOME REST.

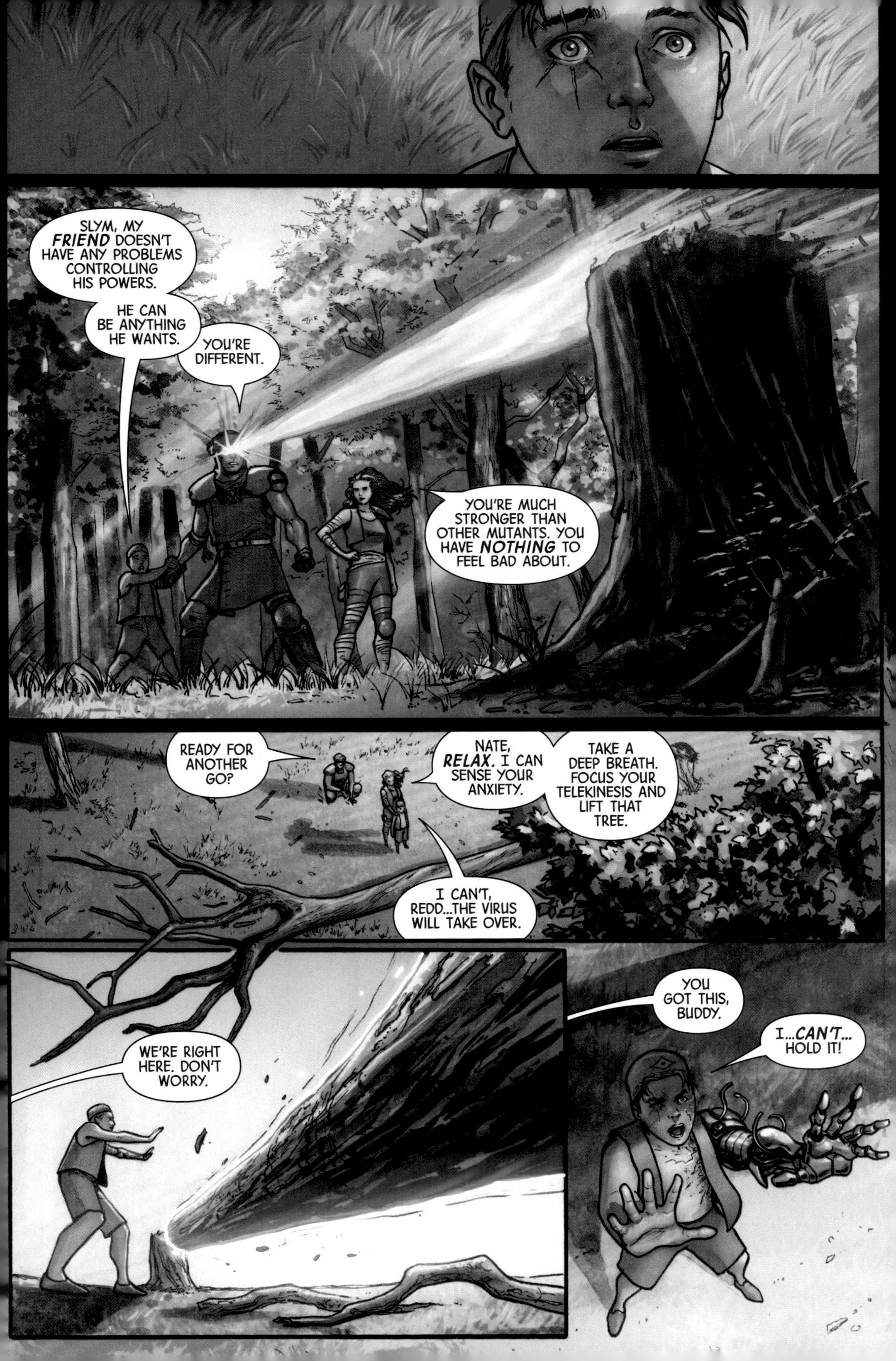
SLYM, MY FRIEND DOESN'T HAVE ANY PROBLEMS CONTROLLING HIS POWERS.
HE CAN BE ANYTHING HE WANTS.
YOU'RE DIFFERENT.
YOU'RE MUCH STRONGER THAN OTHER MUTANTS. YOU HAVE NOTHING TO FEEL BAD ABOUT.
READY FOR ANOTHER GO?
NATE, RELAX. I CAN SENSE YOUR ANXIETY.
TAKE A DEEP BREATH. FOCUS YOUR TELEKINESIS AND LIFT THAT TREE.
I CAN'T, REDD...THE VIRUS WILL TAKE OVER.
WE'RE RIGHT HERE. DON'T WORRY.
YOU GOT THIS, BUDDY.
I...CAN'T... HOLD IT!

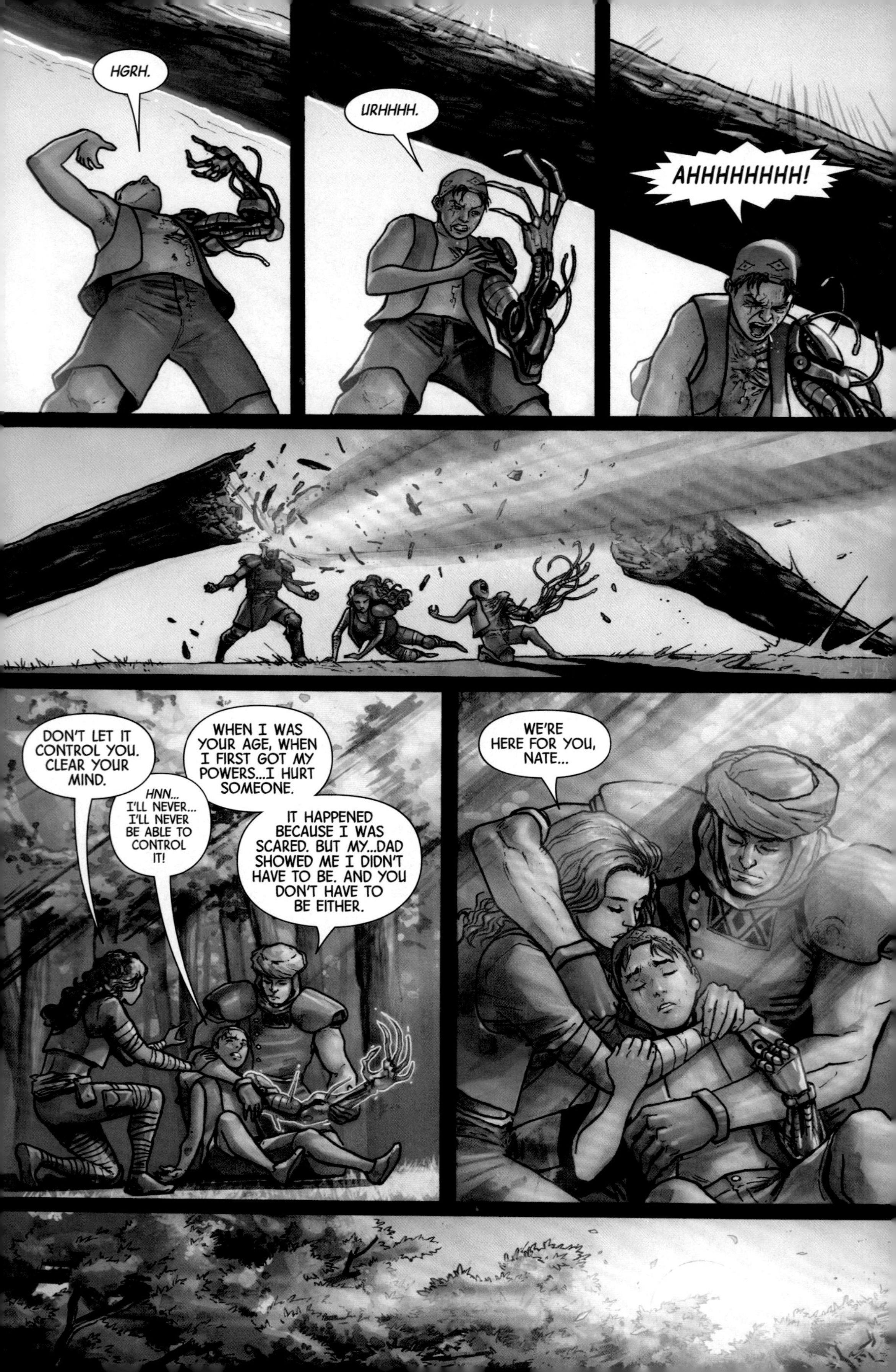
HGRH.
URHHHH.
AHHHHHHHH!
DON'T LET IT CONTROL YOU. CLEAR YOUR MIND.
HNN... I'LL NEVER... I'LL NEVER BE ABLE TO CONTROL IT!
WHEN I WAS YOUR AGE, WHEN I FIRST GOT MY POWERS...I HURT SOMEONE.
IT HAPPENED BECAUSE I WAS SCARED. BUT MY...DAD SHOWED ME I DIDN'T HAVE TO BE. AND YOU DON'T HAVE TO BE EITHER.
WE'RE HERE FOR YOU, NATE...

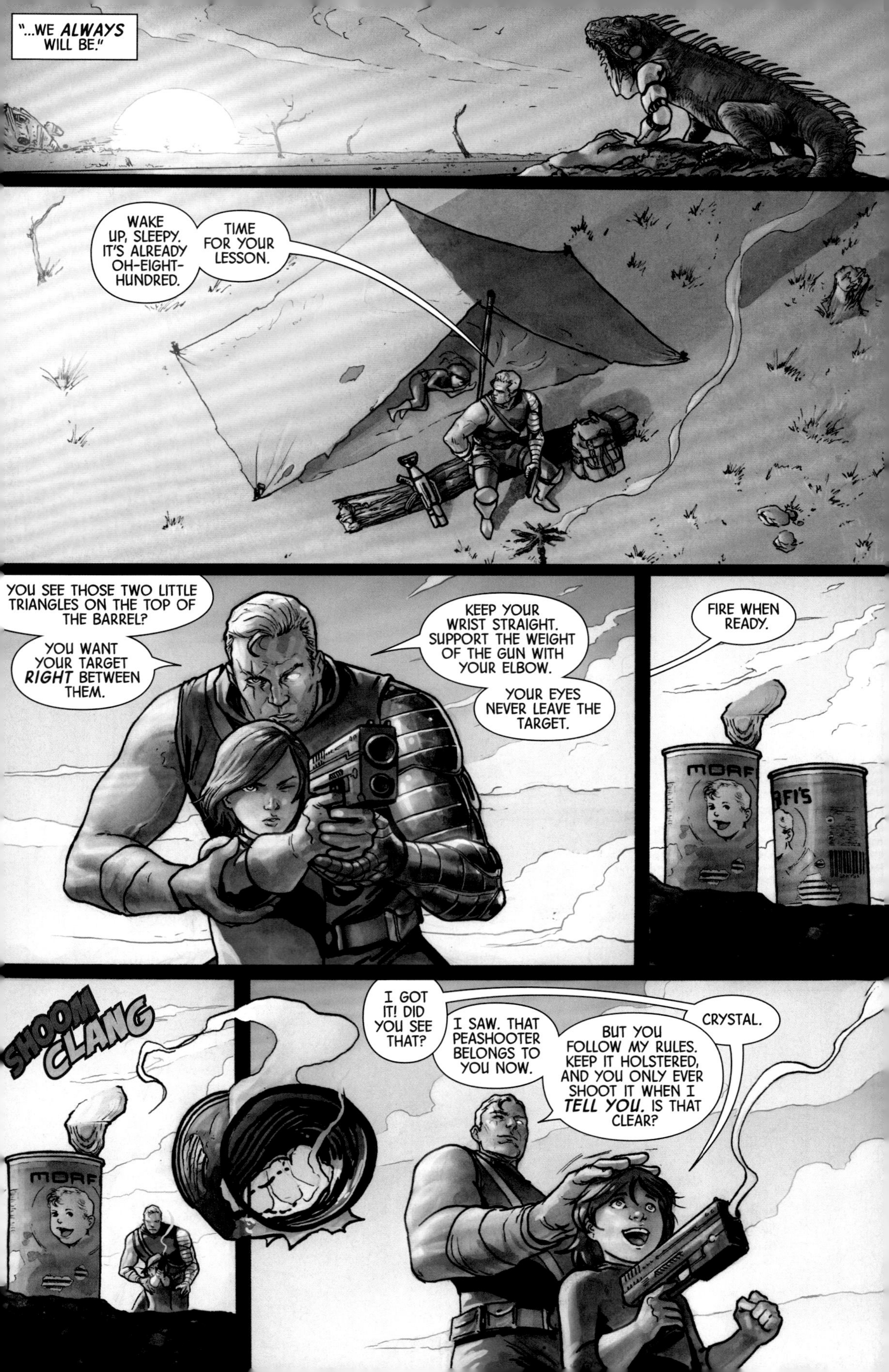
"...WE ALWAYS WILL BE."
WAKE UP, SLEEPY. IT'S ALREADY OH-EIGHT-HUNDRED.
TIME FOR YOUR LESSON.
YOU SEE THOSE TWO LITTLE TRIANGLES ON THE TOP OF THE BARREL?
YOU WANT YOUR TARGET RIGHT BETWEEN THEM.
KEEP YOUR WRIST STRAIGHT. SUPPORT THE WEIGHT OF THE GUN WITH YOUR ELBOW.
YOUR EYES NEVER LEAVE THE TARGET.
FIRE WHEN READY.
MORF
FI'S
SHOOM
CLANG
MORF
I GOT IT! DID YOU SEE THAT?
I SAW. THAT PEASHOOTER BELONGS TO YOU NOW.
BUT YOU FOLLOW MY RULES. KEEP IT HOLSTERED, AND YOU ONLY EVER SHOOT IT WHEN I TELL YOU. IS THAT CLEAR?
CRYSTAL.

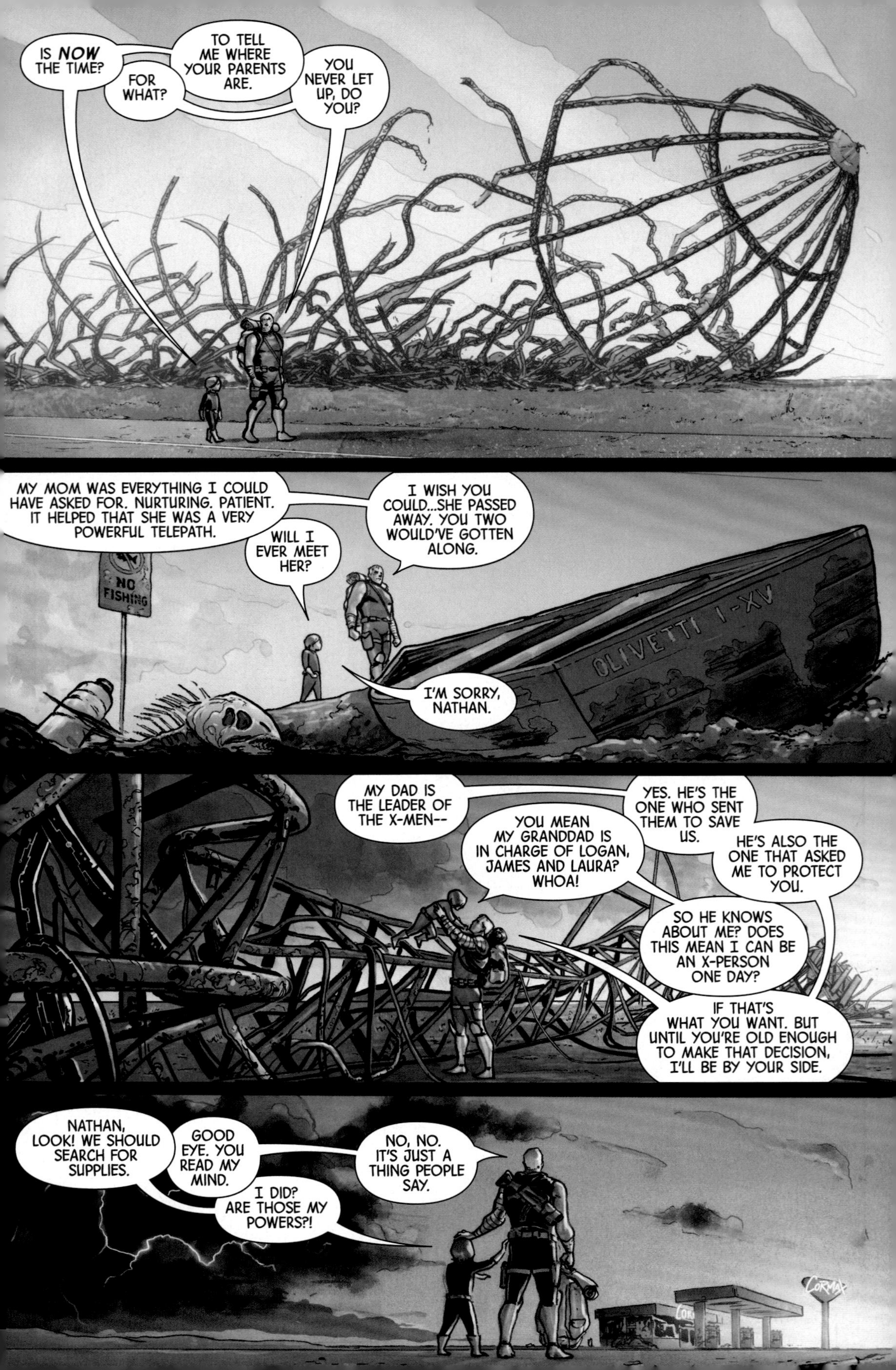
IS NOW THE TIME?
FOR WHAT?
TO TELL ME WHERE YOUR PARENTS ARE.
YOU NEVER LET UP, DO YOU?
MY MOM WAS EVERYTHING I COULD HAVE ASKED FOR. NURTURING. PATIENT. IT HELPED THAT SHE WAS A VERY POWERFUL TELEPATH.
WILL I EVER MEET HER?
I WISH YOU COULD...SHE PASSED AWAY. YOU TWO WOULD'VE GOTTEN ALONG.
NO FISHING
OLIVETTI I-XV
I'M SORRY, NATHAN.
MY DAD IS THE LEADER OF THE X-MEN--
YOU MEAN MY GRANDDAD IS IN CHARGE OF LOGAN, JAMES AND LAURA? WHOA!
YES. HE'S THE ONE WHO SENT THEM TO SAVE US.
HE'S ALSO THE ONE THAT ASKED ME TO PROTECT YOU.
SO HE KNOWS ABOUT ME? DOES THIS MEAN I CAN BE AN X-PERSON ONE DAY?
IF THAT'S WHAT YOU WANT. BUT UNTIL YOU'RE OLD ENOUGH TO MAKE THAT DECISION, I'LL BE BY YOUR SIDE.
NATHAN, LOOK! WE SHOULD SEARCH FOR SUPPLIES.
GOOD EYE. YOU READ MY MIND.
I DID? ARE THOSE MY POWERS?!
NO, NO. IT'S JUST A THING PEOPLE SAY.
CORMAX

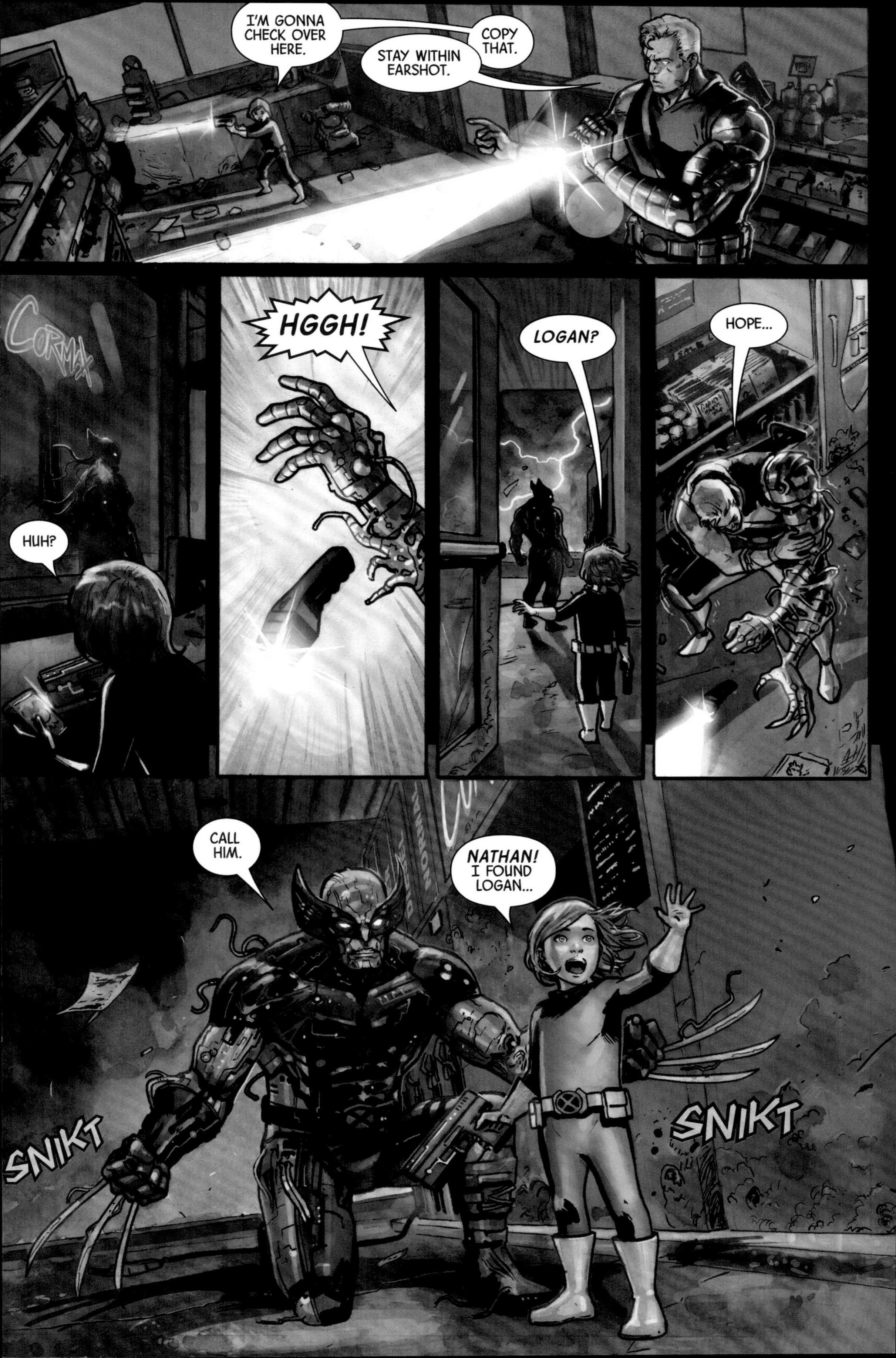
I'M GONNA CHECK OVER HERE.
COPY THAT.
STAY WITHIN EARSHOT.
HUH?
HGGH!
LOGAN?
HOPE...
CALL HIM.
NATHAN! I FOUND LOGAN...
SNIKT
SNIKT

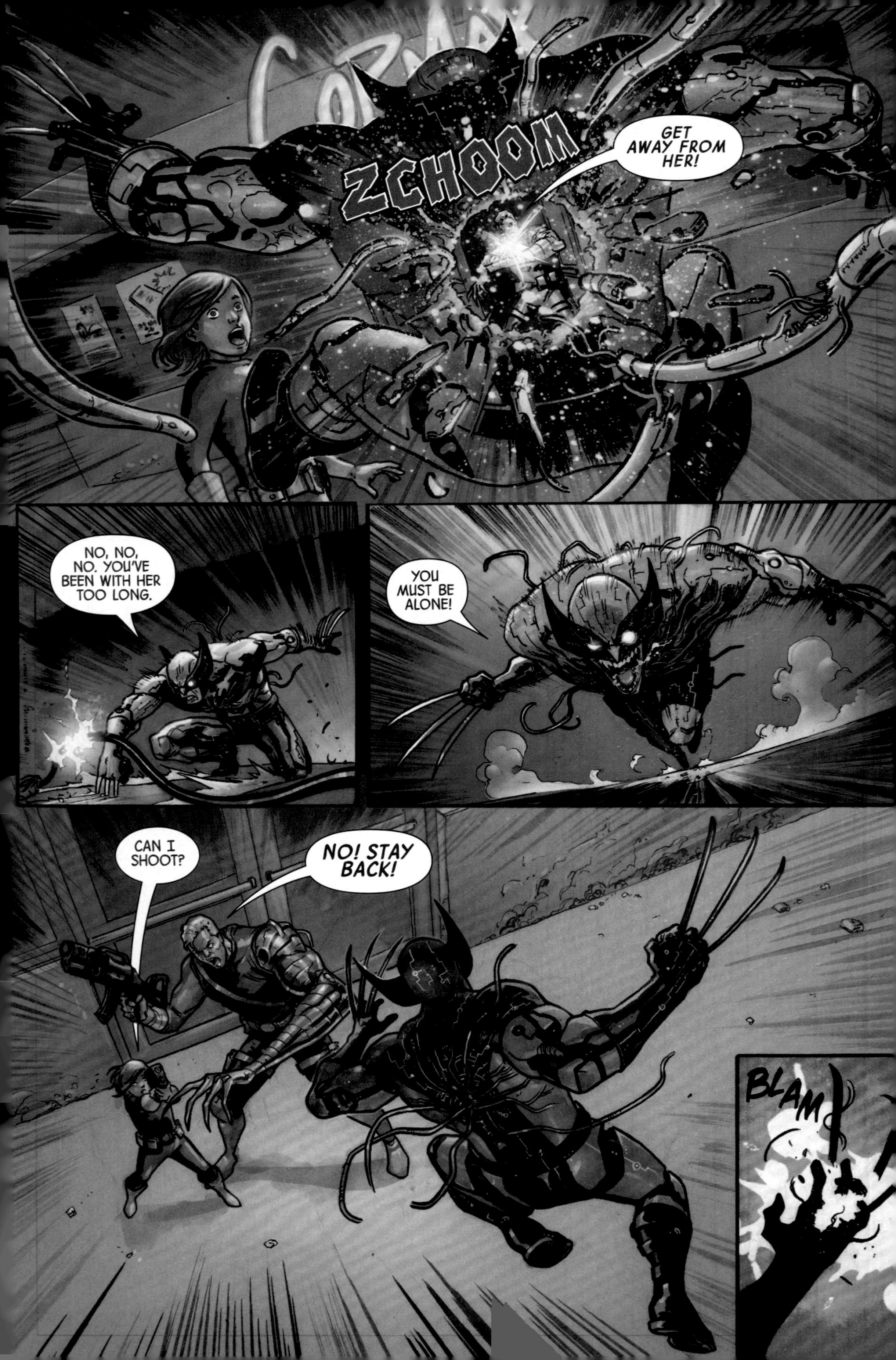
ZCHOOM
GET AWAY FROM HER!
NO, NO, NO. YOU'VE BEEN WITH HER TOO LONG.
YOU MUST BE ALONE!
CAN I SHOOT?
NO! STAY BACK!
BLAM!

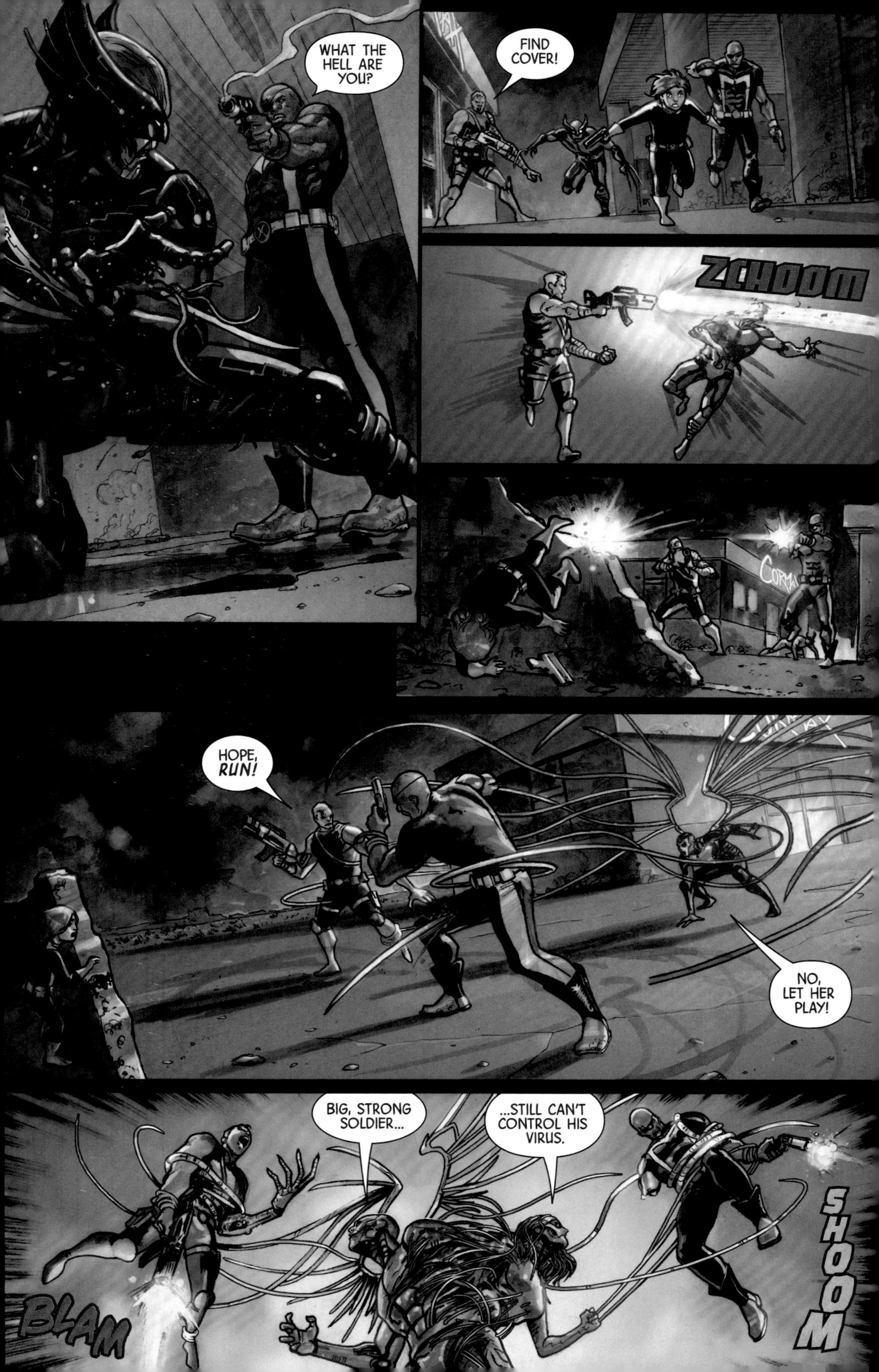

WHAT THE HELL ARE YOU?
FIND COVER!
ZCHOOM
HOPE, RUN!
NO, LET HER PLAY!
BIG, STRONG SOLDIER...
...STILL CAN'T CONTROL HIS VIRUS.
BLAM
SHOOM

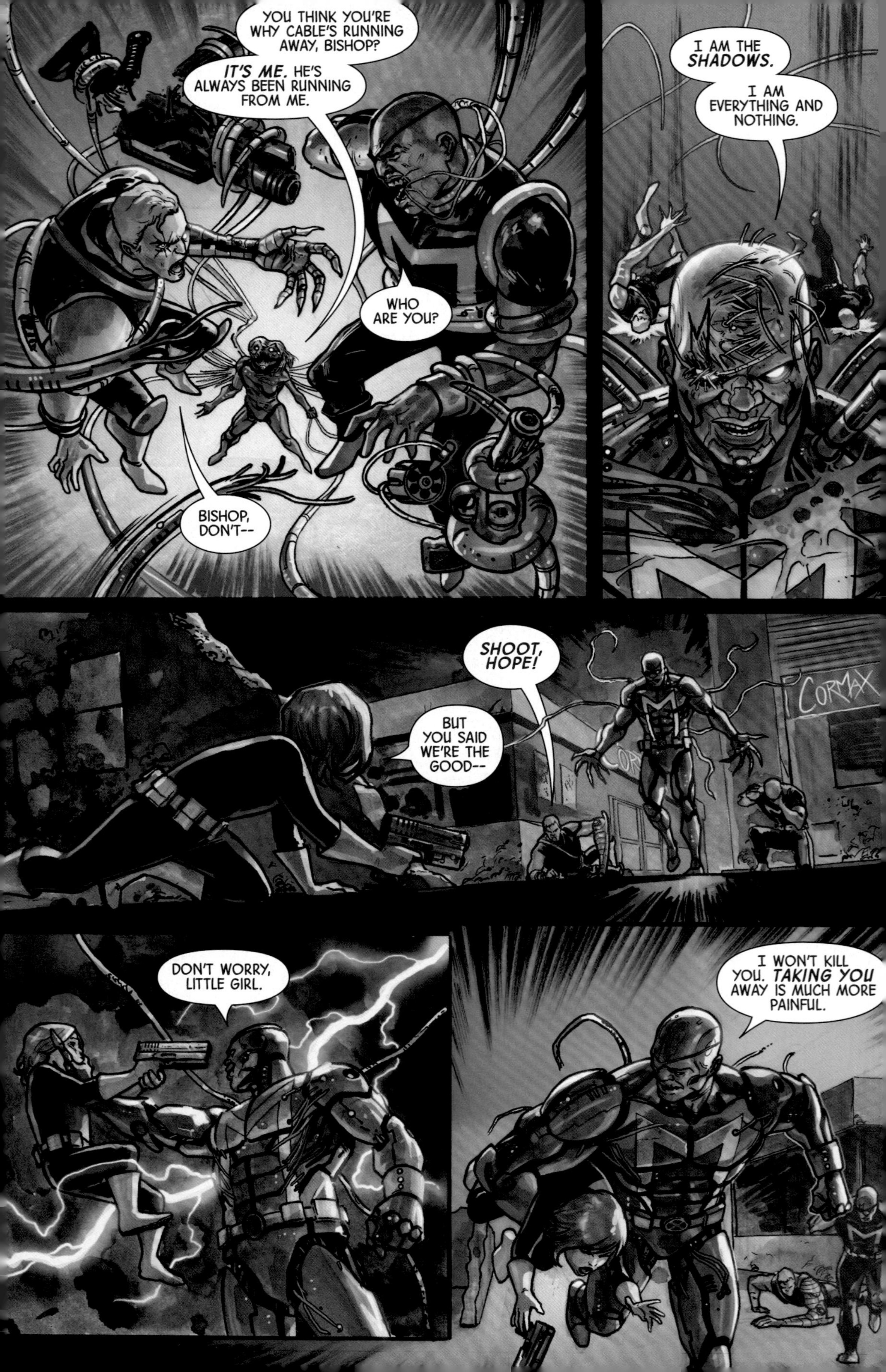
YOU THINK YOU'RE WHY CABLE'S RUNNING AWAY, BISHOP?
IT'S ME. HE'S ALWAYS BEEN RUNNING FROM ME.
WHO ARE YOU?
BISHOP, DON'T--
I AM THE SHADOWS.
I AM EVERYTHING AND NOTHING.
SHOOT, HOPE!
BUT YOU SAID WE'RE THE GOOD--
CORMAX
DON'T WORRY, LITTLE GIRL.
I WON'T KILL YOU. TAKING YOU AWAY IS MUCH MORE PAINFUL.

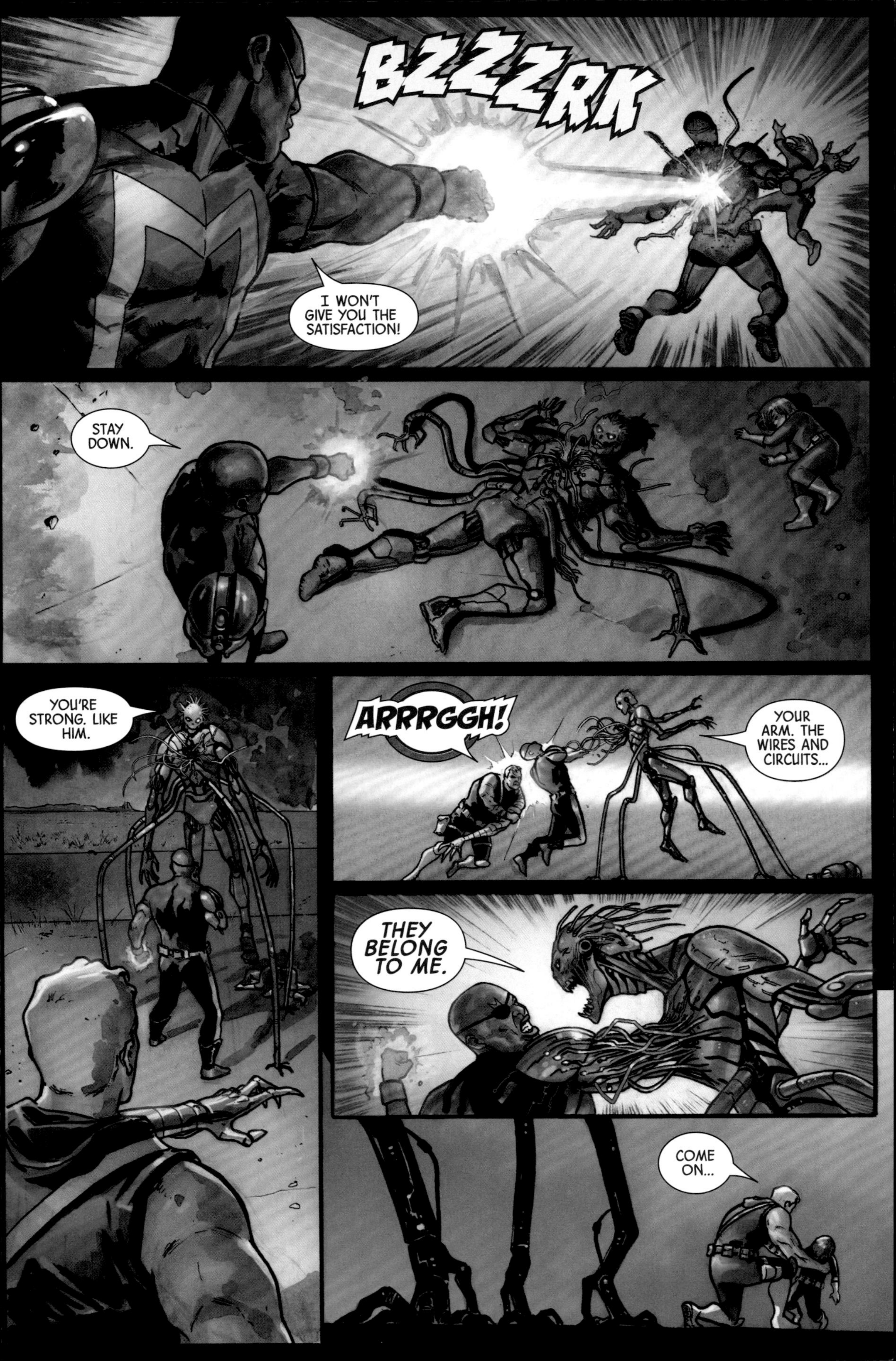
BZZZRK
I WON'T GIVE YOU THE SATISFACTION!
STAY DOWN.
YOU'RE STRONG. LIKE HIM.
ARRRGGH!
YOUR ARM. THE WIRES AND CIRCUITS...
THEY BELONG TO ME.
COME ON...

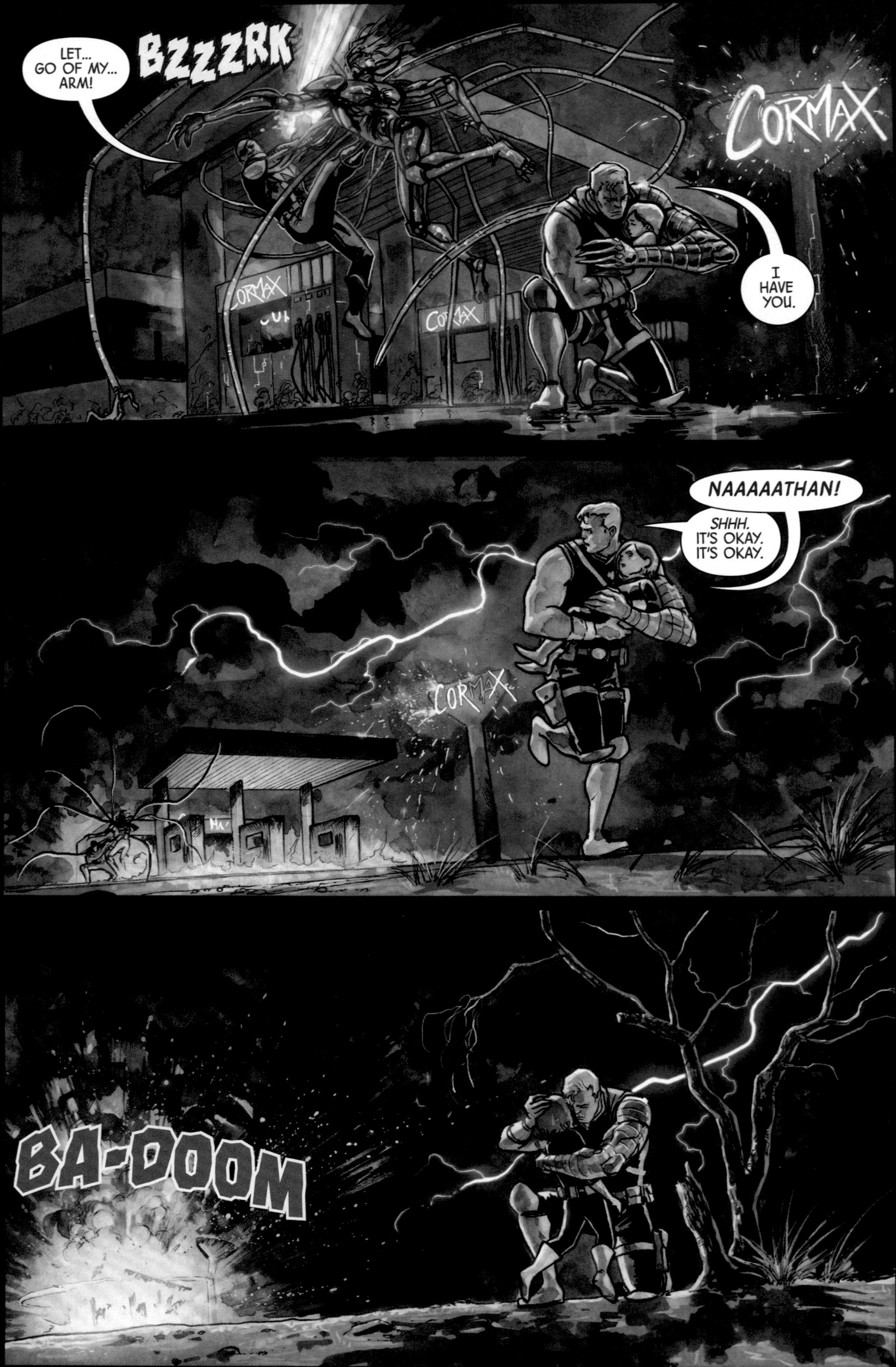
LET... GO OF MY... ARM!
BZZZRK
CORMAX
I HAVE YOU.
NAAAAATHAN!
SHHH. IT'S OKAY. IT'S OKAY.
CORMAX
BA-DOOM

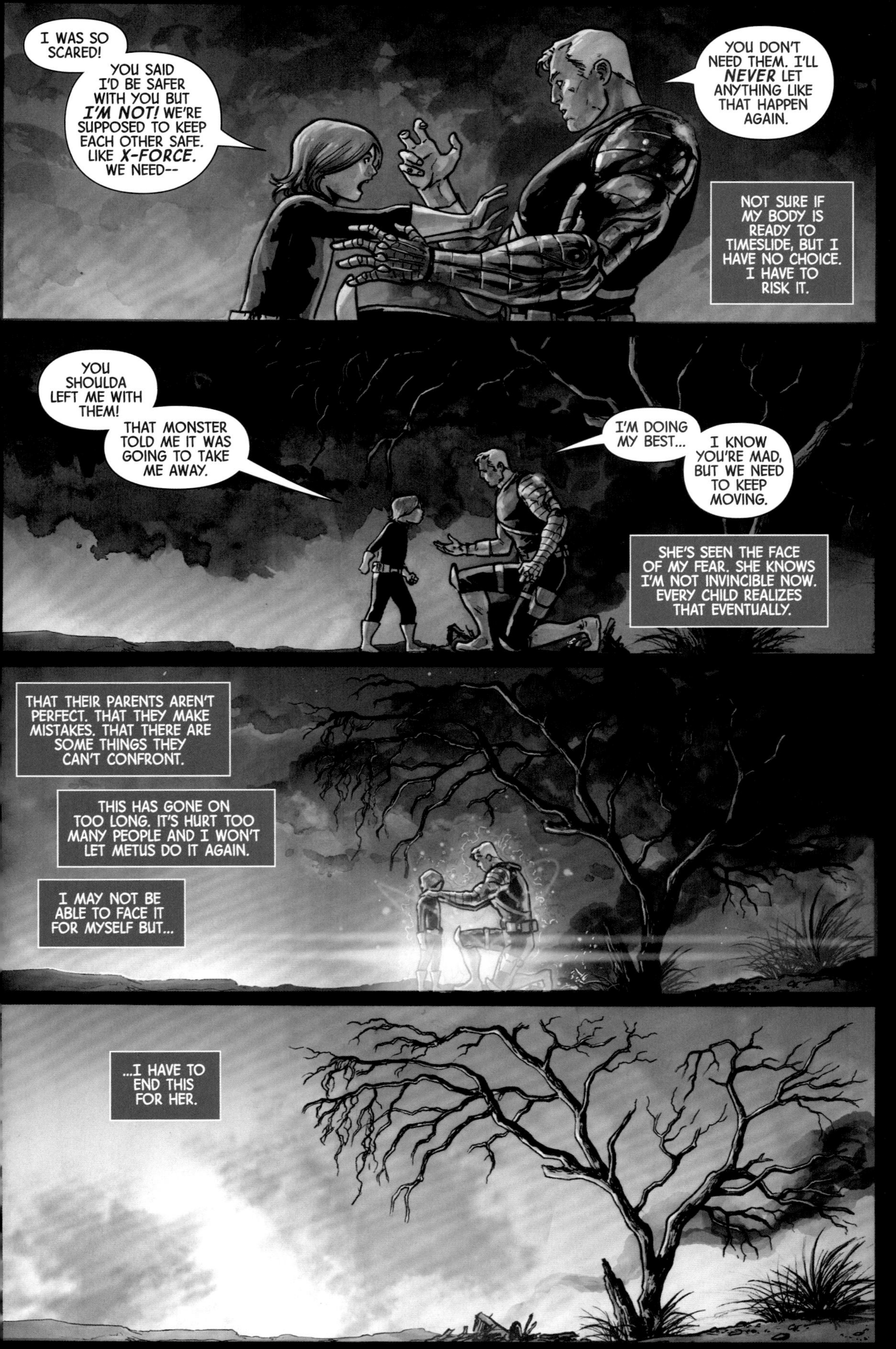
I WAS SO SCARED!
YOU SAID I'D BE SAFER WITH YOU BUT I'M NOT! WE'RE SUPPOSED TO KEEP EACH OTHER SAFE. LIKE X-FORCE. WE NEED--
YOU DON'T NEED THEM. I'LL NEVER LET ANYTHING LIKE THAT HAPPEN AGAIN.
NOT SURE IF MY BODY IS READY TO TIMESLIDE, BUT I HAVE NO CHOICE. I HAVE TO RISK IT.
YOU SHOULDA LEFT ME WITH THEM!
THAT MONSTER TOLD ME IT WAS GOING TO TAKE ME AWAY.
I'M DOING MY BEST...
I KNOW YOU'RE MAD, BUT WE NEED TO KEEP MOVING.
SHE'S SEEN THE FACE OF MY FEAR. SHE KNOWS I'M NOT INVINCIBLE NOW. EVERY CHILD REALIZES THAT EVENTUALLY.
THAT THEIR PARENTS AREN'T PERFECT. THAT THEY MAKE MISTAKES. THAT THERE ARE SOME THINGS THEY CAN'T CONFRONT.
THIS HAS GONE ON TOO LONG. IT'S HURT TOO MANY PEOPLE AND I WON'T LET METUS DO IT AGAIN.
I MAY NOT BE ABLE TO FACE IT FOR MYSELF BUT...
...I HAVE TO END THIS FOR HER.

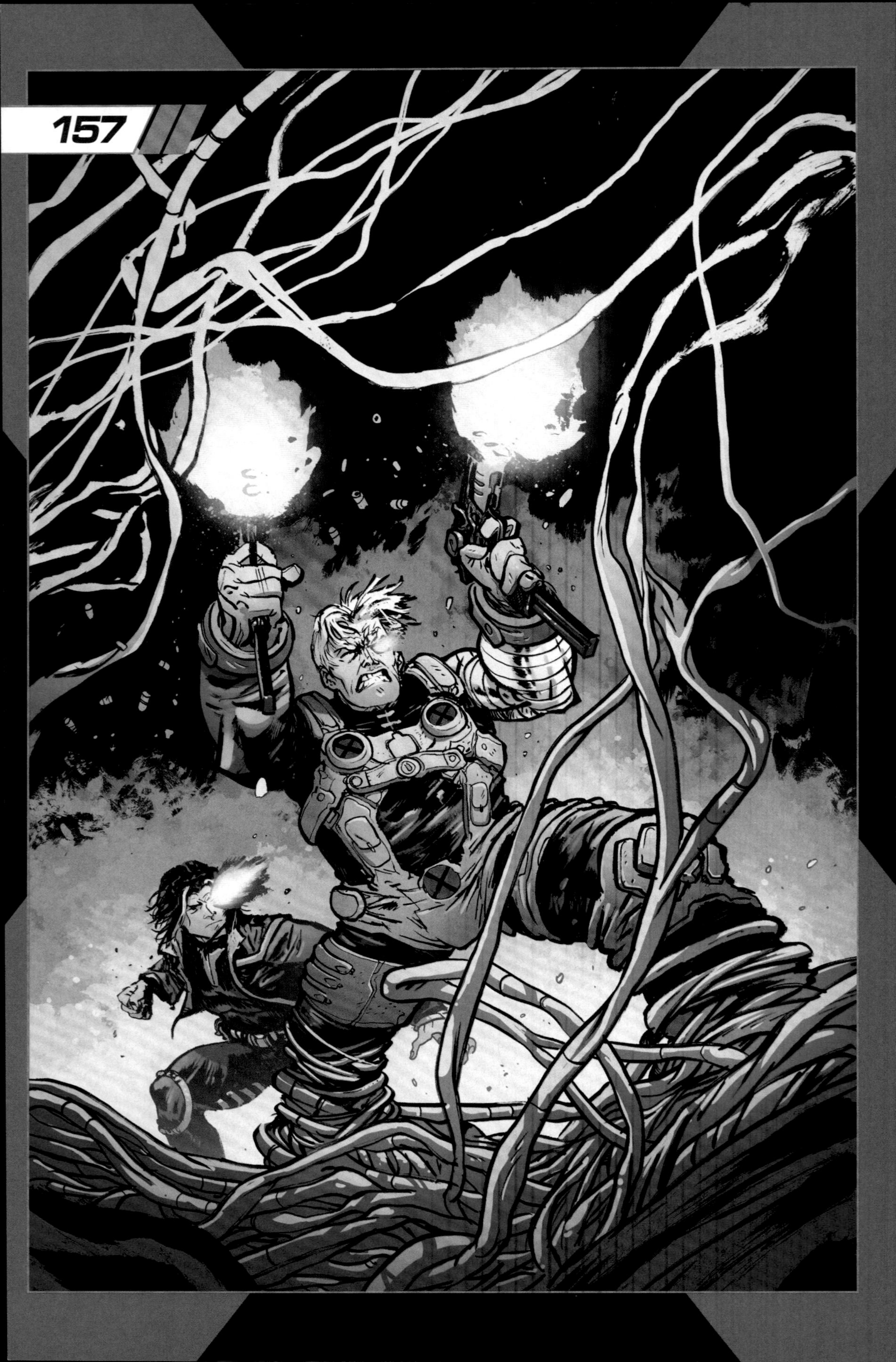
157

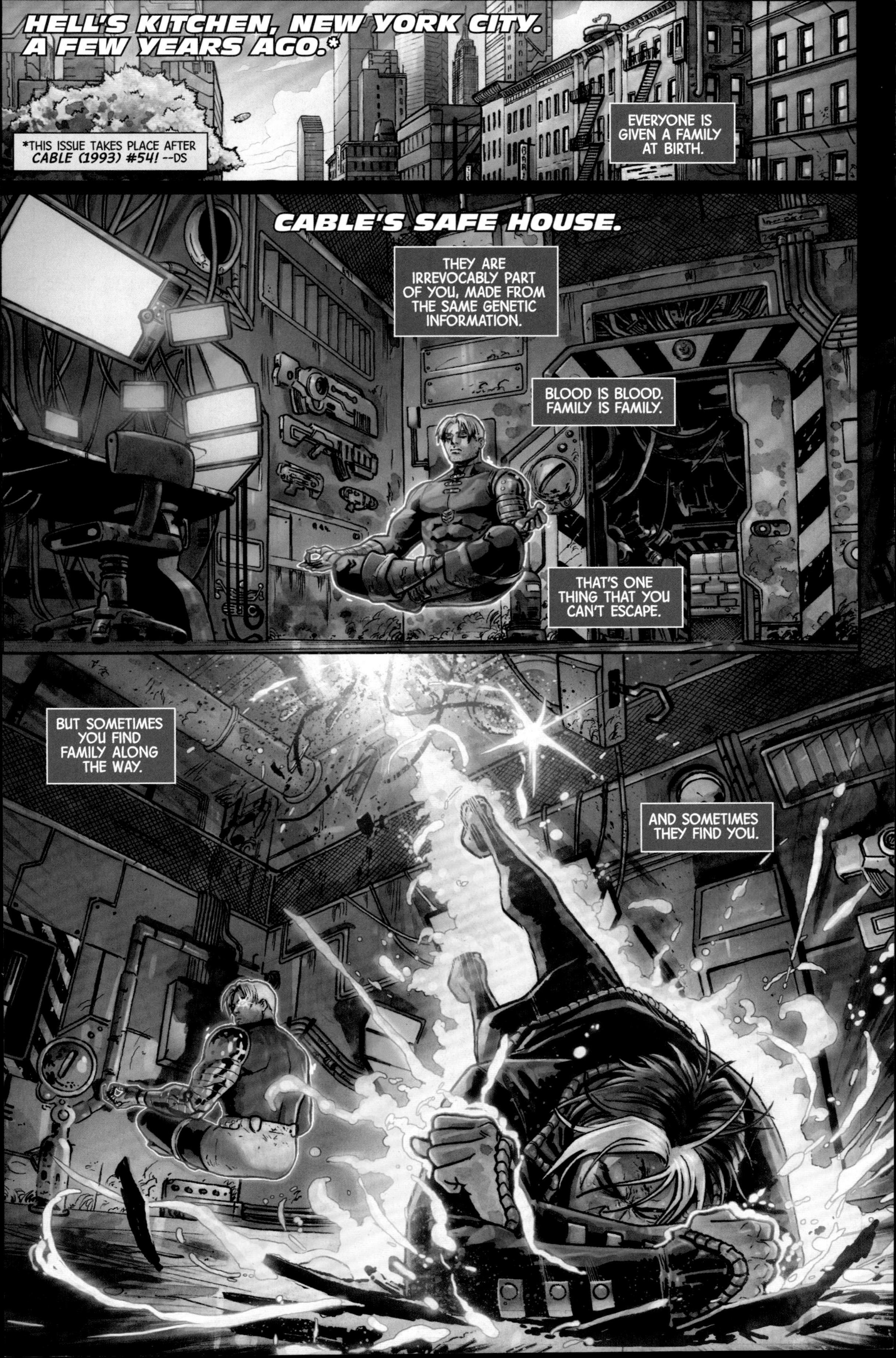
HELL'S KITCHEN, NEW YORK CITY. A FEW YEARS AGO.*
*THIS ISSUE TAKES PLACE AFTER CABLE (1993) #54! --DS
EVERYONE IS GIVEN A FAMILY AT BIRTH.
CABLE'S SAFE HOUSE.
THEY ARE IRREVOCABLY PART OF YOU, MADE FROM THE SAME GENETIC INFORMATION.
BLOOD IS BLOOD. FAMILY IS FAMILY.
THAT'S ONE THING THAT YOU CAN'T ESCAPE.
BUT SOMETIMES YOU FIND FAMILY ALONG THE WAY.
AND SOMETIMES THEY FIND YOU.

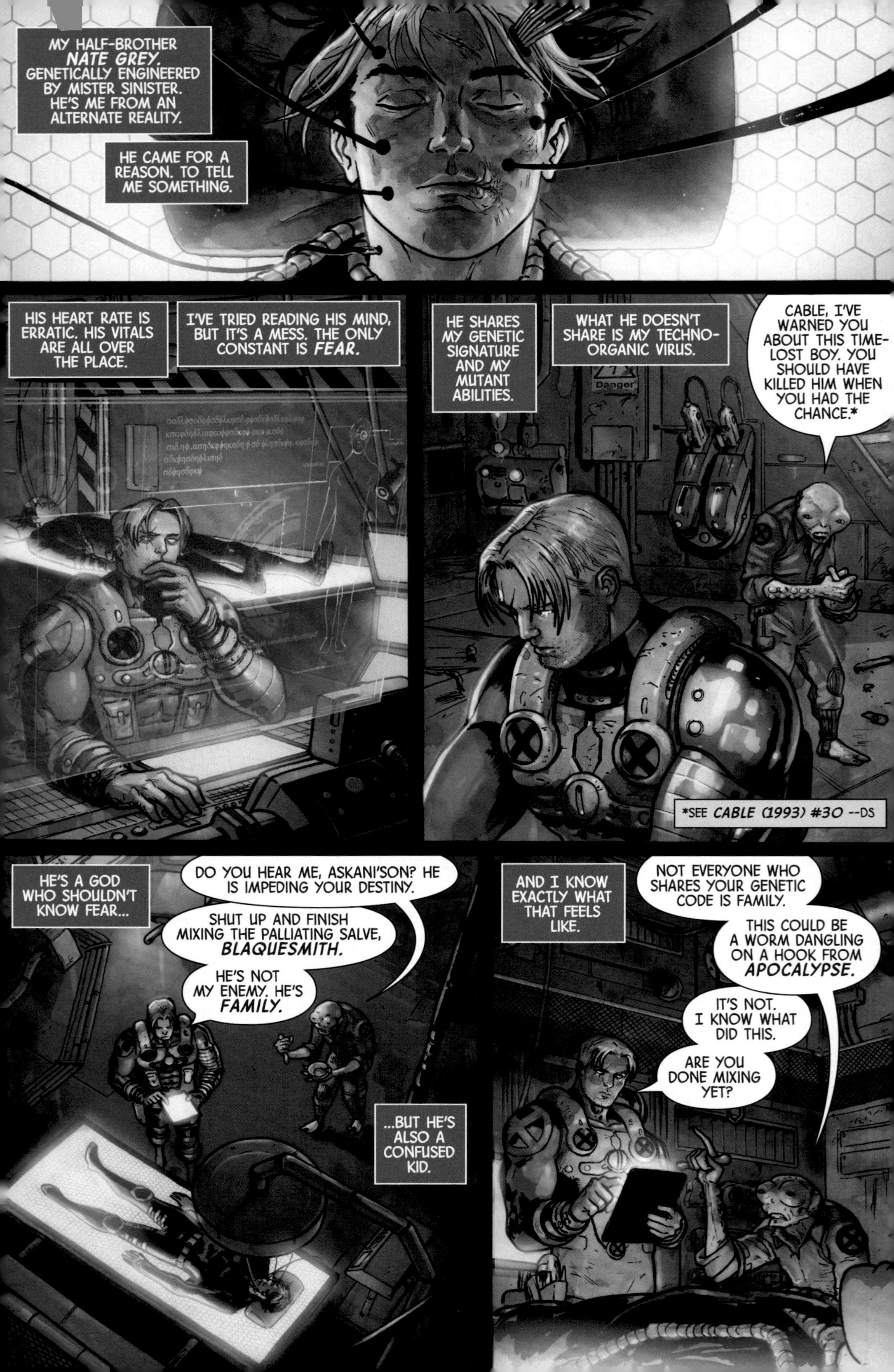
MY HALF-BROTHER NATE GREY. GENETICALLY ENGINEERED BY MISTER SINISTER. HE'S ME FROM AN ALTERNATE REALITY.
HE CAME FOR A REASON. TO TELL ME SOMETHING.
HIS HEART RATE IS ERRATIC. HIS VITALS ARE ALL OVER THE PLACE.
I'VE TRIED READING HIS MIND, BUT IT'S A MESS. THE ONLY CONSTANT IS FEAR.
HE SHARES MY GENETIC SIGNATURE AND MY MUTANT ABILITIES.
WHAT HE DOESN'T SHARE IS MY TECHNO-ORGANIC VIRUS.
Danger
CABLE, I'VE WARNED YOU ABOUT THIS TIME-LOST BOY. YOU SHOULD HAVE KILLED HIM WHEN YOU HAD THE CHANCE.*
*SEE CABLE (1993) #30 --DS
HE'S A GOD WHO SHOULDN'T KNOW FEAR...
DO YOU HEAR ME, ASKANI'SON? HE IS IMPEDING YOUR DESTINY.
SHUT UP AND FINISH MIXING THE PALLIATING SALVE, BLAQUESMITH.
HE'S NOT MY ENEMY. HE'S FAMILY.
...BUT HE'S ALSO A CONFUSED KID.
AND I KNOW EXACTLY WHAT THAT FEELS LIKE.
NOT EVERYONE WHO SHARES YOUR GENETIC CODE IS FAMILY.
THIS COULD BE A WORM DANGLING ON A HOOK FROM APOCALYPSE.
IT'S NOT. I KNOW WHAT DID THIS.
ARE YOU DONE MIXING YET?

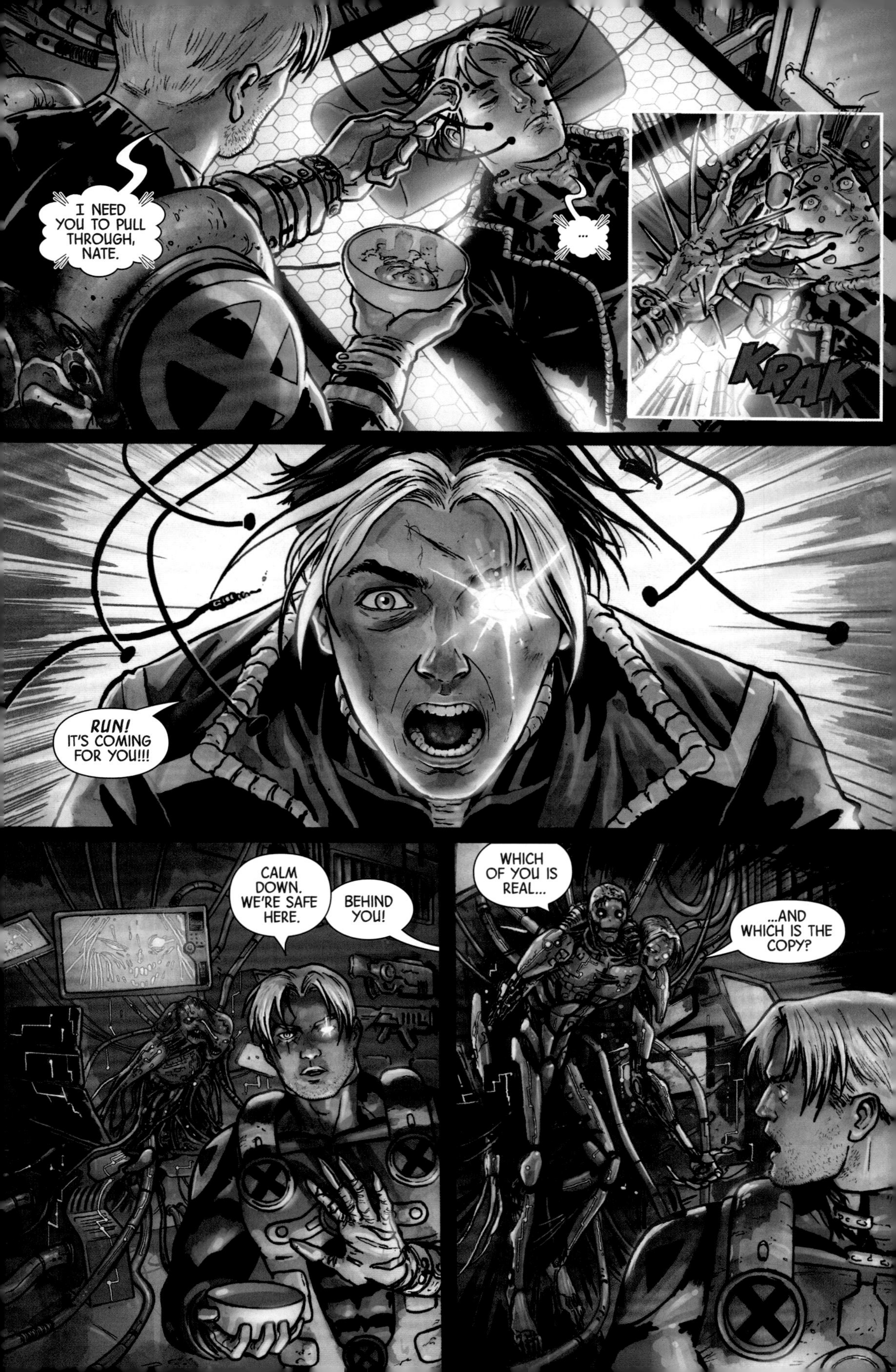
I NEED YOU TO PULL THROUGH, NATE.
...
KRAK
RUN! IT'S COMING FOR YOU!!!
CALM DOWN. WE'RE SAFE HERE.
BEHIND YOU!
WHICH OF YOU IS REAL...
...AND WHICH IS THE COPY?

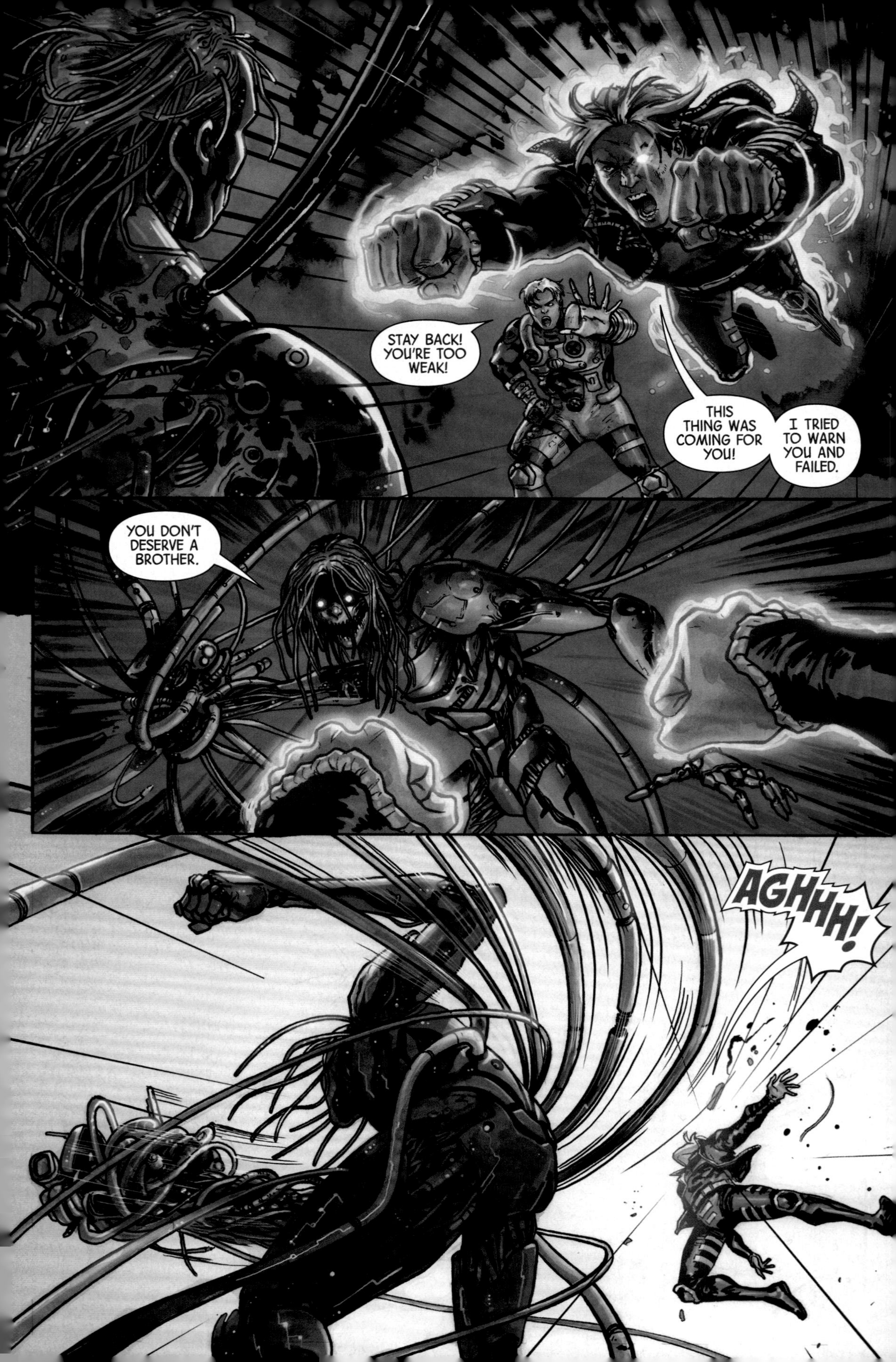
STAY BACK! YOU'RE TOO WEAK!
THIS THING WAS COMING FOR YOU!
I TRIED TO WARN YOU AND FAILED.
YOU DON'T DESERVE A BROTHER.
AGHHH!

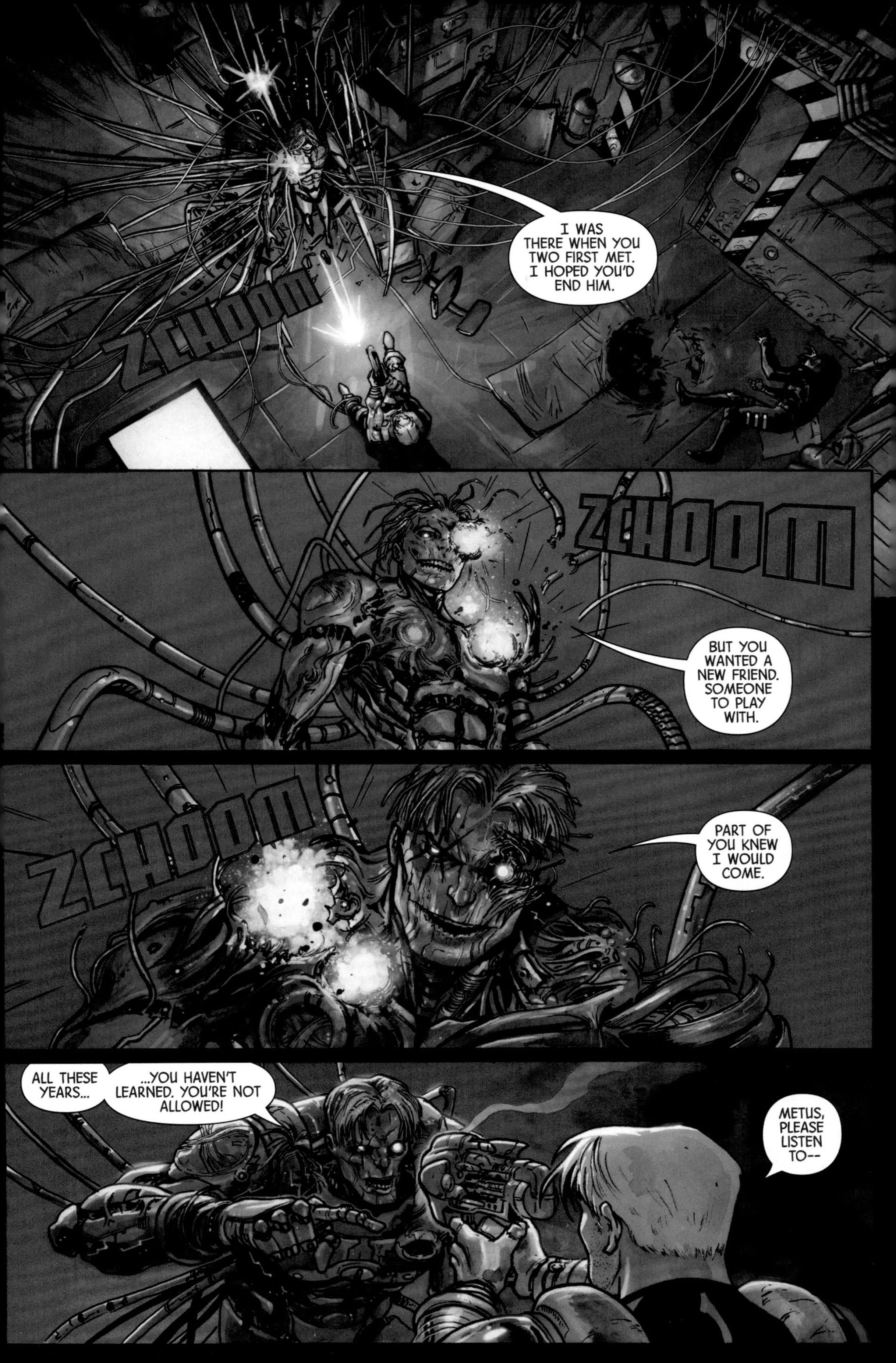
ZCHOOM
I WAS THERE WHEN YOU TWO FIRST MET. I HOPED YOU'D END HIM.
ZCHOOM
BUT YOU WANTED A NEW FRIEND. SOMEONE TO PLAY WITH.
ZCHOOM
PART OF YOU KNEW I WOULD COME.
ALL THESE YEARS...
...YOU HAVEN'T LEARNED. YOU'RE NOT ALLOWED!
METUS, PLEASE LISTEN TO--

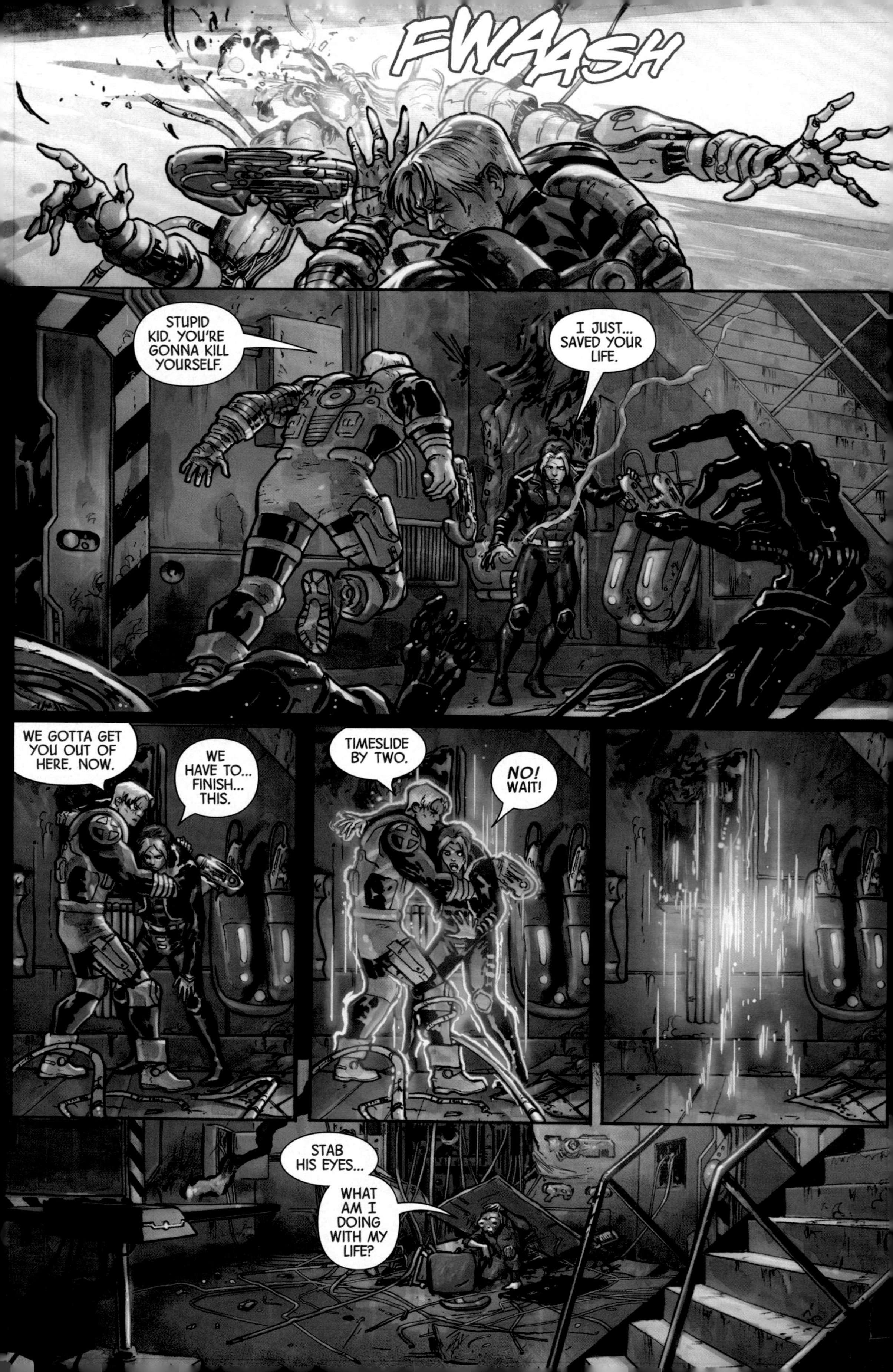
FWAAASH
STUPID KID. YOU'RE GONNA KILL YOURSELF.
I JUST... SAVED YOUR LIFE.
WE GOTTA GET YOU OUT OF HERE. NOW.
WE HAVE TO... FINISH... THIS.
TIMESLIDE BY TWO.
NO! WAIT!
STAB HIS EYES...
WHAT AM I DOING WITH MY LIFE?

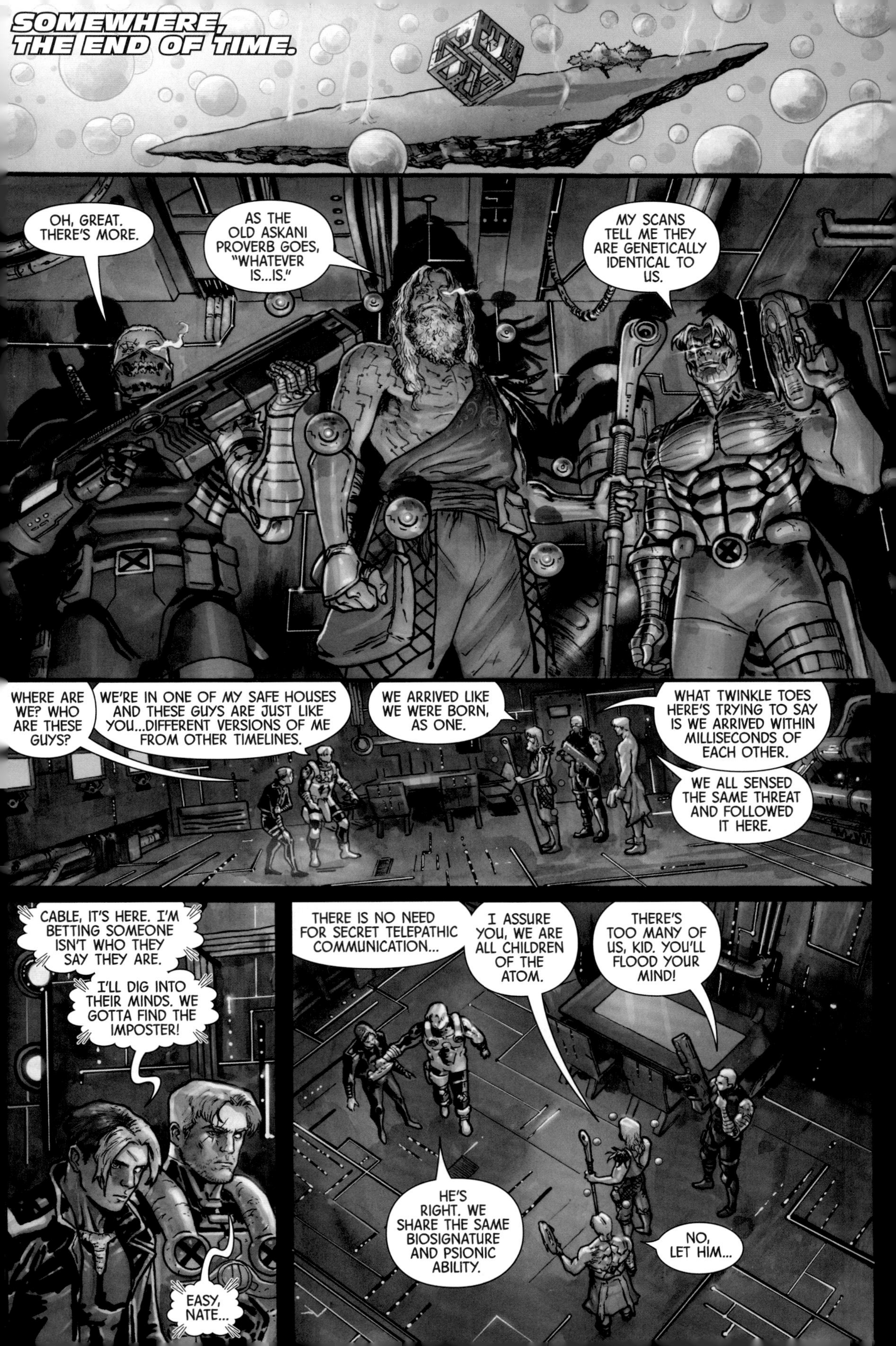
SOMEWHERE, THE END OF TIME.
OH, GREAT. THERE'S MORE.
AS THE OLD ASKANI PROVERB GOES, "WHATEVER IS...IS."
MY SCANS TELL ME THEY ARE GENETICALLY IDENTICAL TO US.
WHERE ARE WE? WHO ARE THESE GUYS?
WE'RE IN ONE OF MY SAFE HOUSES AND THESE GUYS ARE JUST LIKE YOU...DIFFERENT VERSIONS OF ME FROM OTHER TIMELINES.
WE ARRIVED LIKE WE WERE BORN, AS ONE.
WHAT TWINKLE TOES HERE'S TRYING TO SAY IS WE ARRIVED WITHIN MILLISECONDS OF EACH OTHER.
WE ALL SENSED THE SAME THREAT AND FOLLOWED IT HERE.
CABLE, IT'S HERE. I'M BETTING SOMEONE ISN'T WHO THEY SAY THEY ARE.
I'LL DIG INTO THEIR MINDS. WE GOTTA FIND THE IMPOSTER!
EASY, NATE...
THERE IS NO NEED FOR SECRET TELEPATHIC COMMUNICATION...
I ASSURE YOU, WE ARE ALL CHILDREN OF THE ATOM.
THERE'S TOO MANY OF US, KID. YOU'LL FLOOD YOUR MIND!
HE'S RIGHT. WE SHARE THE SAME BIOSIGNATURE AND PSIONIC ABILITY.
NO, LET HIM...

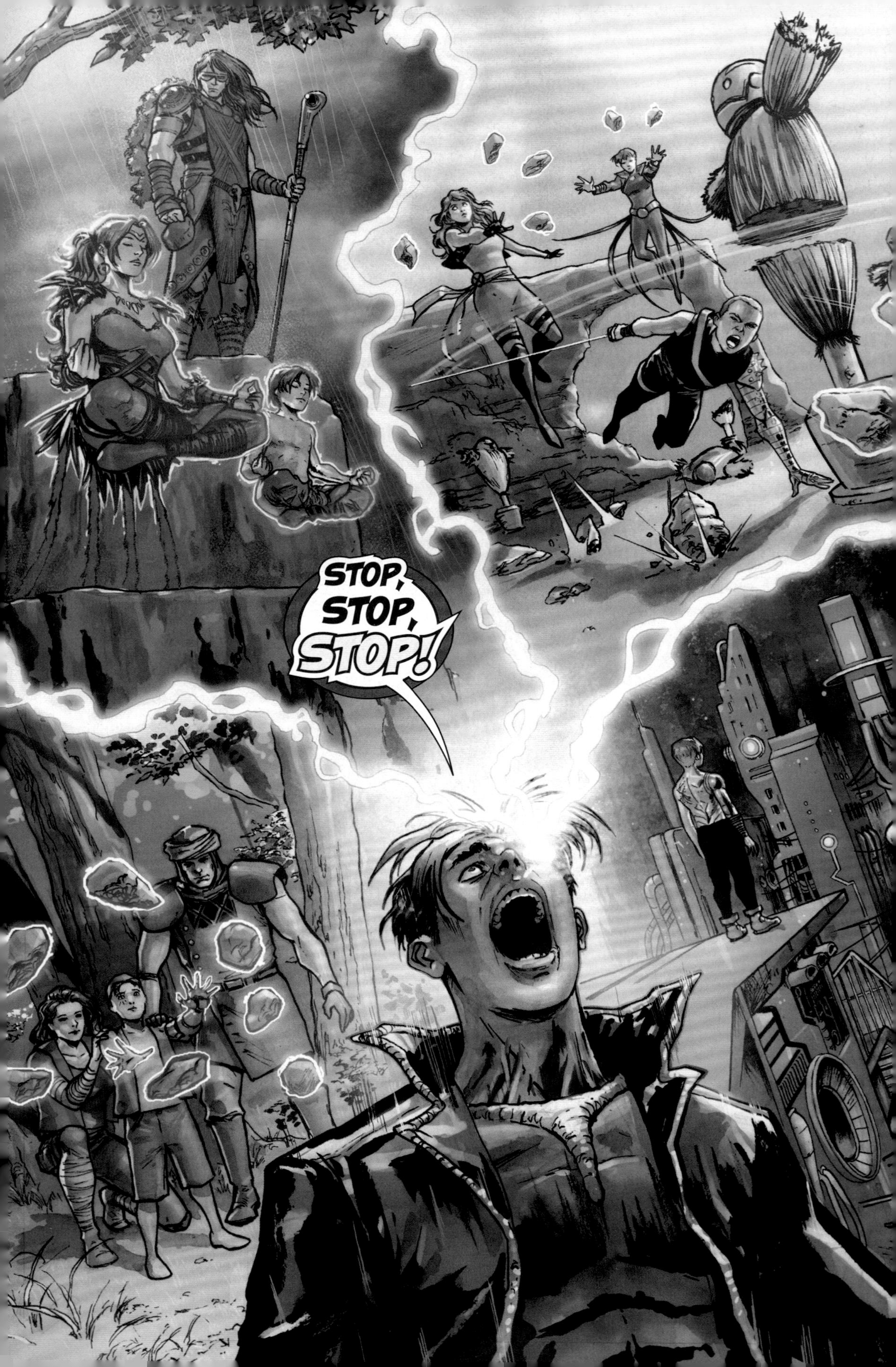
STOP, STOP, STOP!

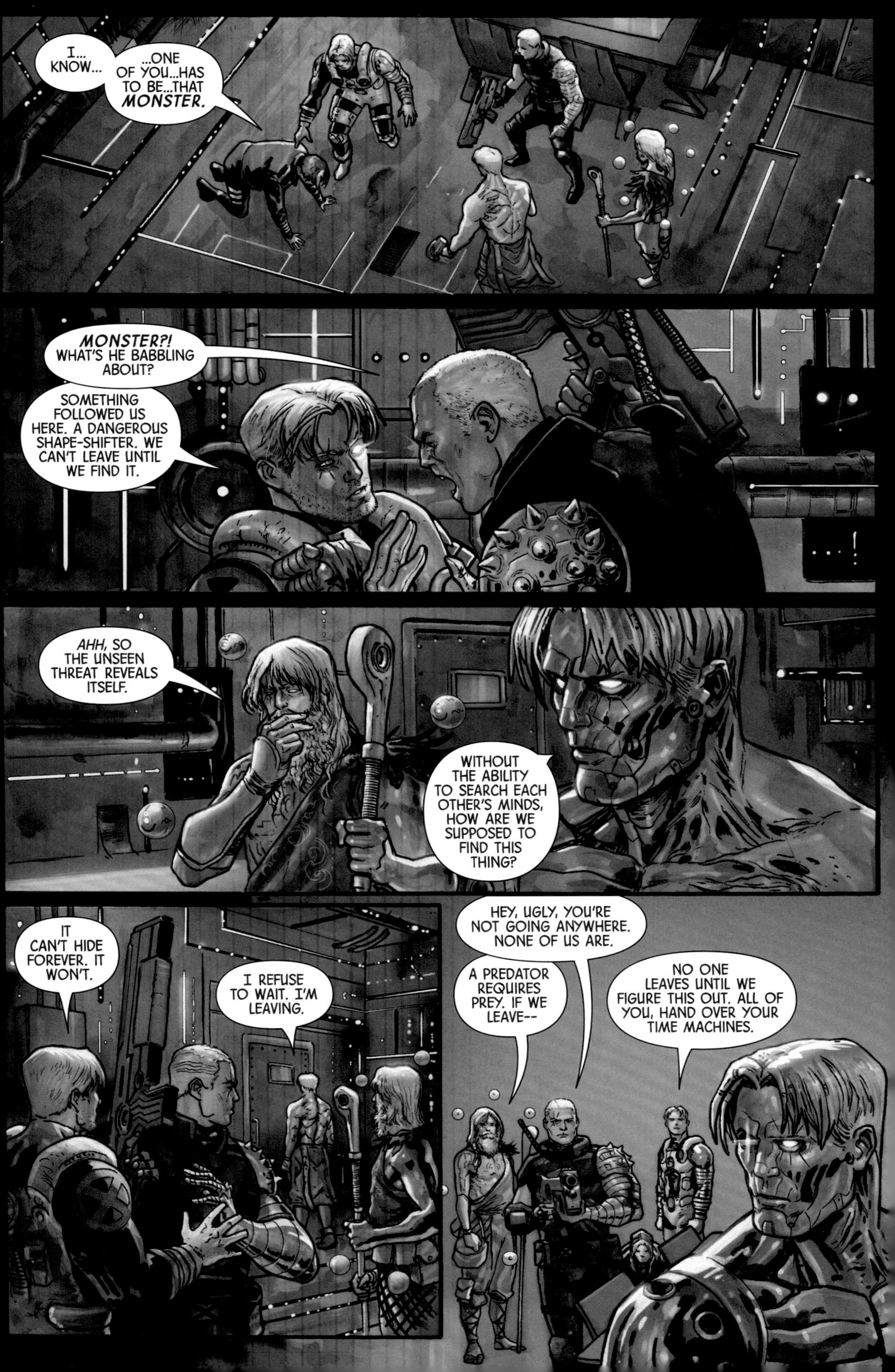
I... KNOW...
...ONE OF YOU...HAS TO BE...THAT MONSTER.
MONSTER?! WHAT'S HE BABBLING ABOUT?
SOMETHING FOLLOWED US HERE. A DANGEROUS SHAPE-SHIFTER. WE CAN'T LEAVE UNTIL WE FIND IT.
AHH, SO THE UNSEEN THREAT REVEALS ITSELF.
WITHOUT THE ABILITY TO SEARCH EACH OTHER'S MINDS, HOW ARE WE SUPPOSED TO FIND THIS THING?
IT CAN'T HIDE FOREVER. IT WON'T.
I REFUSE TO WAIT. I'M LEAVING.
HEY, UGLY, YOU'RE NOT GOING ANYWHERE. NONE OF US ARE.
A PREDATOR REQUIRES PREY. IF WE LEAVE--
NO ONE LEAVES UNTIL WE FIGURE THIS OUT. ALL OF YOU, HAND OVER YOUR TIME MACHINES.

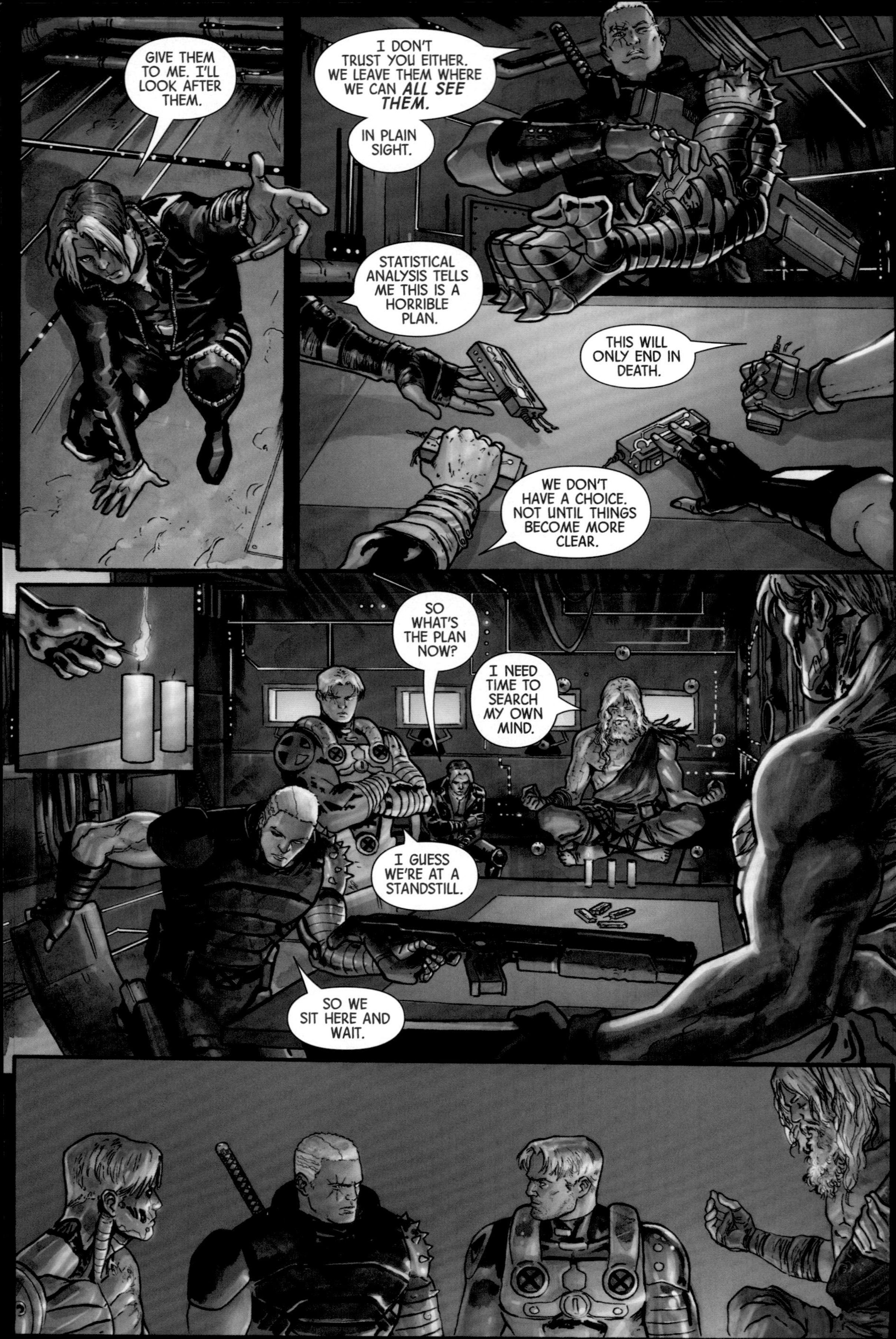
GIVE THEM TO ME. I'LL LOOK AFTER THEM.
I DON'T TRUST YOU EITHER. WE LEAVE THEM WHERE WE CAN ALL SEE THEM.
IN PLAIN SIGHT.
STATISTICAL ANALYSIS TELLS ME THIS IS A HORRIBLE PLAN.
THIS WILL ONLY END IN DEATH.
WE DON'T HAVE A CHOICE. NOT UNTIL THINGS BECOME MORE CLEAR.
SO WHAT'S THE PLAN NOW?
I NEED TIME TO SEARCH MY OWN MIND.
I GUESS WE'RE AT A STANDSTILL.
SO WE SIT HERE AND WAIT.

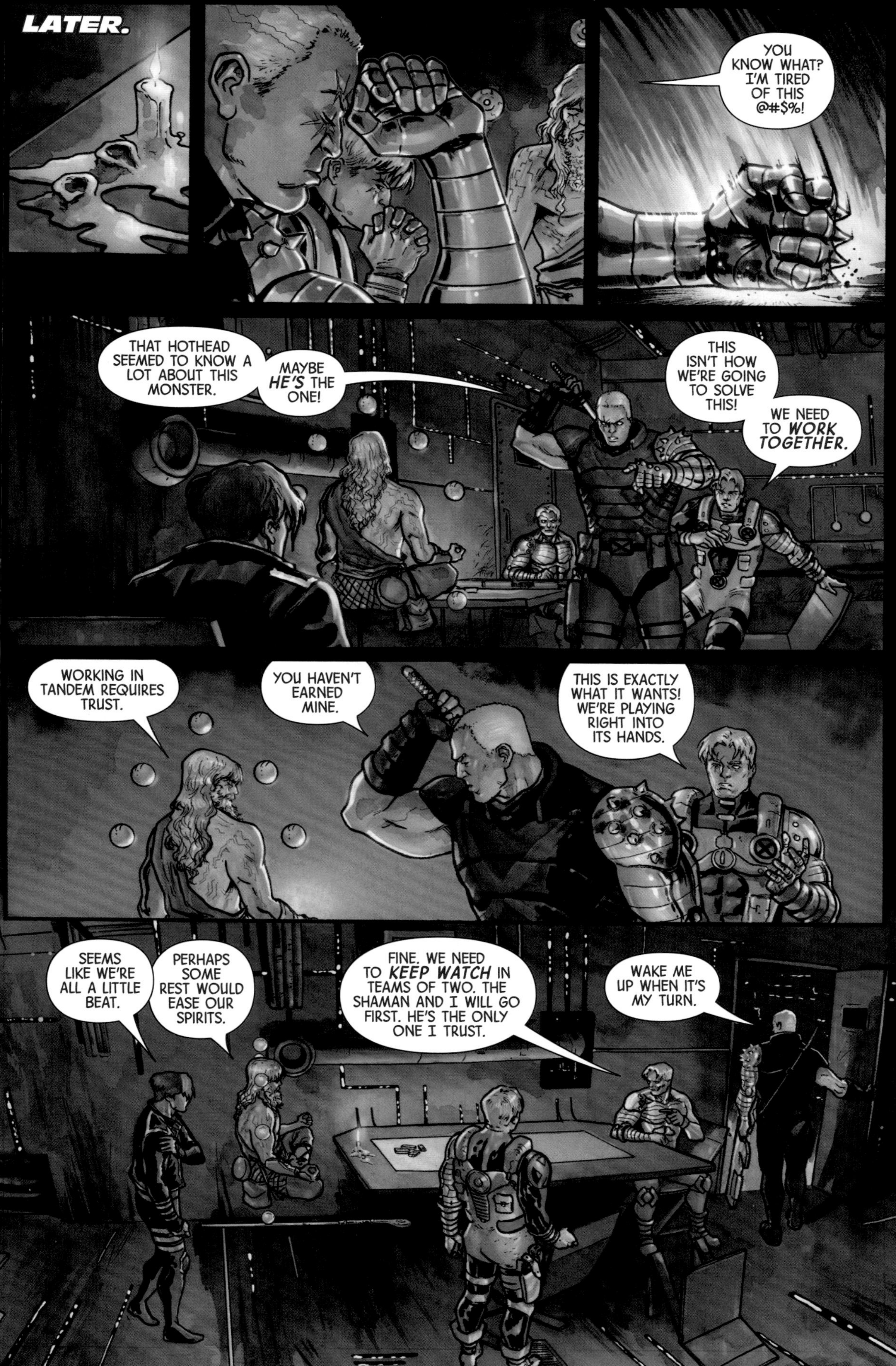
LATER.
YOU KNOW WHAT? I'M TIRED OF THIS @#$%!
THAT HOTHEAD SEEMED TO KNOW A LOT ABOUT THIS MONSTER.
MAYBE HE'S THE ONE!
THIS ISN'T HOW WE'RE GOING TO SOLVE THIS!
WE NEED TO WORK TOGETHER.
WORKING IN TANDEM REQUIRES TRUST.
YOU HAVEN'T EARNED MINE.
THIS IS EXACTLY WHAT IT WANTS! WE'RE PLAYING RIGHT INTO ITS HANDS.
SEEMS LIKE WE'RE ALL A LITTLE BEAT.
PERHAPS SOME REST WOULD EASE OUR SPIRITS.
FINE. WE NEED TO KEEP WATCH IN TEAMS OF TWO. THE SHAMAN AND I WILL GO FIRST. HE'S THE ONLY ONE I TRUST.
WAKE ME UP WHEN IT'S MY TURN.

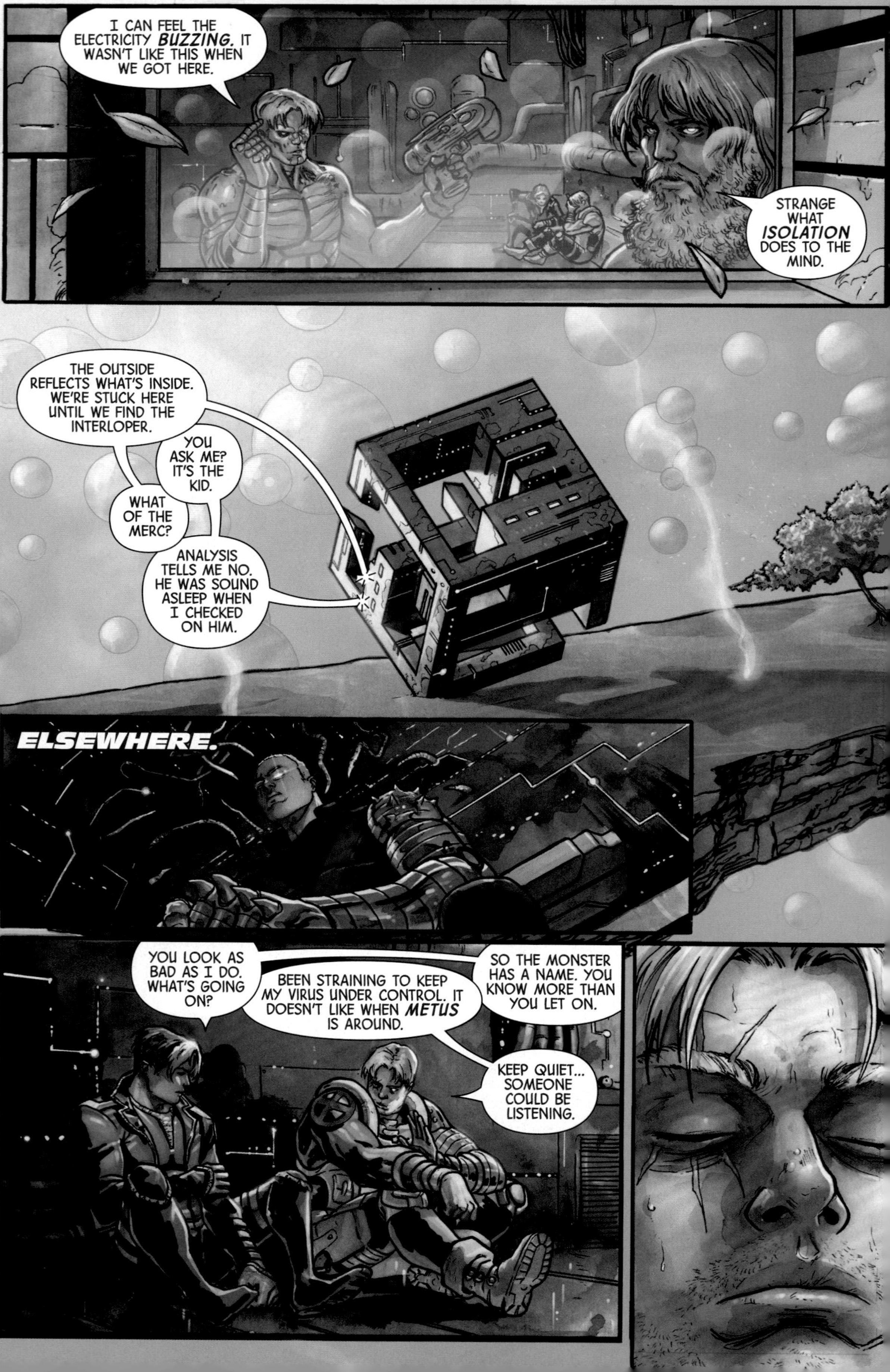
I CAN FEEL THE ELECTRICITY BUZZING. IT WASN'T LIKE THIS WHEN WE GOT HERE.
STRANGE WHAT ISOLATION DOES TO THE MIND.
THE OUTSIDE REFLECTS WHAT'S INSIDE. WE'RE STUCK HERE UNTIL WE FIND THE INTERLOPER.
WHAT OF THE MERC?
YOU ASK ME? IT'S THE KID.
ANALYSIS TELLS ME NO. HE WAS SOUND ASLEEP WHEN I CHECKED ON HIM.
ELSEWHERE.
YOU LOOK AS BAD AS I DO. WHAT'S GOING ON?
BEEN STRAINING TO KEEP MY VIRUS UNDER CONTROL. IT DOESN'T LIKE WHEN METUS IS AROUND.
SO THE MONSTER HAS A NAME. YOU KNOW MORE THAN YOU LET ON.
KEEP QUIET... SOMEONE COULD BE LISTENING.

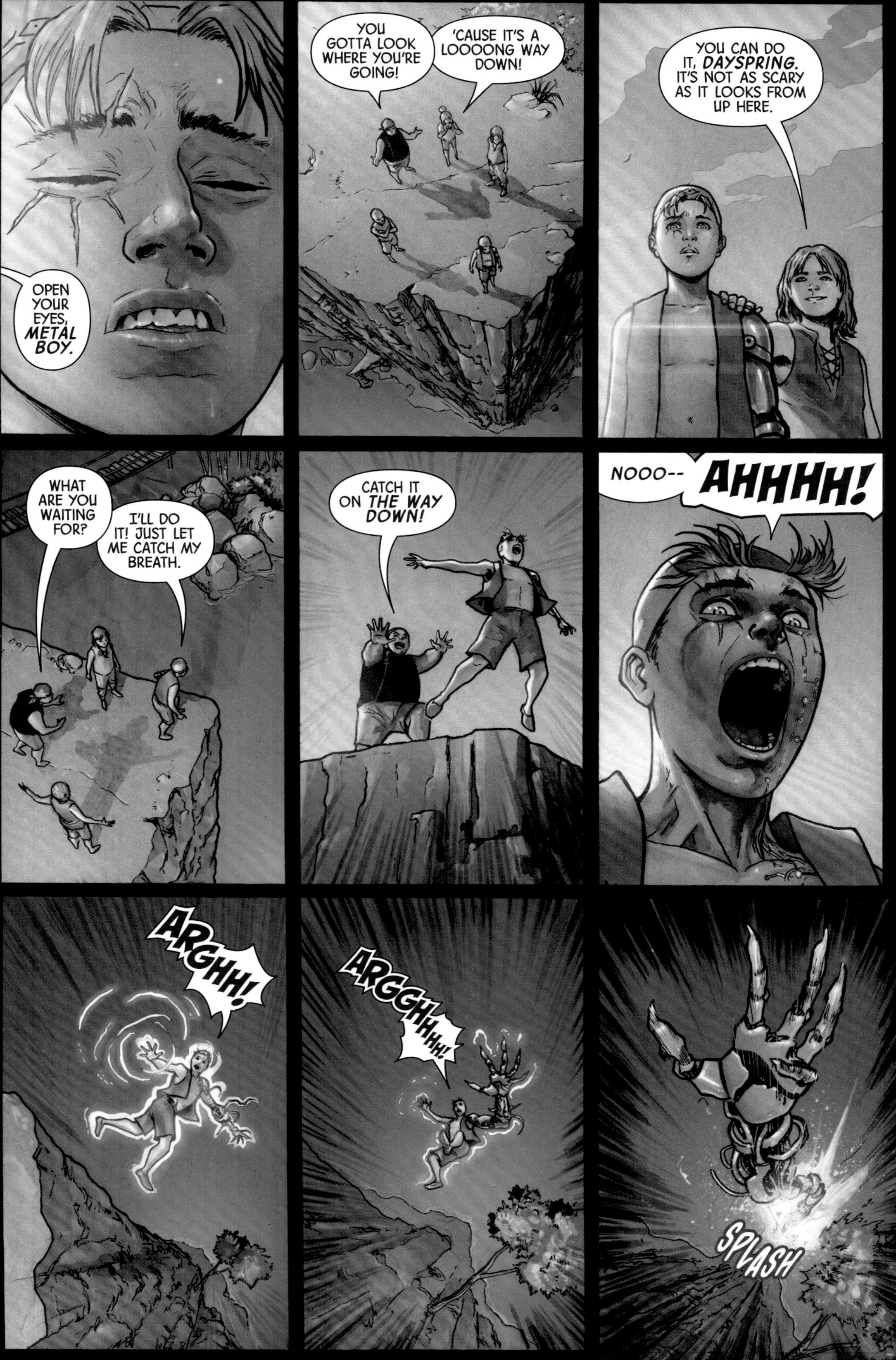
OPEN YOUR EYES, *METAL BOY.*
YOU GOTTA LOOK WHERE YOU'RE GOING!
'CAUSE IT'S A LOOOONG WAY DOWN!
YOU CAN DO IT, *DAYSPRING.* IT'S NOT AS SCARY AS IT LOOKS FROM UP HERE.
WHAT ARE YOU WAITING FOR?
I'LL DO IT! JUST LET ME CATCH MY BREATH.
CATCH IT ON *THE WAY DOWN!*
NOOO--
AHHHH!
ARGHH!
ARGGHHHH!
SPLASH

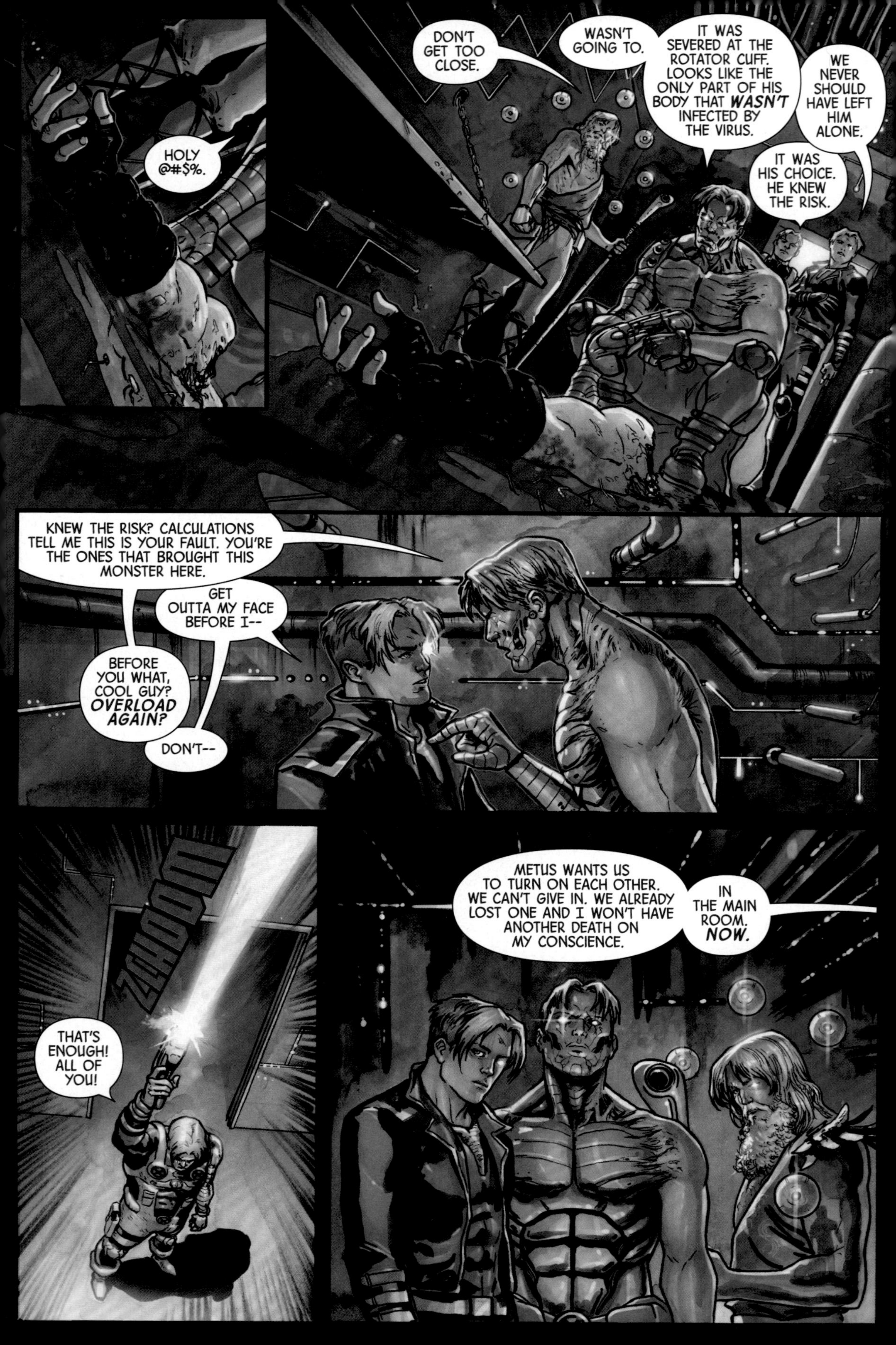
HOLY @#$%.
DON'T GET TOO CLOSE.
WASN'T GOING TO.
IT WAS SEVERED AT THE ROTATOR CUFF. LOOKS LIKE THE ONLY PART OF HIS BODY THAT ***WASN'T*** INFECTED BY THE VIRUS.
WE NEVER SHOULD HAVE LEFT HIM ALONE.
IT WAS HIS CHOICE. HE KNEW THE RISK.
KNEW THE RISK? CALCULATIONS TELL ME THIS IS YOUR FAULT. YOU'RE THE ONES THAT BROUGHT THIS MONSTER HERE.
GET OUTTA MY FACE BEFORE I--
BEFORE YOU WHAT, COOL GUY? ***OVERLOAD AGAIN?***
DON'T--
ZZHOOM
THAT'S ENOUGH! ALL OF YOU!
METUS WANTS US TO TURN ON EACH OTHER. WE CAN'T GIVE IN. WE ALREADY LOST ONE AND I WON'T HAVE ANOTHER DEATH ON MY CONSCIENCE.
IN THE MAIN ROOM. ***NOW.***

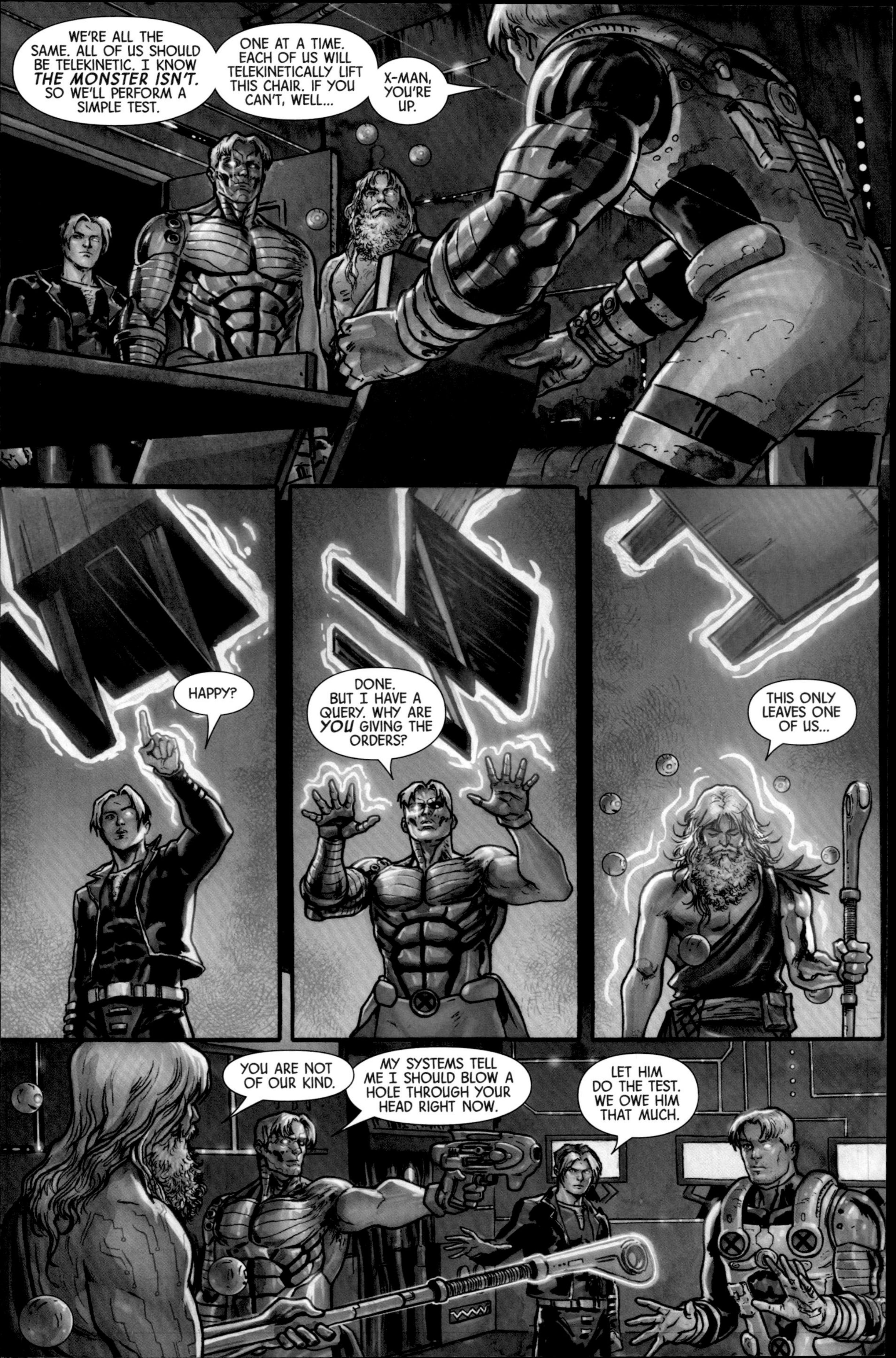
WE'RE ALL THE SAME. ALL OF US SHOULD BE TELEKINETIC. I KNOW ***THE MONSTER ISN'T.*** SO WE'LL PERFORM A SIMPLE TEST.
ONE AT A TIME. EACH OF US WILL TELEKINETICALLY LIFT THIS CHAIR. IF YOU CAN'T, WELL...
X-MAN, YOU'RE UP.
HAPPY?
DONE. BUT I HAVE A QUERY. WHY ARE ***YOU*** GIVING THE ORDERS?
THIS ONLY LEAVES ONE OF US...
YOU ARE NOT OF OUR KIND.
MY SYSTEMS TELL ME I SHOULD BLOW A HOLE THROUGH YOUR HEAD RIGHT NOW.
LET HIM DO THE TEST. WE OWE HIM THAT MUCH.

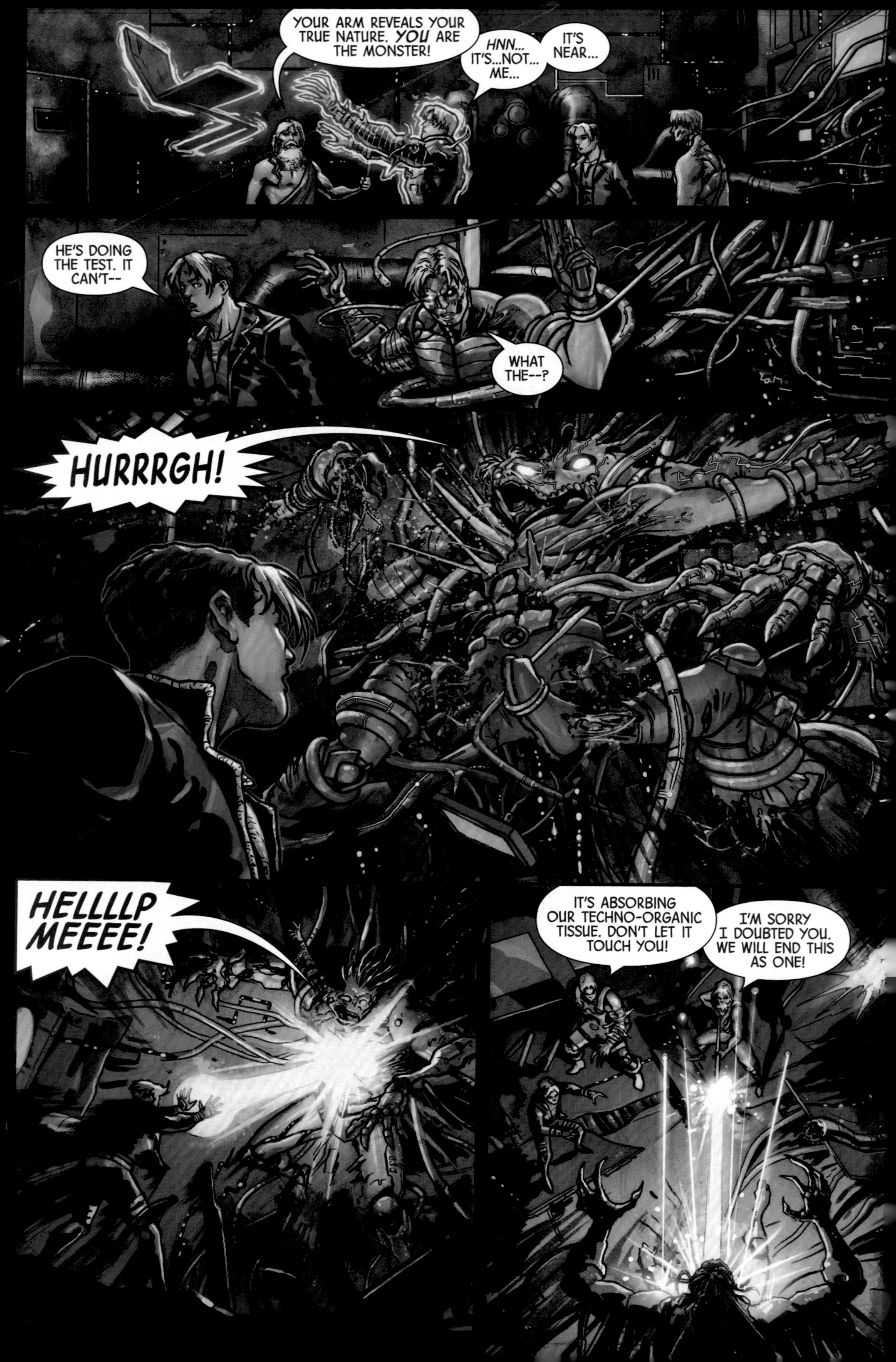
YOUR ARM REVEALS YOUR TRUE NATURE. YOU ARE THE MONSTER!
HNN... IT'S...NOT... ME...
IT'S NEAR...
HE'S DOING THE TEST. IT CAN'T--
WHAT THE--?
HURRRGH!
HELLLLP MEEEE!
IT'S ABSORBING OUR TECHNO-ORGANIC TISSUE. DON'T LET IT TOUCH YOU!
I'M SORRY I DOUBTED YOU. WE WILL END THIS AS ONE!

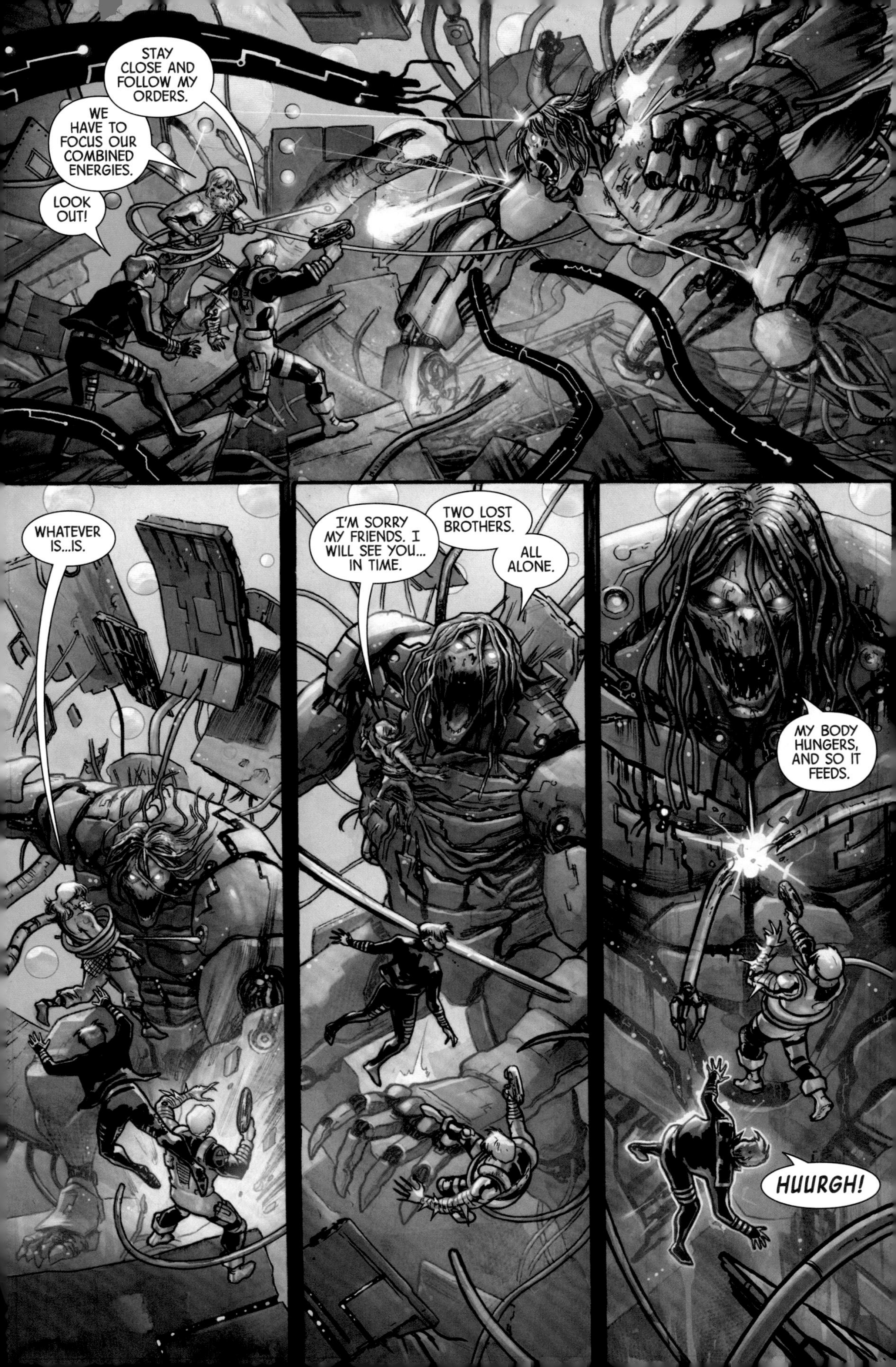

STAY CLOSE AND FOLLOW MY ORDERS.
WE HAVE TO FOCUS OUR COMBINED ENERGIES.
LOOK OUT!
WHATEVER IS...IS.
I'M SORRY MY FRIENDS. I WILL SEE YOU... IN TIME.
TWO LOST BROTHERS.
ALL ALONE.
MY BODY HUNGERS, AND SO IT FEEDS.
HUURGH!

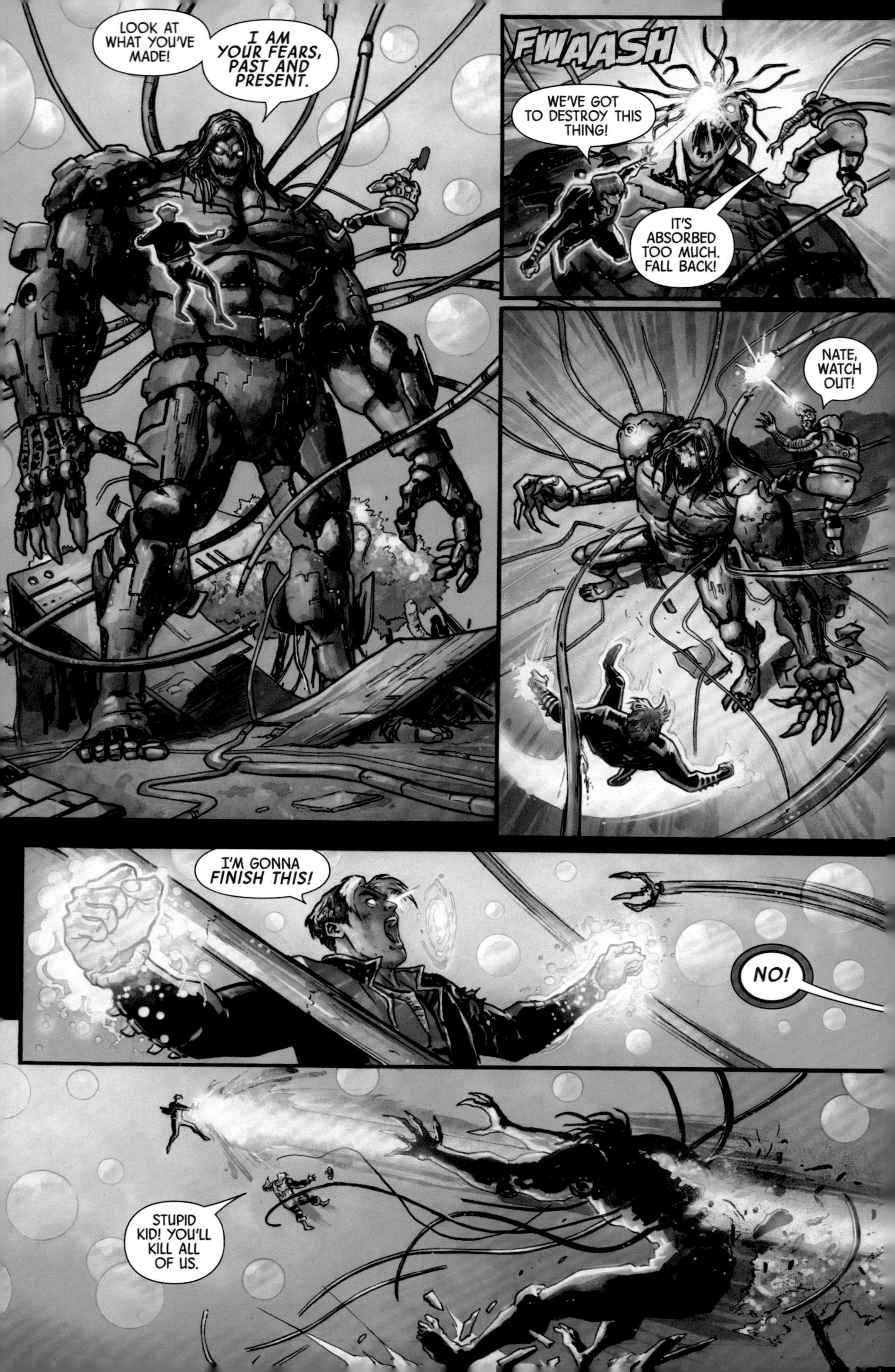
LOOK AT WHAT YOU'VE MADE!
I AM YOUR FEARS, PAST AND PRESENT.
FWAASH
WE'VE GOT TO DESTROY THIS THING!
IT'S ABSORBED TOO MUCH. FALL BACK!
NATE, WATCH OUT!
I'M GONNA FINISH THIS!
NO!
STUPID KID! YOU'LL KILL ALL OF US.

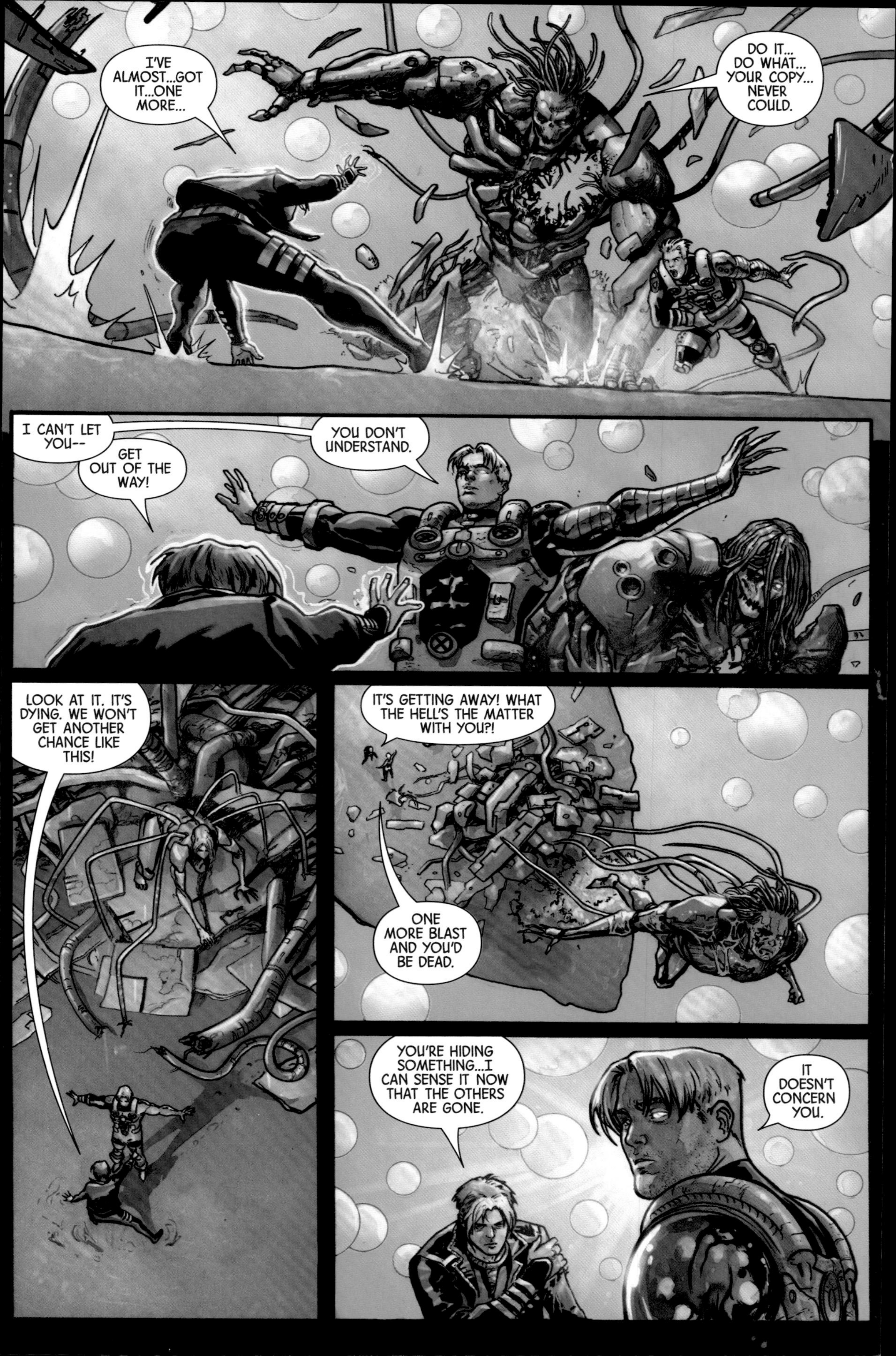
I'VE ALMOST...GOT IT...ONE MORE...
DO IT... DO WHAT... YOUR COPY... NEVER COULD.
I CAN'T LET YOU--
YOU DON'T UNDERSTAND.
GET OUT OF THE WAY!
LOOK AT IT. IT'S DYING. WE WON'T GET ANOTHER CHANCE LIKE THIS!
IT'S GETTING AWAY! WHAT THE HELL'S THE MATTER WITH YOU?!
ONE MORE BLAST AND YOU'D BE DEAD.
YOU'RE HIDING SOMETHING...I CAN SENSE IT NOW THAT THE OTHERS ARE GONE.
IT DOESN'T CONCERN YOU.

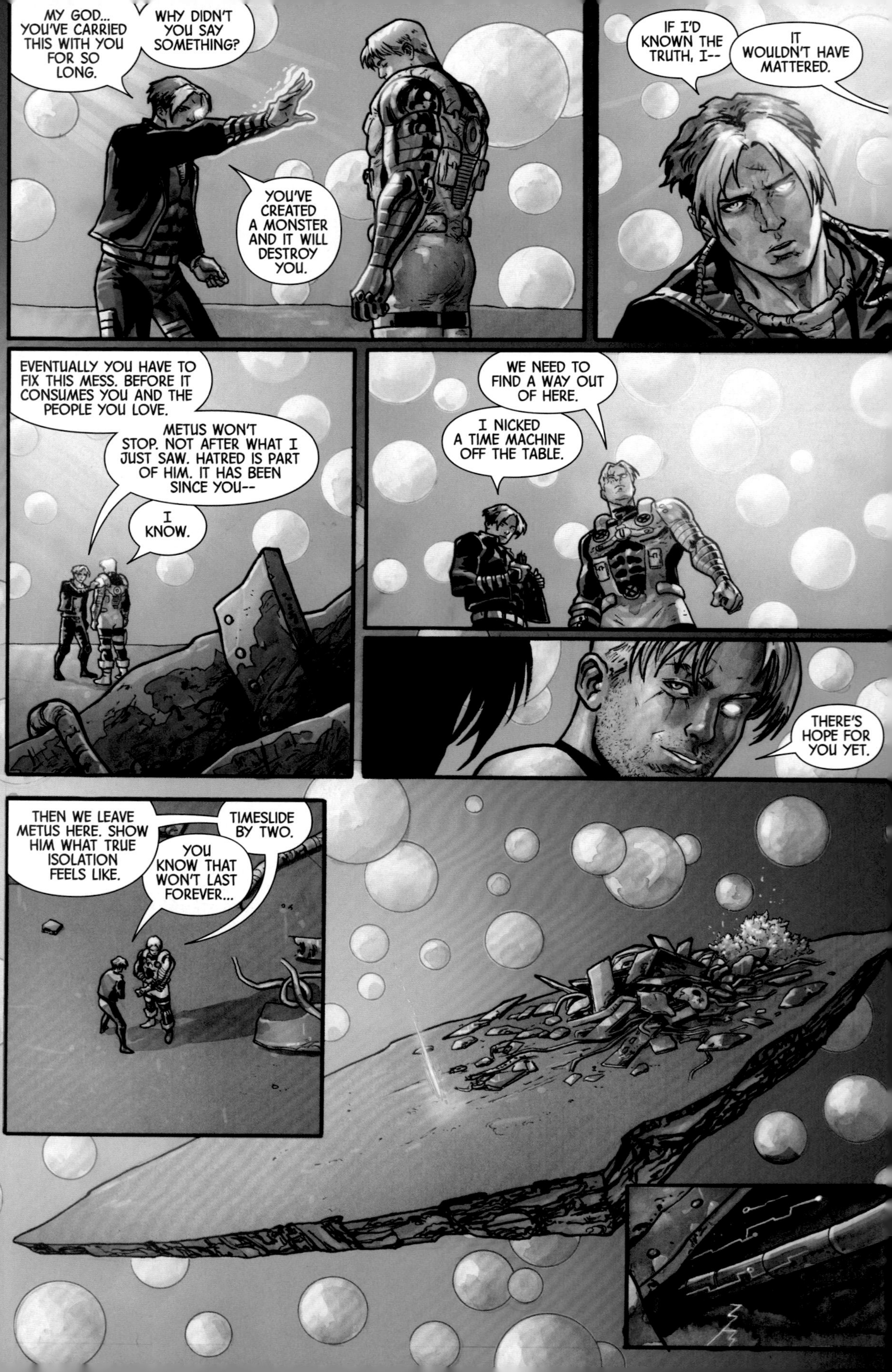
MY GOD... YOU'VE CARRIED THIS WITH YOU FOR SO LONG.
WHY DIDN'T YOU SAY SOMETHING?
YOU'VE CREATED A MONSTER AND IT WILL DESTROY YOU.
IF I'D KNOWN THE TRUTH, I--
IT WOULDN'T HAVE MATTERED.
EVENTUALLY YOU HAVE TO FIX THIS MESS. BEFORE IT CONSUMES YOU AND THE PEOPLE YOU LOVE.
METUS WON'T STOP. NOT AFTER WHAT I JUST SAW. HATRED IS PART OF HIM. IT HAS BEEN SINCE YOU--
I KNOW.
WE NEED TO FIND A WAY OUT OF HERE.
I NICKED A TIME MACHINE OFF THE TABLE.
THERE'S HOPE FOR YOU YET.
THEN WE LEAVE METUS HERE. SHOW HIM WHAT TRUE ISOLATION FEELS LIKE.
TIMESLIDE BY TWO.
YOU KNOW THAT WON'T LAST FOREVER...

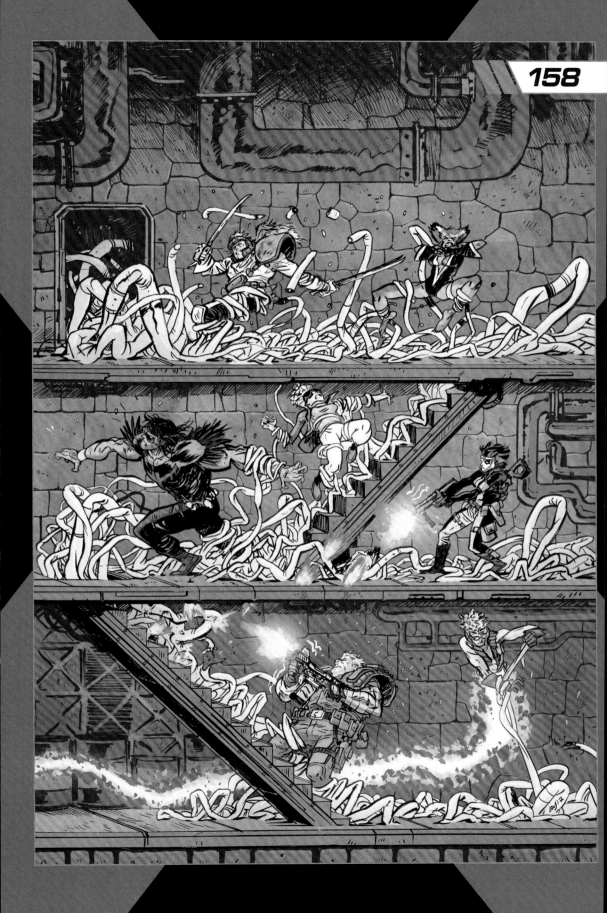

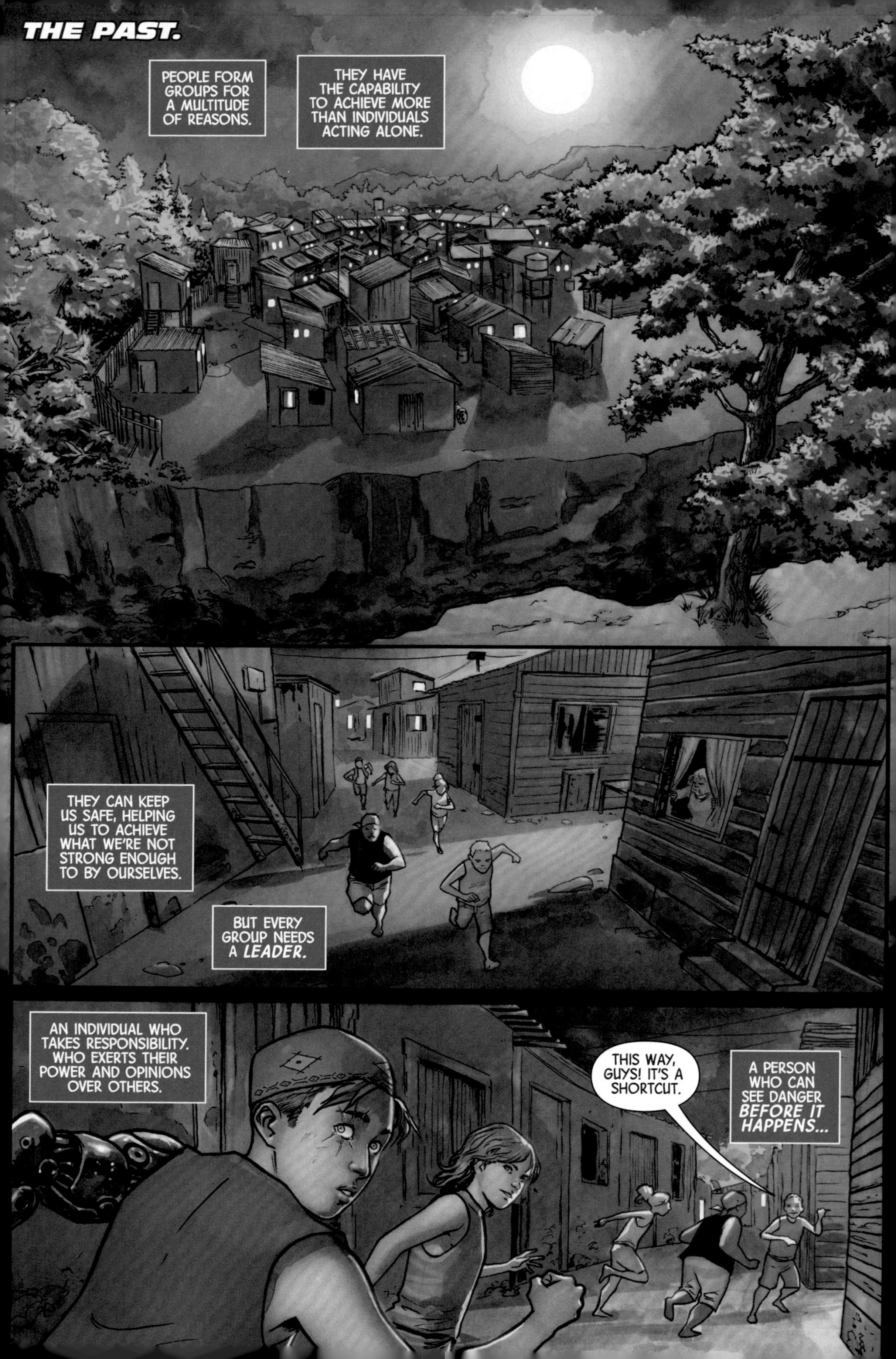
THE PAST.
PEOPLE FORM GROUPS FOR A MULTITUDE OF REASONS.
THEY HAVE THE CAPABILITY TO ACHIEVE MORE THAN INDIVIDUALS ACTING ALONE.
THEY CAN KEEP US SAFE, HELPING US TO ACHIEVE WHAT WE'RE NOT STRONG ENOUGH TO BY OURSELVES.
BUT EVERY GROUP NEEDS A *LEADER.*
AN INDIVIDUAL WHO TAKES RESPONSIBILITY. WHO EXERTS THEIR POWER AND OPINIONS OVER OTHERS.
THIS WAY, GUYS! IT'S A SHORTCUT.
A PERSON WHO CAN SEE DANGER *BEFORE IT HAPPENS...*

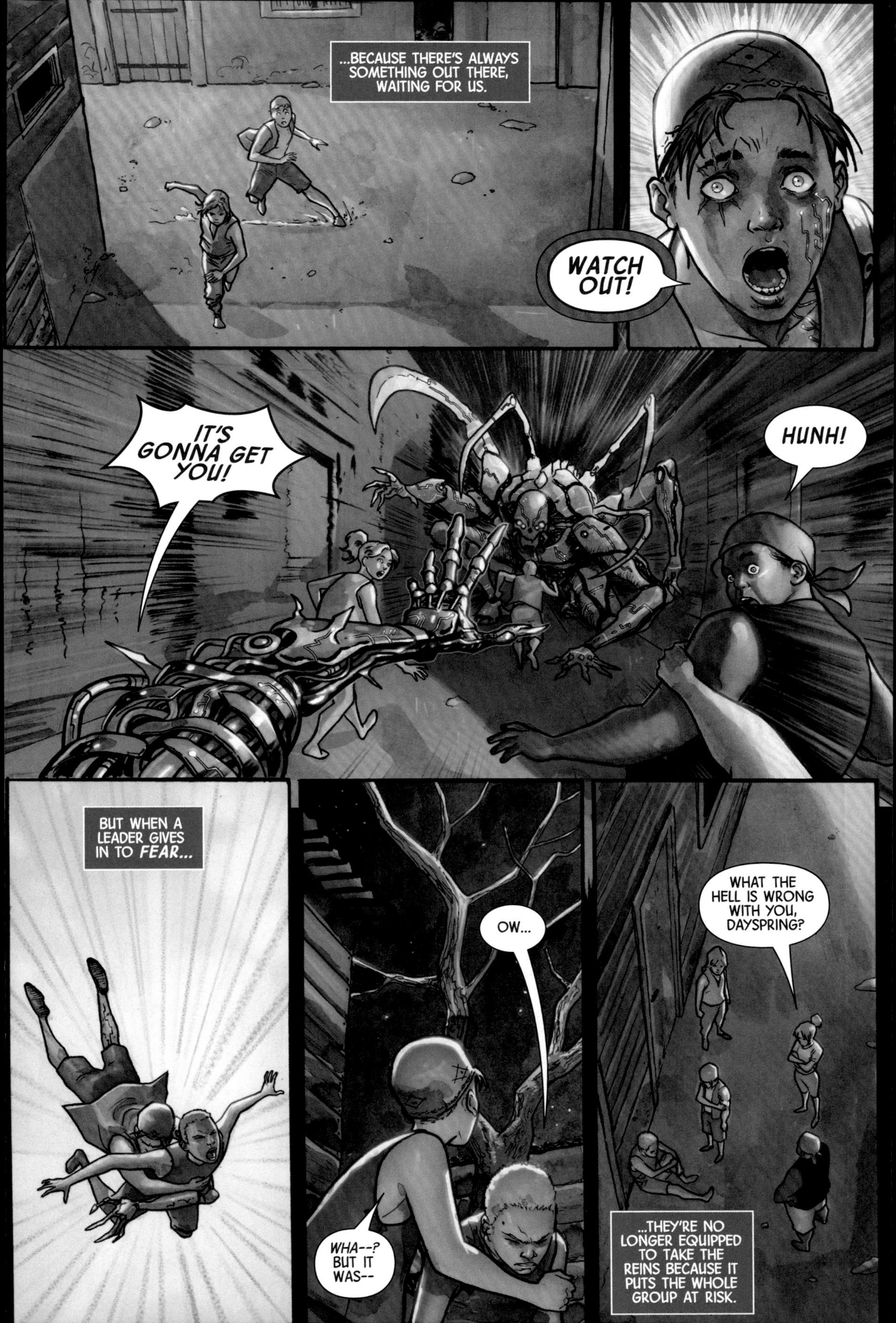
...BECAUSE THERE'S ALWAYS SOMETHING OUT THERE, WAITING FOR US.
WATCH OUT!
IT'S GONNA GET YOU!
HUNH!
BUT WHEN A LEADER GIVES IN TO FEAR...
OW...
WHA--? BUT IT WAS--
WHAT THE HELL IS WRONG WITH YOU, DAYSPRING?
...THEY'RE NO LONGER EQUIPPED TO TAKE THE REINS BECAUSE IT PUTS THE WHOLE GROUP AT RISK.

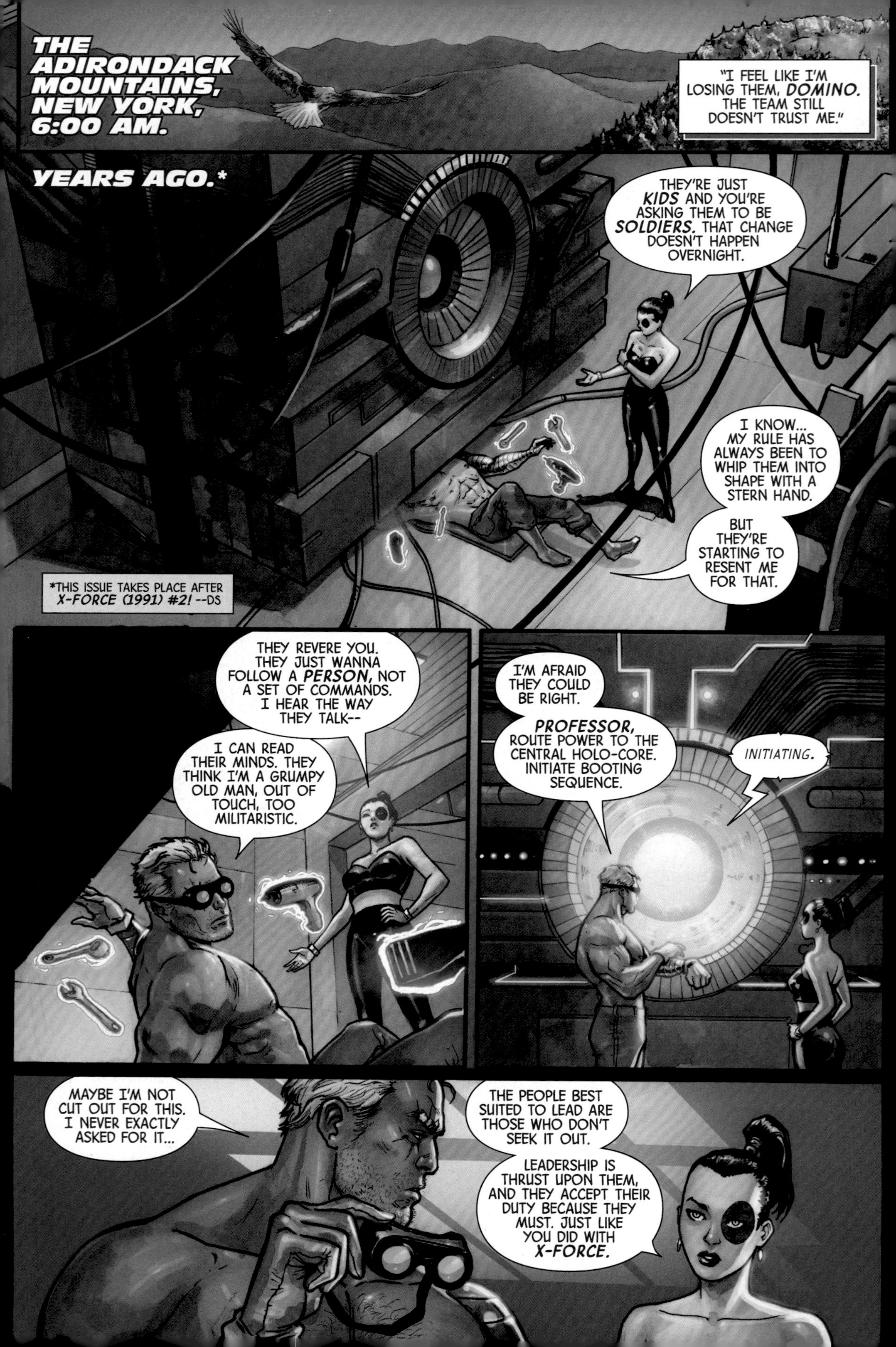
THE ADIRONDACK MOUNTAINS, NEW YORK, 6:00 AM.
"I FEEL LIKE I'M LOSING THEM, DOMINO. THE TEAM STILL DOESN'T TRUST ME."
YEARS AGO.*
THEY'RE JUST KIDS AND YOU'RE ASKING THEM TO BE SOLDIERS. THAT CHANGE DOESN'T HAPPEN OVERNIGHT.
I KNOW... MY RULE HAS ALWAYS BEEN TO WHIP THEM INTO SHAPE WITH A STERN HAND.
BUT THEY'RE STARTING TO RESENT ME FOR THAT.
*THIS ISSUE TAKES PLACE AFTER X-FORCE (1991) #2! --DS
THEY REVERE YOU. THEY JUST WANNA FOLLOW A PERSON, NOT A SET OF COMMANDS. I HEAR THE WAY THEY TALK--
I CAN READ THEIR MINDS. THEY THINK I'M A GRUMPY OLD MAN, OUT OF TOUCH, TOO MILITARISTIC.
I'M AFRAID THEY COULD BE RIGHT.
PROFESSOR, ROUTE POWER TO THE CENTRAL HOLO-CORE. INITIATE BOOTING SEQUENCE.
INITIATING.
MAYBE I'M NOT CUT OUT FOR THIS. I NEVER EXACTLY ASKED FOR IT...
THE PEOPLE BEST SUITED TO LEAD ARE THOSE WHO DON'T SEEK IT OUT.
LEADERSHIP IS THRUST UPON THEM, AND THEY ACCEPT THEIR DUTY BECAUSE THEY MUST. JUST LIKE YOU DID WITH X-FORCE.

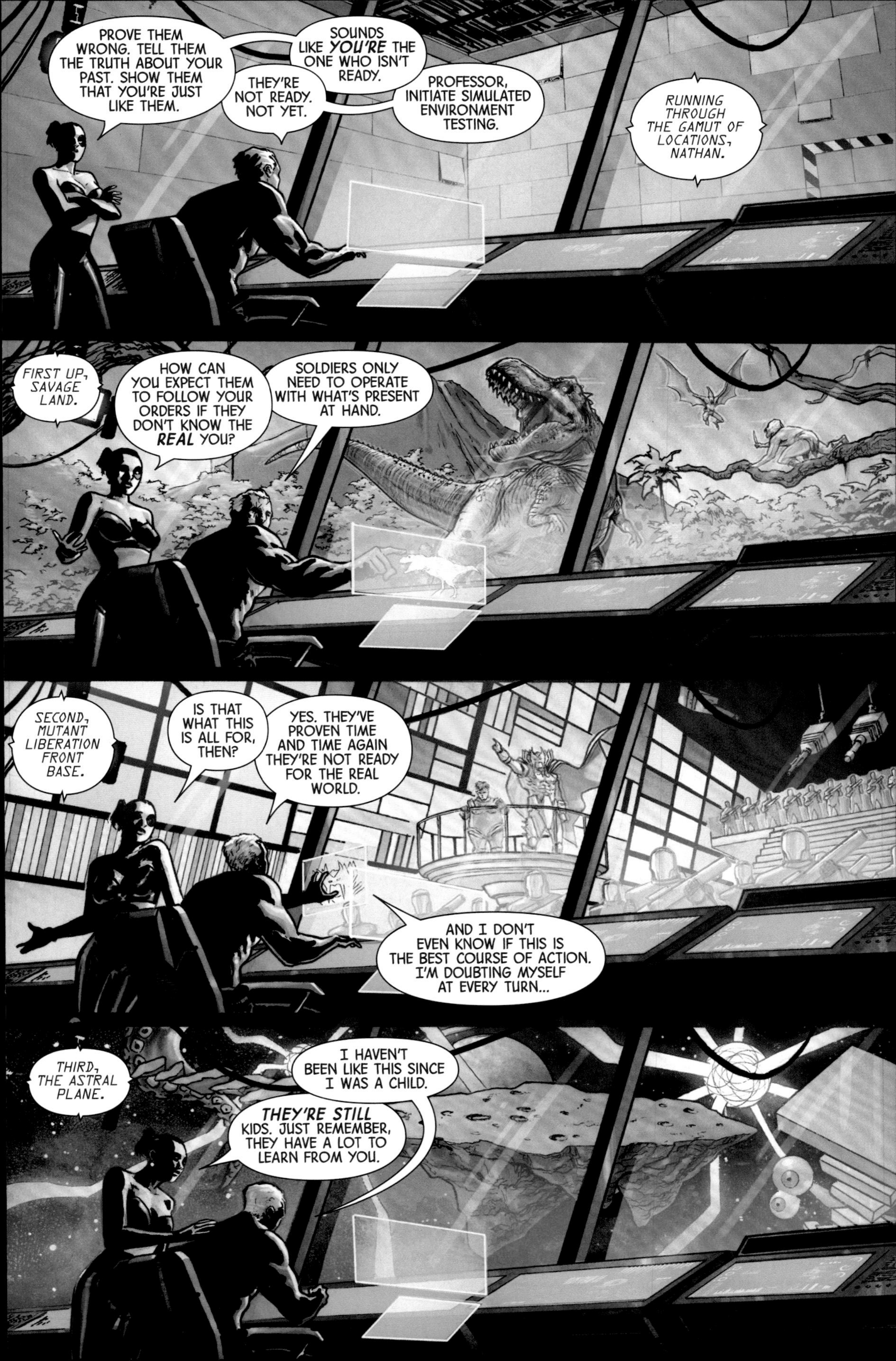
PROVE THEM WRONG. TELL THEM THE TRUTH ABOUT YOUR PAST. SHOW THEM THAT YOU'RE JUST LIKE THEM.
THEY'RE NOT READY. NOT YET.
SOUNDS LIKE YOU'RE THE ONE WHO ISN'T READY.
PROFESSOR, INITIATE SIMULATED ENVIRONMENT TESTING.
RUNNING THROUGH THE GAMUT OF LOCATIONS, NATHAN.
FIRST UP, SAVAGE LAND.
HOW CAN YOU EXPECT THEM TO FOLLOW YOUR ORDERS IF THEY DON'T KNOW THE REAL YOU?
SOLDIERS ONLY NEED TO OPERATE WITH WHAT'S PRESENT AT HAND.
SECOND, MUTANT LIBERATION FRONT BASE.
IS THAT WHAT THIS IS ALL FOR, THEN?
YES. THEY'VE PROVEN TIME AND TIME AGAIN THEY'RE NOT READY FOR THE REAL WORLD.
AND I DON'T EVEN KNOW IF THIS IS THE BEST COURSE OF ACTION. I'M DOUBTING MYSELF AT EVERY TURN...
THIRD, THE ASTRAL PLANE.
I HAVEN'T BEEN LIKE THIS SINCE I WAS A CHILD.
THEY'RE STILL KIDS. JUST REMEMBER, THEY HAVE A LOT TO LEARN FROM YOU.

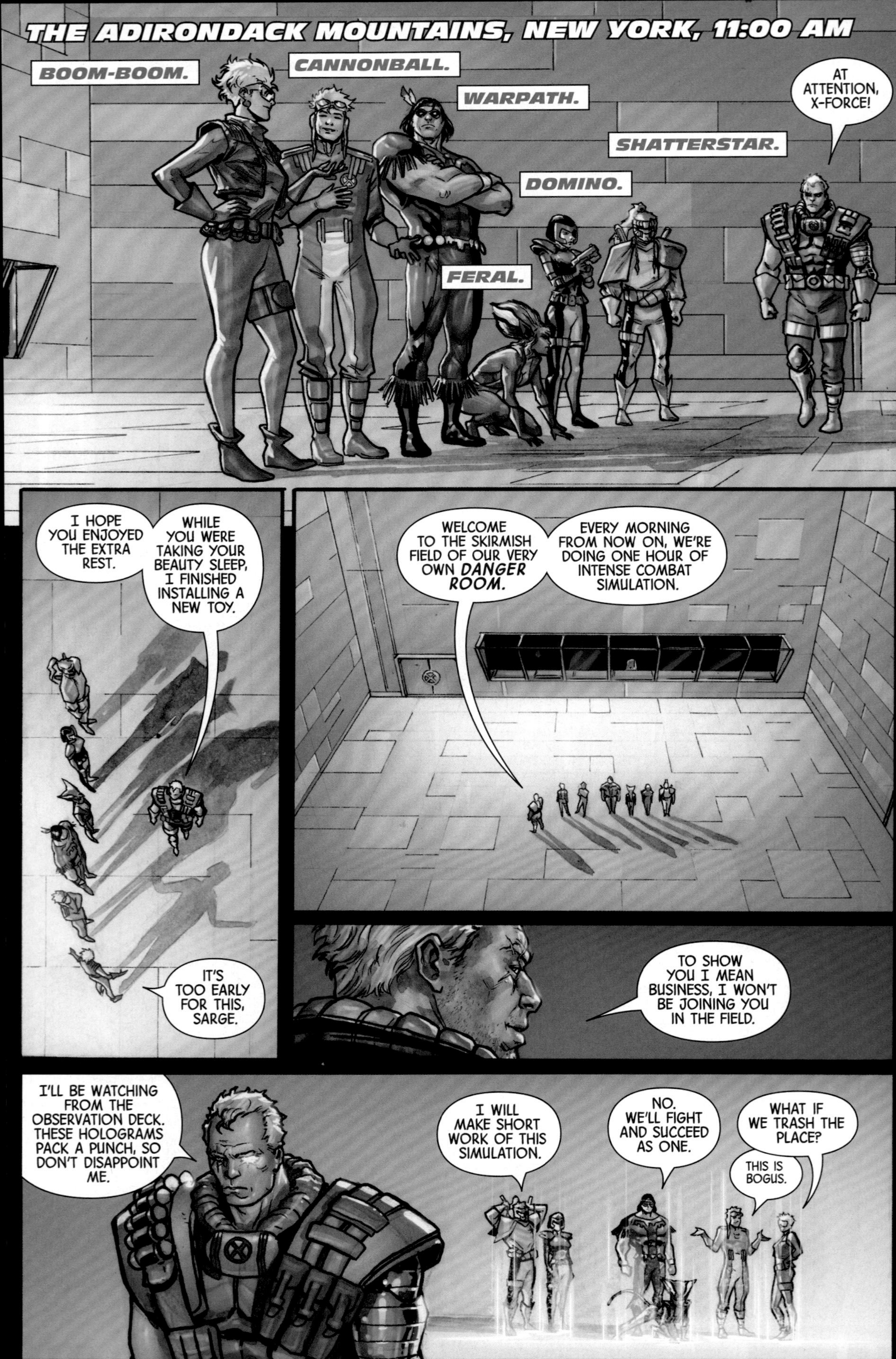
THE ADIRONDACK MOUNTAINS, NEW YORK, 11:00 AM
BOOM-BOOM.
CANNONBALL.
WARPATH.
SHATTERSTAR.
DOMINO.
FERAL.
AT ATTENTION, X-FORCE!
I HOPE YOU ENJOYED THE EXTRA REST.
WHILE YOU WERE TAKING YOUR BEAUTY SLEEP, I FINISHED INSTALLING A NEW TOY.
IT'S TOO EARLY FOR THIS, SARGE.
WELCOME TO THE SKIRMISH FIELD OF OUR VERY OWN DANGER ROOM.
EVERY MORNING FROM NOW ON, WE'RE DOING ONE HOUR OF INTENSE COMBAT SIMULATION.
TO SHOW YOU I MEAN BUSINESS, I WON'T BE JOINING YOU IN THE FIELD.
I'LL BE WATCHING FROM THE OBSERVATION DECK. THESE HOLOGRAMS PACK A PUNCH, SO DON'T DISAPPOINT ME.
I WILL MAKE SHORT WORK OF THIS SIMULATION.
NO. WE'LL FIGHT AND SUCCEED AS ONE.
WHAT IF WE TRASH THE PLACE?
THIS IS BOGUS.

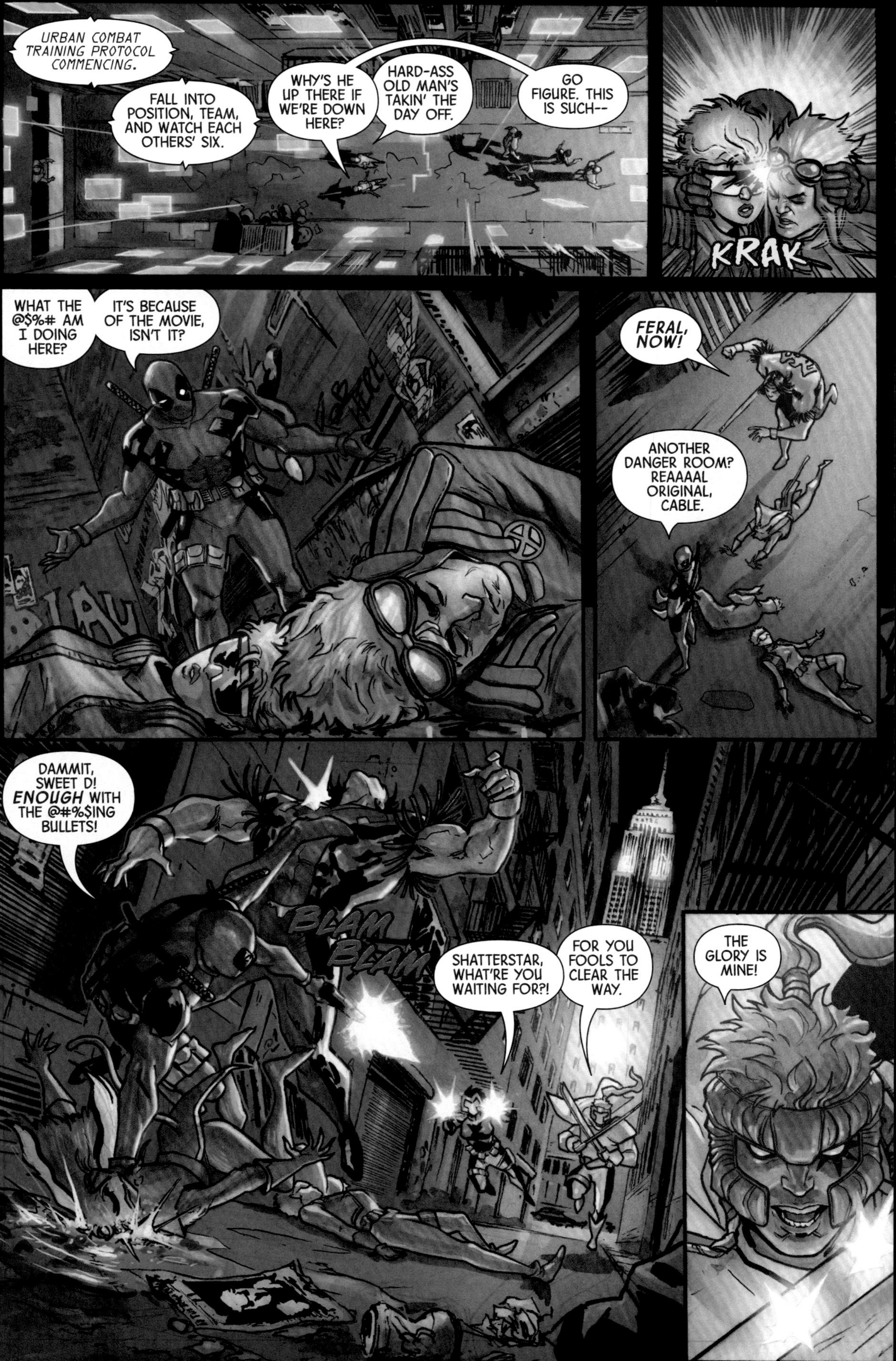
URBAN COMBAT TRAINING PROTOCOL COMMENCING.
FALL INTO POSITION, TEAM, AND WATCH EACH OTHERS' SIX.
WHY'S HE UP THERE IF WE'RE DOWN HERE?
HARD-ASS OLD MAN'S TAKIN' THE DAY OFF.
GO FIGURE. THIS IS SUCH--
KRAK
WHAT THE @$%# AM I DOING HERE?
IT'S BECAUSE OF THE MOVIE, ISN'T IT?
FERAL, NOW!
ANOTHER DANGER ROOM? REAAAAL ORIGINAL, CABLE.
DAMMIT, SWEET D! ENOUGH WITH THE @#%$ING BULLETS!
BLAM BLAM
SHATTERSTAR, WHAT'RE YOU WAITING FOR?!
FOR YOU FOOLS TO CLEAR THE WAY.
THE GLORY IS MINE!

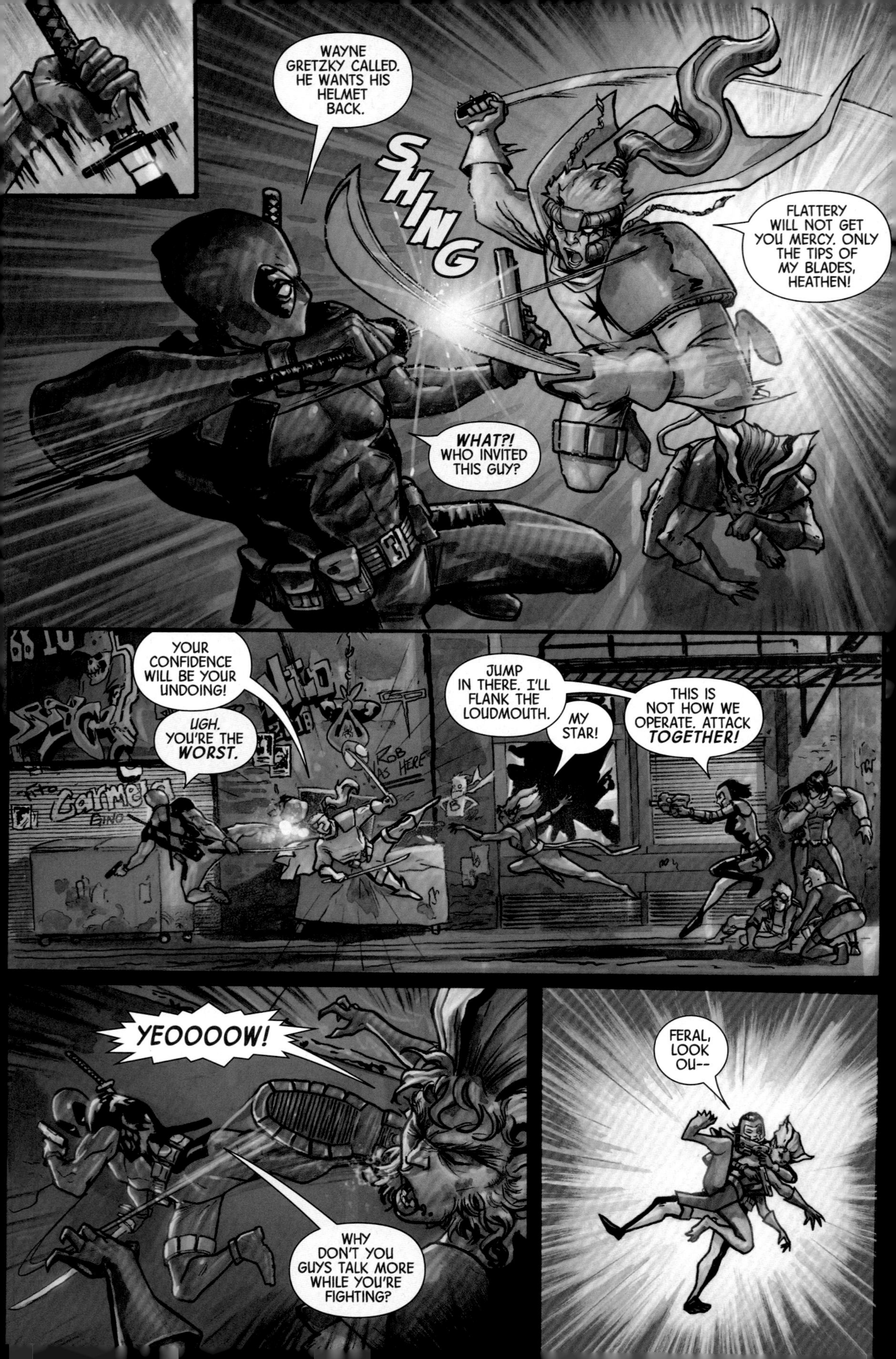
WAYNE GRETZKY CALLED. HE WANTS HIS HELMET BACK.
SHING
FLATTERY WILL NOT GET YOU MERCY. ONLY THE TIPS OF MY BLADES, HEATHEN!
WHAT?! WHO INVITED THIS GUY?
YOUR CONFIDENCE WILL BE YOUR UNDOING!
UGH. YOU'RE THE WORST.
JUMP IN THERE. I'LL FLANK THE LOUDMOUTH.
MY STAR!
THIS IS NOT HOW WE OPERATE. ATTACK TOGETHER!
ROB WAS HERE
YEOOOOW!
WHY DON'T YOU GUYS TALK MORE WHILE YOU'RE FIGHTING?
FERAL, LOOK OU--

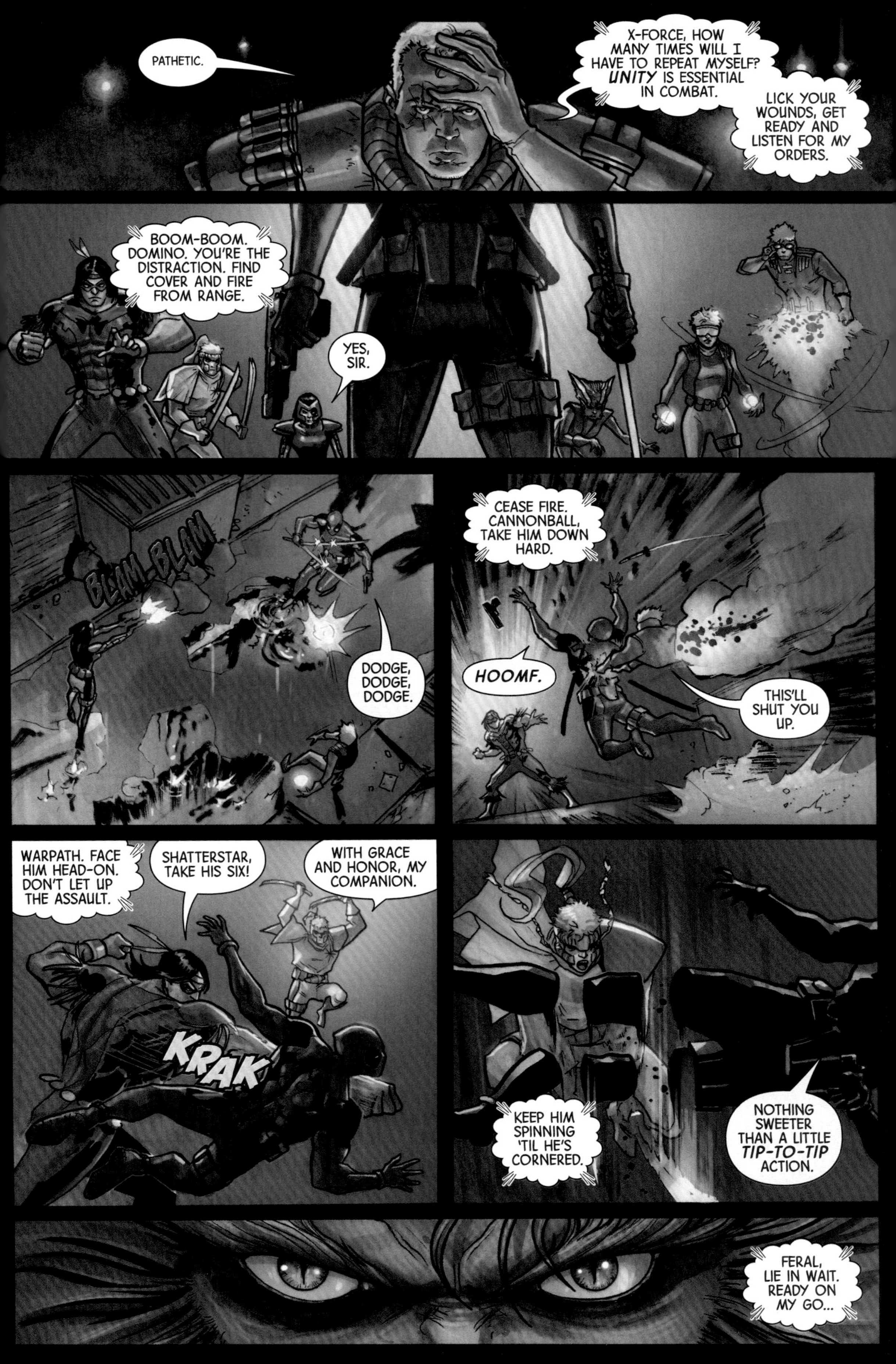
PATHETIC.
X-FORCE, HOW MANY TIMES WILL I HAVE TO REPEAT MYSELF? UNITY IS ESSENTIAL IN COMBAT.
LICK YOUR WOUNDS, GET READY AND LISTEN FOR MY ORDERS.
BOOM-BOOM. DOMINO. YOU'RE THE DISTRACTION. FIND COVER AND FIRE FROM RANGE.
YES, SIR.
BLAM-BLAM
DODGE, DODGE, DODGE.
CEASE FIRE. CANNONBALL, TAKE HIM DOWN HARD.
HOOMF.
THIS'LL SHUT YOU UP.
WARPATH. FACE HIM HEAD-ON. DON'T LET UP THE ASSAULT.
SHATTERSTAR, TAKE HIS SIX!
WITH GRACE AND HONOR, MY COMPANION.
KRAK
KEEP HIM SPINNING 'TIL HE'S CORNERED.
NOTHING SWEETER THAN A LITTLE TIP-TO-TIP ACTION.
FERAL, LIE IN WAIT. READY ON MY GO...

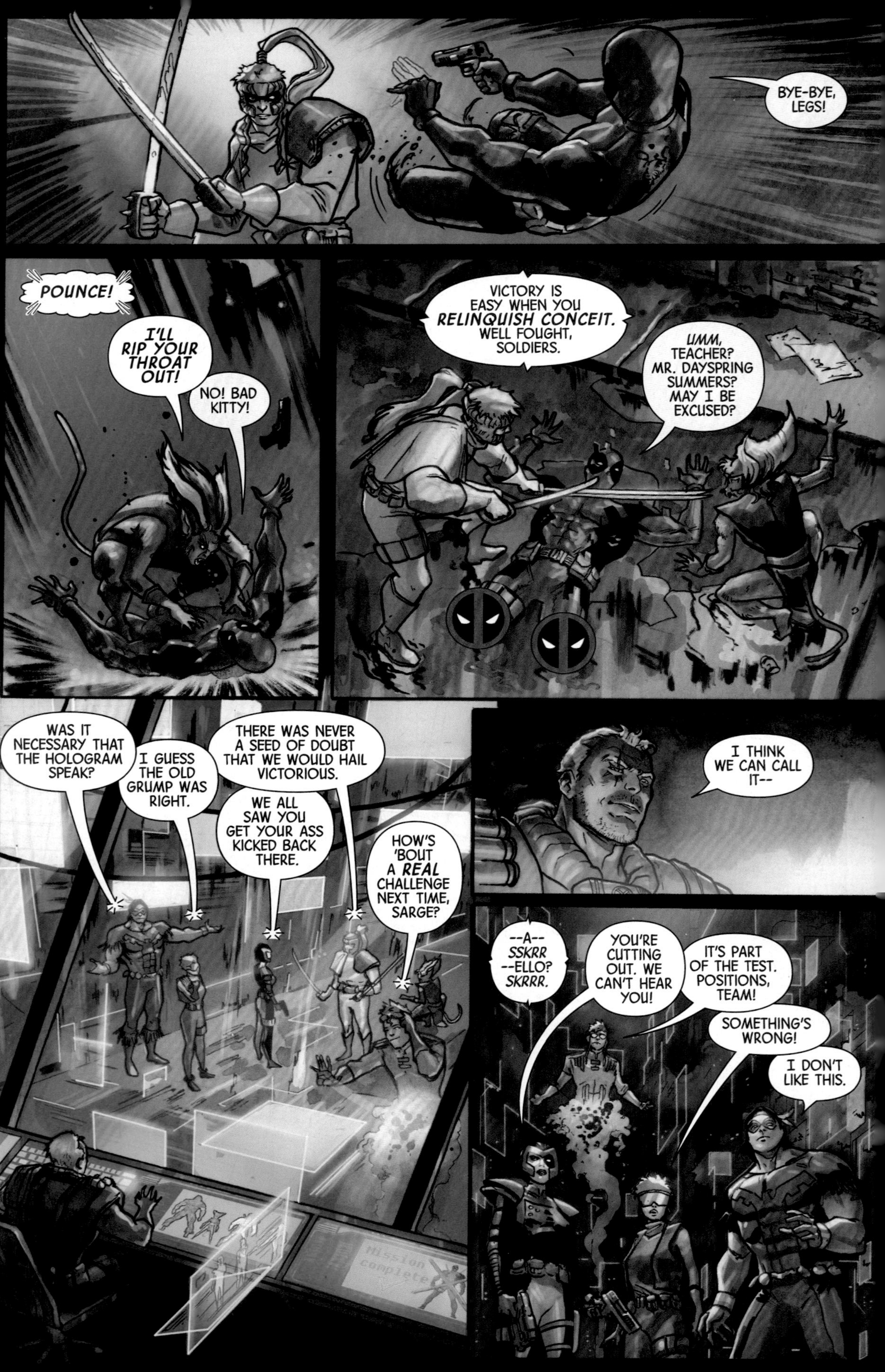
BYE-BYE, LEGS!
POUNCE!
I'LL RIP YOUR THROAT OUT!
NO! BAD KITTY!
VICTORY IS EASY WHEN YOU RELINQUISH CONCEIT. WELL FOUGHT, SOLDIERS.
UMM, TEACHER? MR. DAYSPRING SUMMERS? MAY I BE EXCUSED?
WAS IT NECESSARY THAT THE HOLOGRAM SPEAK?
I GUESS THE OLD GRUMP WAS RIGHT.
THERE WAS NEVER A SEED OF DOUBT THAT WE WOULD HAIL VICTORIOUS.
WE ALL SAW YOU GET YOUR ASS KICKED BACK THERE.
HOW'S 'BOUT A REAL CHALLENGE NEXT TIME, SARGE?
Mission complete
I THINK WE CAN CALL IT--
--A-- SSKRR --ELLO? SKRRR.
YOU'RE CUTTING OUT. WE CAN'T HEAR YOU!
IT'S PART OF THE TEST. POSITIONS, TEAM!
SOMETHING'S WRONG!
I DON'T LIKE THIS.

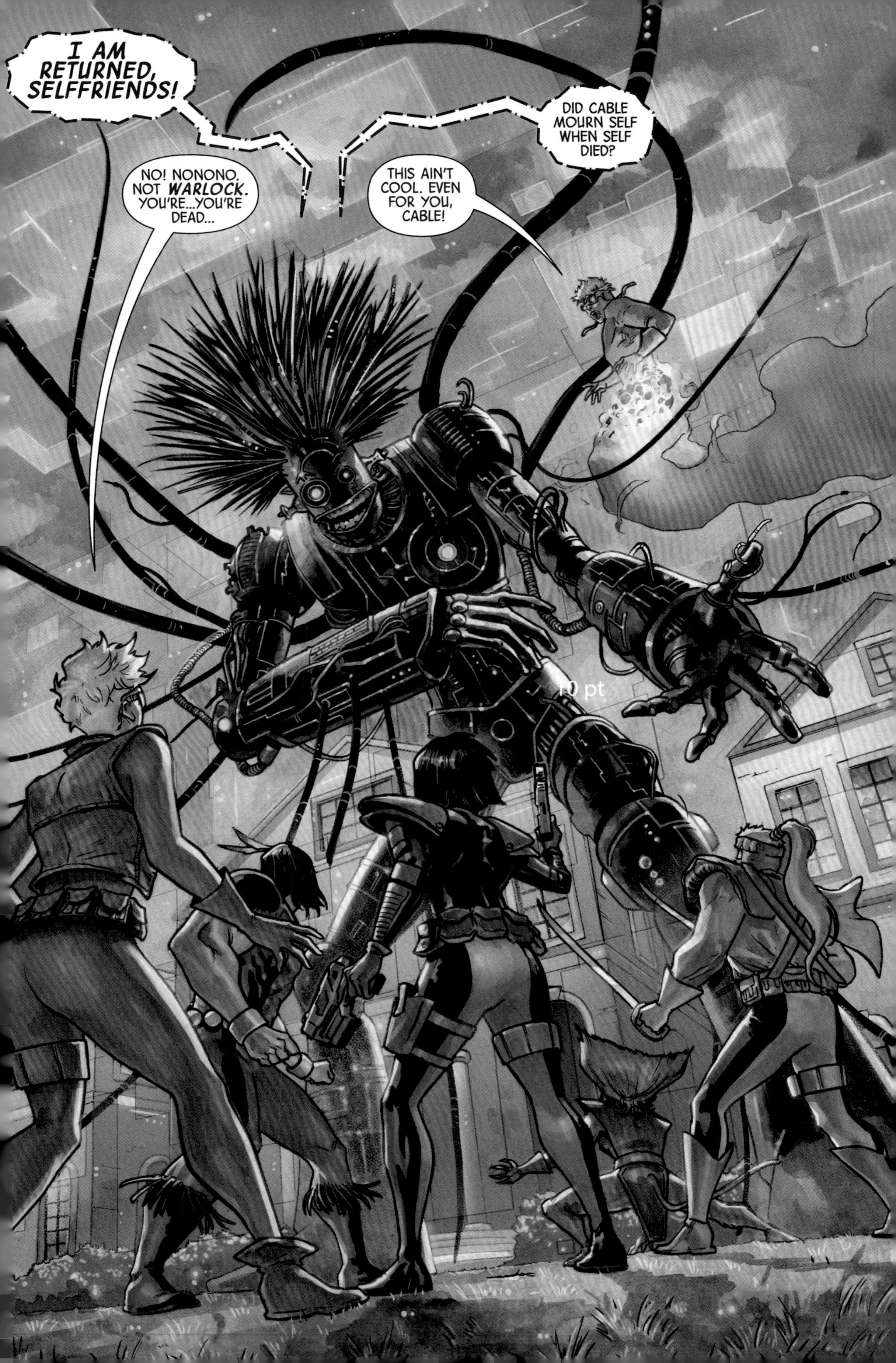
I AM RETURNED, SELFFRIENDS!
NO! NONONO. NOT *WARLOCK*. YOU'RE...YOU'RE DEAD...
THIS AIN'T COOL. EVEN FOR YOU, CABLE!
DID CABLE MOURN SELF WHEN SELF DIED?

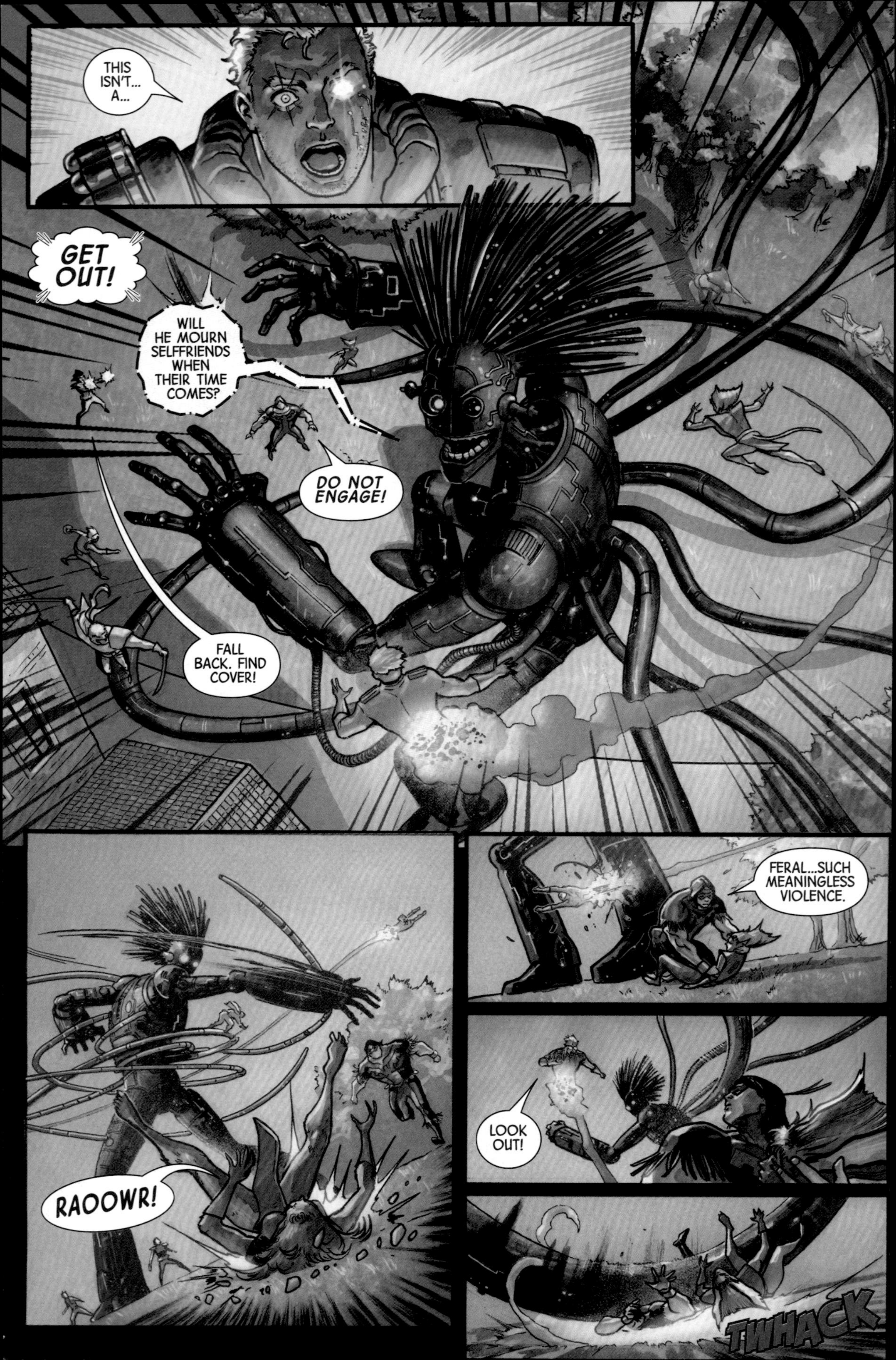
THIS ISN'T... A...
GET OUT!
WILL HE MOURN SELFFRIENDS WHEN THEIR TIME COMES?
DO NOT ENGAGE!
FALL BACK. FIND COVER!
RAOOWR!
FERAL...SUCH MEANINGLESS VIOLENCE.
LOOK OUT!
TWHACK

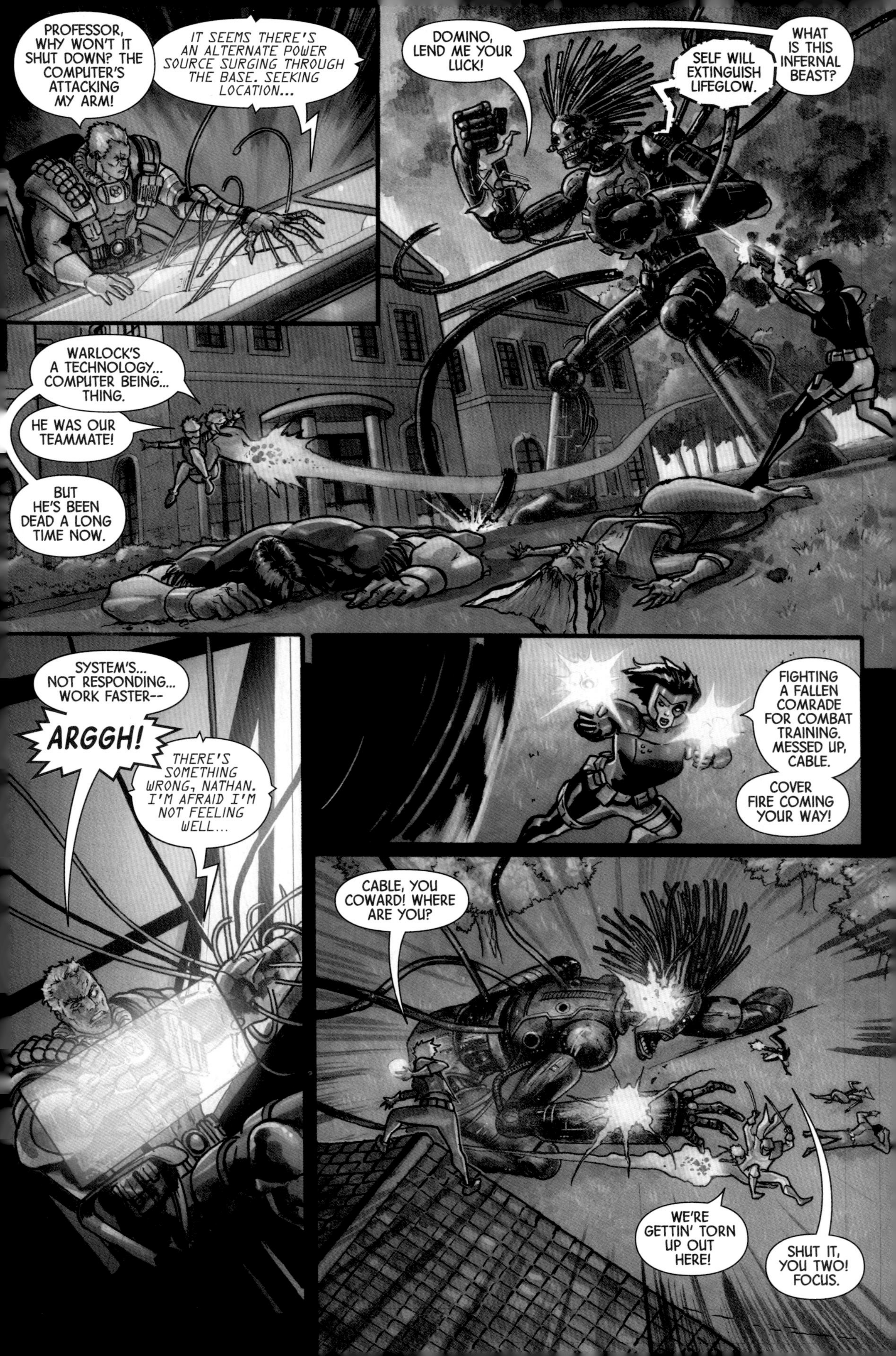
PROFESSOR, WHY WON'T IT SHUT DOWN? THE COMPUTER'S ATTACKING MY ARM!
IT SEEMS THERE'S AN ALTERNATE POWER SOURCE SURGING THROUGH THE BASE. SEEKING LOCATION...
DOMINO, LEND ME YOUR LUCK!
WHAT IS THIS INFERNAL BEAST?
SELF WILL EXTINGUISH LIFEGLOW.
WARLOCK'S A TECHNOLOGY... COMPUTER BEING... THING.
HE WAS OUR TEAMMATE!
BUT HE'S BEEN DEAD A LONG TIME NOW.
SYSTEM'S... NOT RESPONDING... WORK FASTER--
ARGGH!
THERE'S SOMETHING WRONG, NATHAN. I'M AFRAID I'M NOT FEELING WELL...
FIGHTING A FALLEN COMRADE FOR COMBAT TRAINING. MESSED UP, CABLE.
COVER FIRE COMING YOUR WAY!
CABLE, YOU COWARD! WHERE ARE YOU?
WE'RE GETTIN' TORN UP OUT HERE!
SHUT IT, YOU TWO! FOCUS.

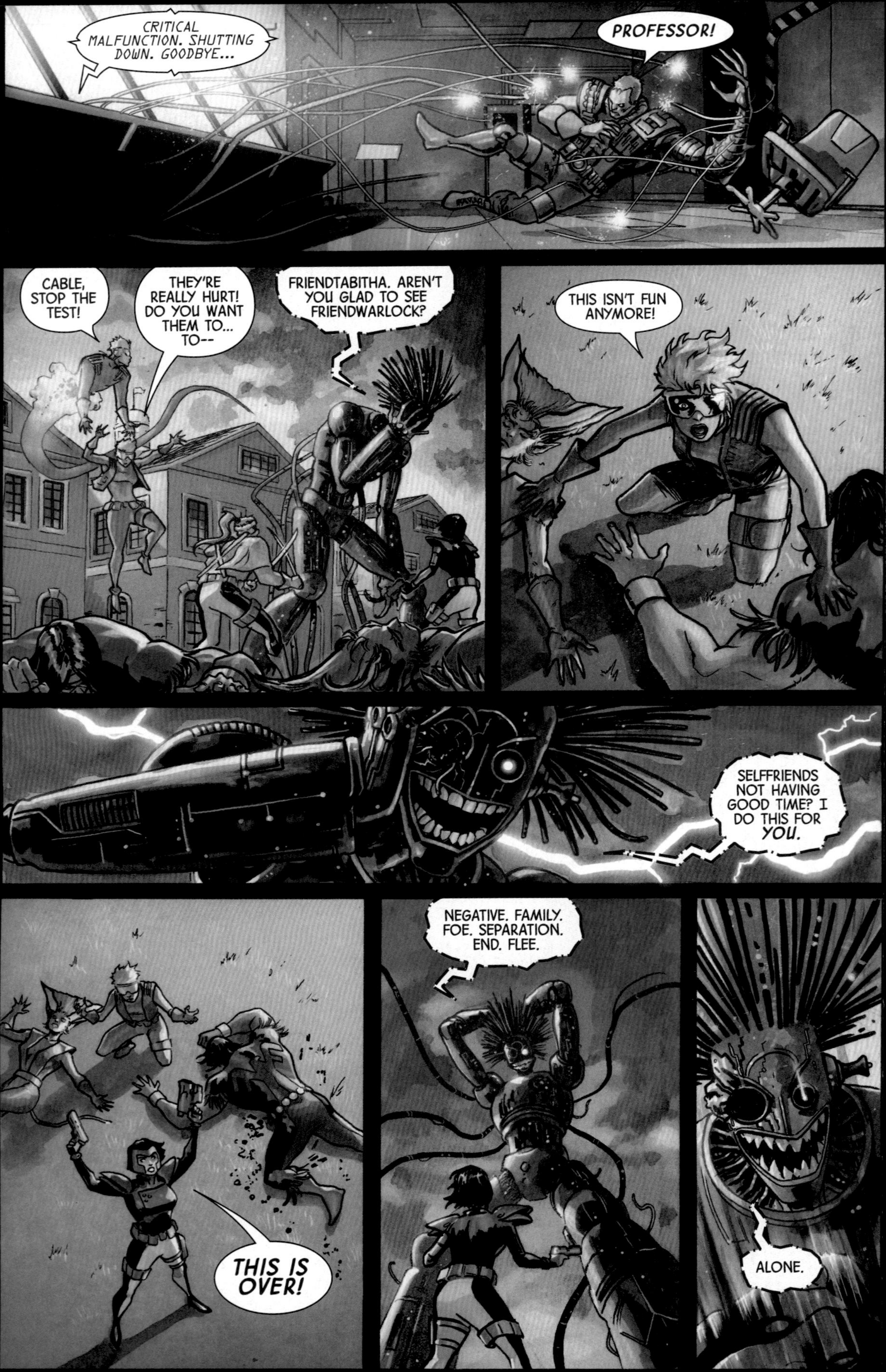
CRITICAL MALFUNCTION. SHUTTING DOWN. GOODBYE...
PROFESSOR!
CABLE, STOP THE TEST!
THEY'RE REALLY HURT! DO YOU WANT THEM TO... TO--
FRIENDTABITHA. AREN'T YOU GLAD TO SEE FRIENDWARLOCK?
THIS ISN'T FUN ANYMORE!
SELFFRIENDS NOT HAVING GOOD TIME? I DO THIS FOR YOU.
THIS IS OVER!
NEGATIVE. FAMILY. FOE. SEPARATION. END. FLEE.
ALONE.

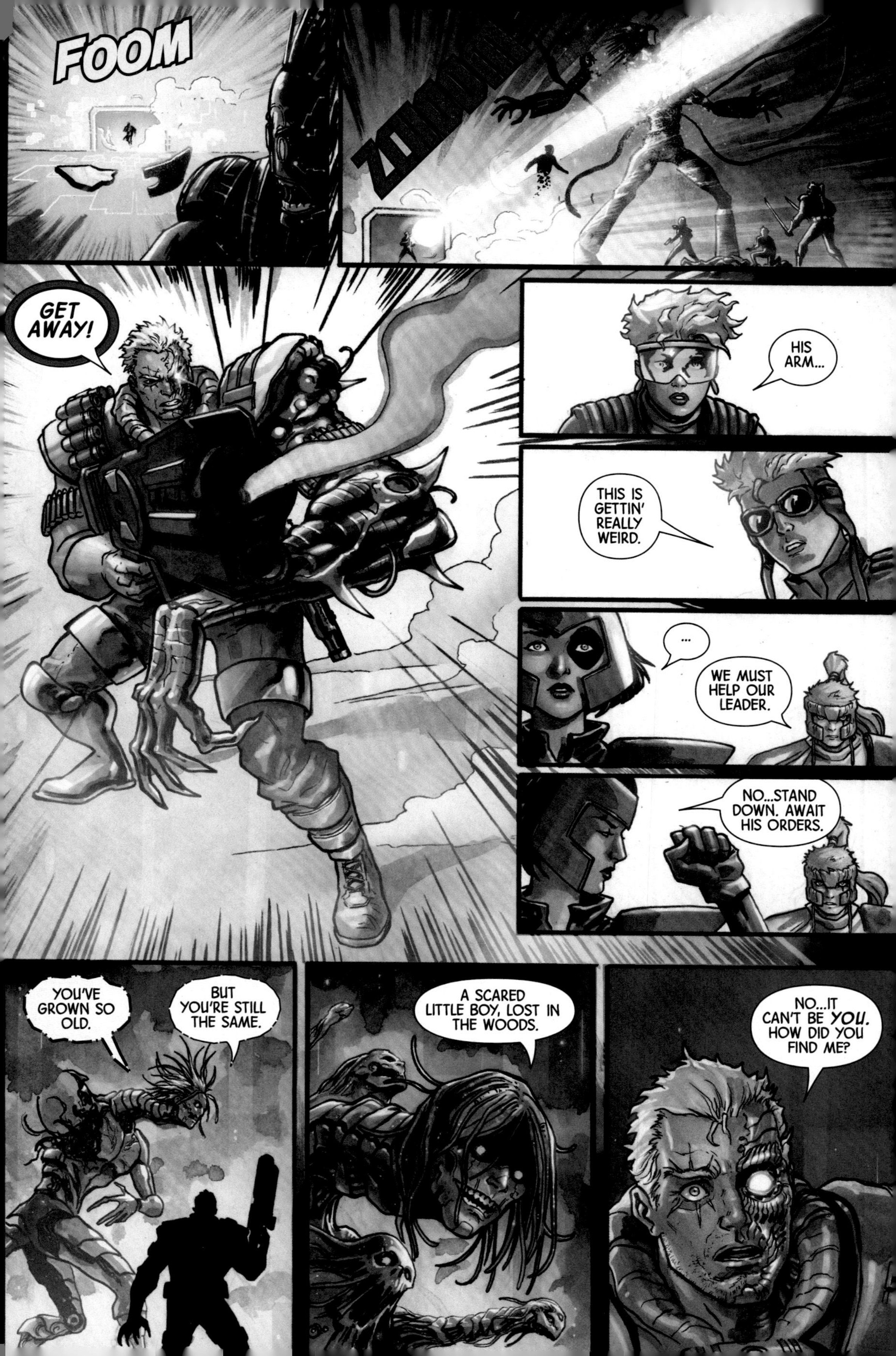
FOOM
GET AWAY!
HIS ARM...
THIS IS GETTIN' REALLY WEIRD.
...
WE MUST HELP OUR LEADER.
NO...STAND DOWN. AWAIT HIS ORDERS.
YOU'VE GROWN SO OLD.
BUT YOU'RE STILL THE SAME.
A SCARED LITTLE BOY, LOST IN THE WOODS.
NO...IT CAN'T BE YOU. HOW DID YOU FIND ME?

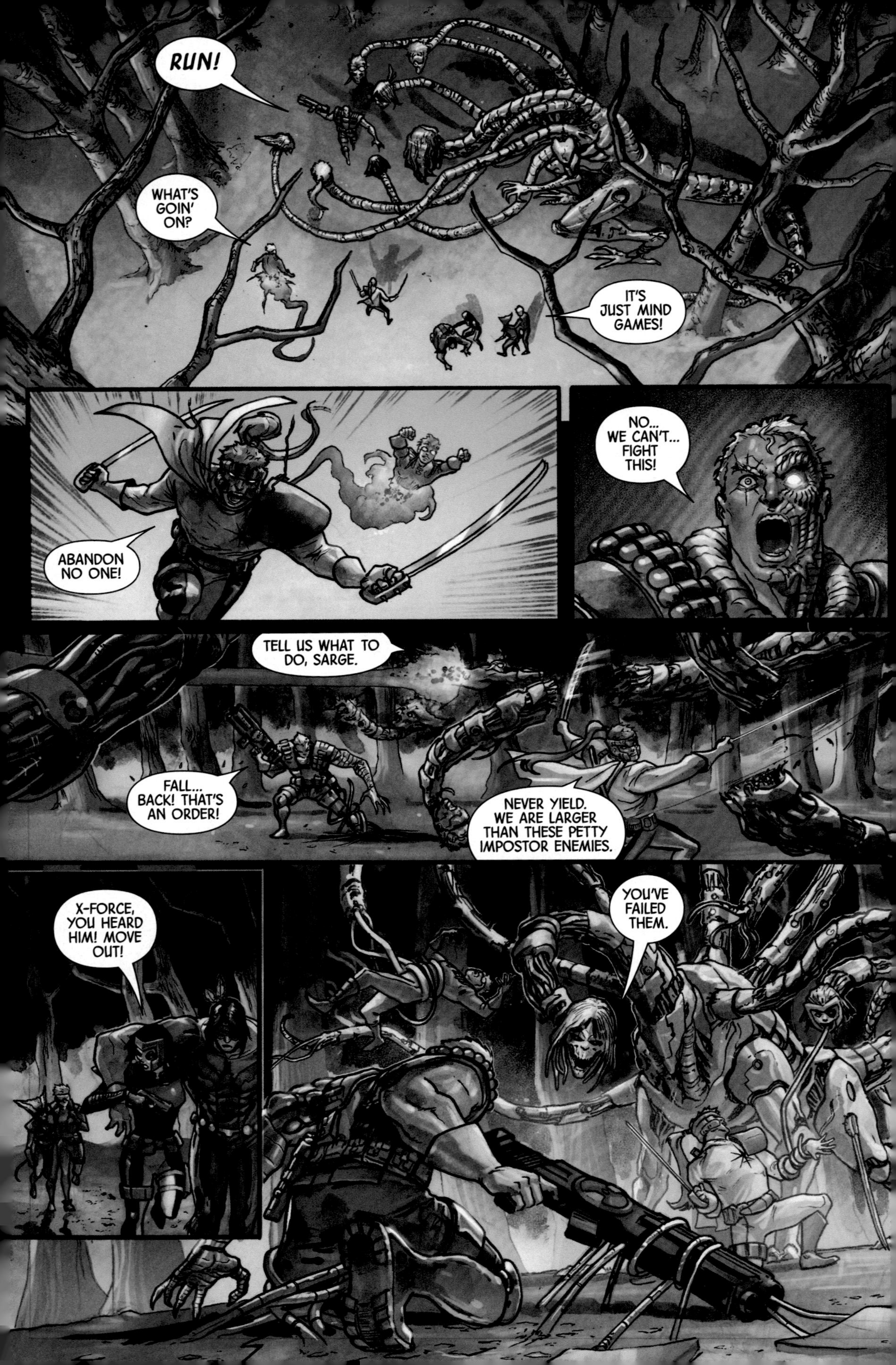
RUN!
WHAT'S GOIN' ON?
IT'S JUST MIND GAMES!
ABANDON NO ONE!
NO... WE CAN'T... FIGHT THIS!
TELL US WHAT TO DO, SARGE.
FALL... BACK! THAT'S AN ORDER!
NEVER YIELD. WE ARE LARGER THAN THESE PETTY IMPOSTOR ENEMIES.
X-FORCE, YOU HEARD HIM! MOVE OUT!
YOU'VE FAILED THEM.

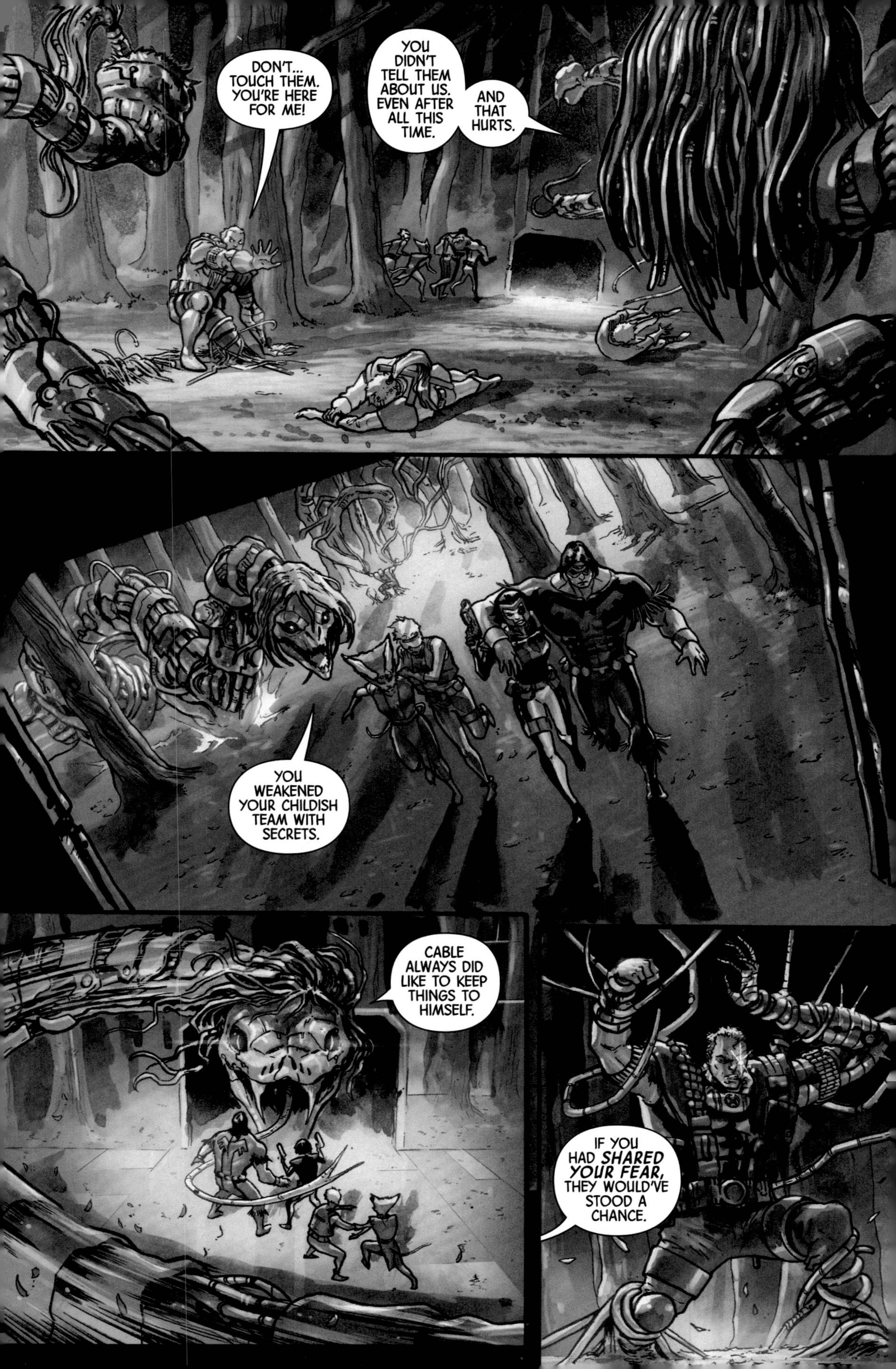
DON'T... TOUCH THEM. YOU'RE HERE FOR ME!
YOU DIDN'T TELL THEM ABOUT US. EVEN AFTER ALL THIS TIME.
AND THAT HURTS.
YOU WEAKENED YOUR CHILDISH TEAM WITH SECRETS.
CABLE ALWAYS DID LIKE TO KEEP THINGS TO HIMSELF.
IF YOU HAD SHARED YOUR FEAR, THEY WOULD'VE STOOD A CHANCE.

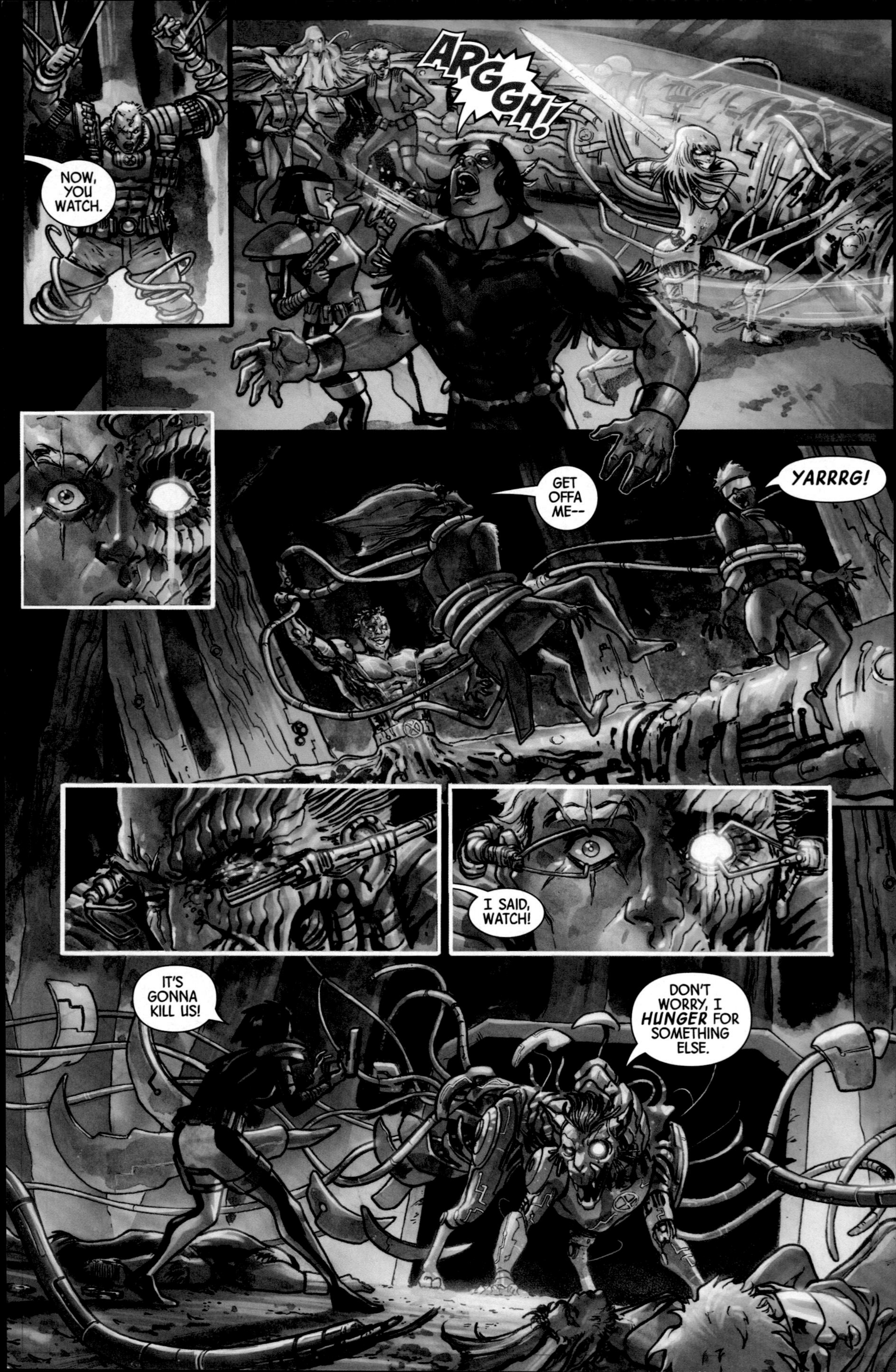
NOW, YOU WATCH.
ARGGH!
GET OFFA ME--
YARRRG!
I SAID, WATCH!
IT'S GONNA KILL US!
DON'T WORRY, I HUNGER FOR SOMETHING ELSE.

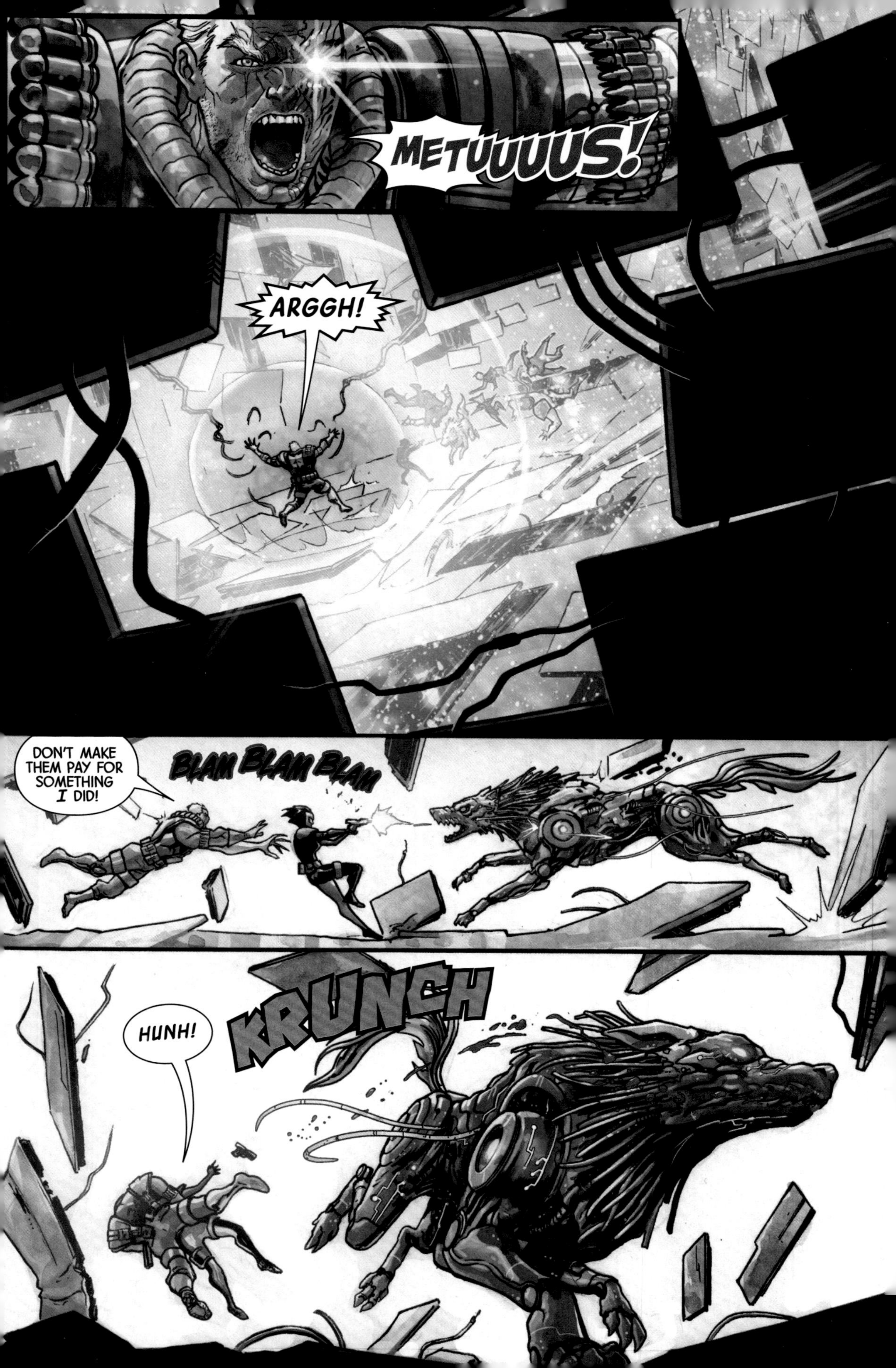
METUUUUS!
ARGGH!
DON'T MAKE THEM PAY FOR SOMETHING *I* DID!
BLAM BLAM BLAM
HUNH!
KRUNCH

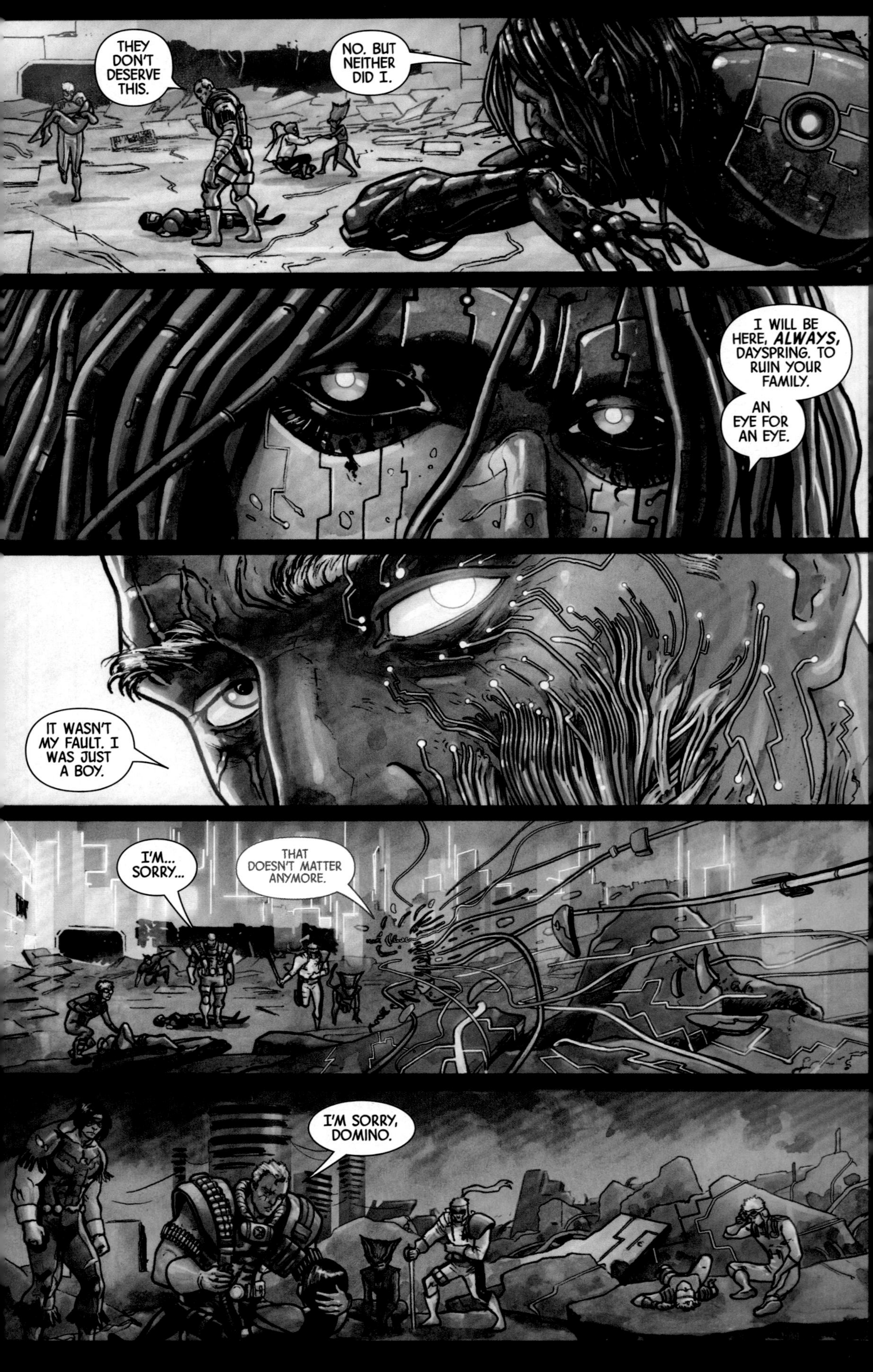
THEY DON'T DESERVE THIS.
NO. BUT NEITHER DID I.
I WILL BE HERE, ALWAYS, DAYSPRING. TO RUIN YOUR FAMILY.
AN EYE FOR AN EYE.
IT WASN'T MY FAULT. I WAS JUST A BOY.
I'M... SORRY...
THAT DOESN'T MATTER ANYMORE.
I'M SORRY, DOMINO.

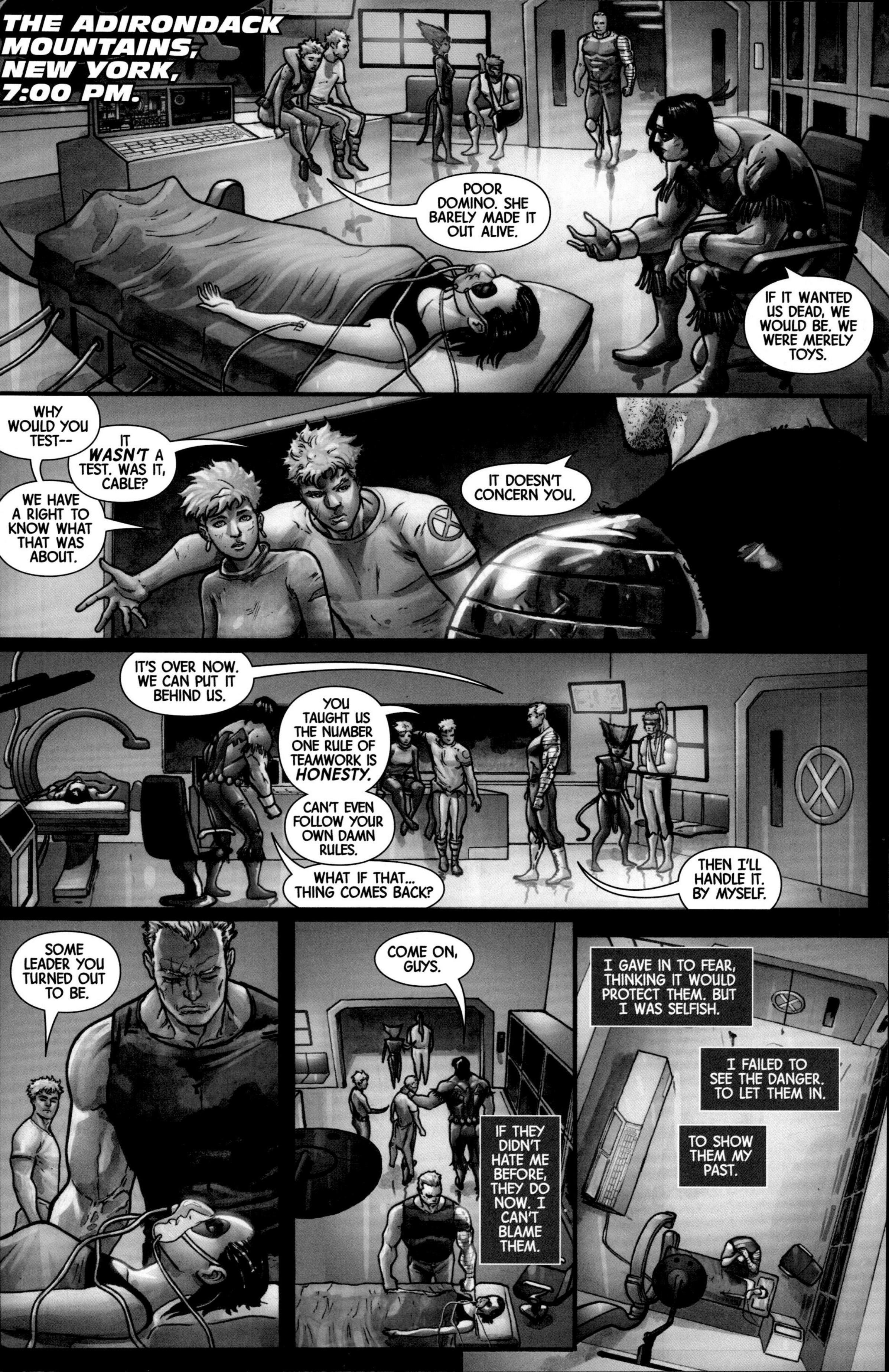
THE ADIRONDACK MOUNTAINS, NEW YORK, 7:00 PM.
POOR DOMINO. SHE BARELY MADE IT OUT ALIVE.
IF IT WANTED US DEAD, WE WOULD BE. WE WERE MERELY TOYS.
WHY WOULD YOU TEST--
IT WASN'T A TEST. WAS IT, CABLE?
WE HAVE A RIGHT TO KNOW WHAT THAT WAS ABOUT.
IT DOESN'T CONCERN YOU.
IT'S OVER NOW. WE CAN PUT IT BEHIND US.
YOU TAUGHT US THE NUMBER ONE RULE OF TEAMWORK IS HONESTY.
CAN'T EVEN FOLLOW YOUR OWN DAMN RULES.
WHAT IF THAT... THING COMES BACK?
THEN I'LL HANDLE IT. BY MYSELF.
SOME LEADER YOU TURNED OUT TO BE.
COME ON, GUYS.
IF THEY DIDN'T HATE ME BEFORE, THEY DO NOW. I CAN'T BLAME THEM.
I GAVE IN TO FEAR, THINKING IT WOULD PROTECT THEM. BUT I WAS SELFISH.
I FAILED TO SEE THE DANGER. TO LET THEM IN.
TO SHOW THEM MY PAST.

159

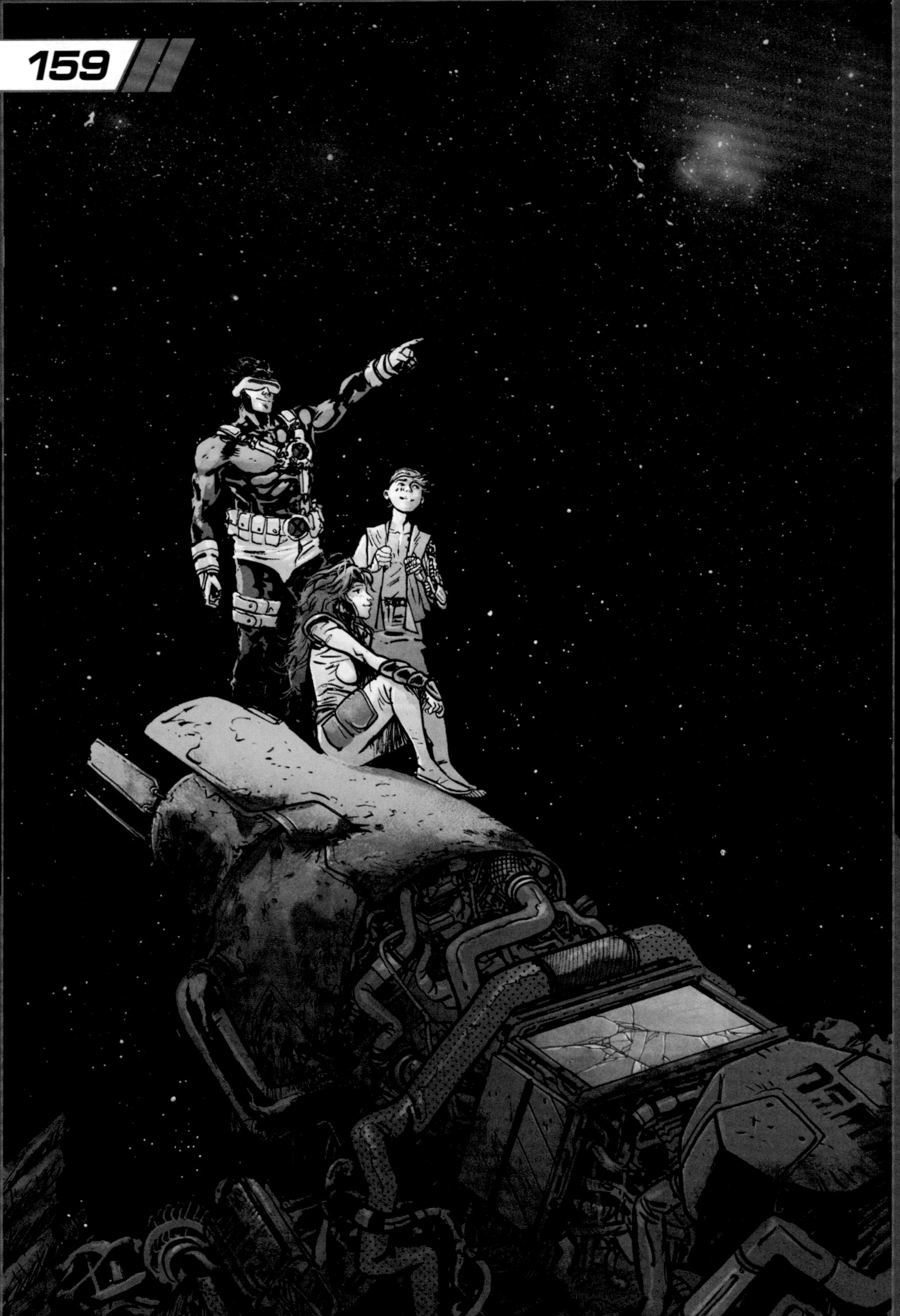

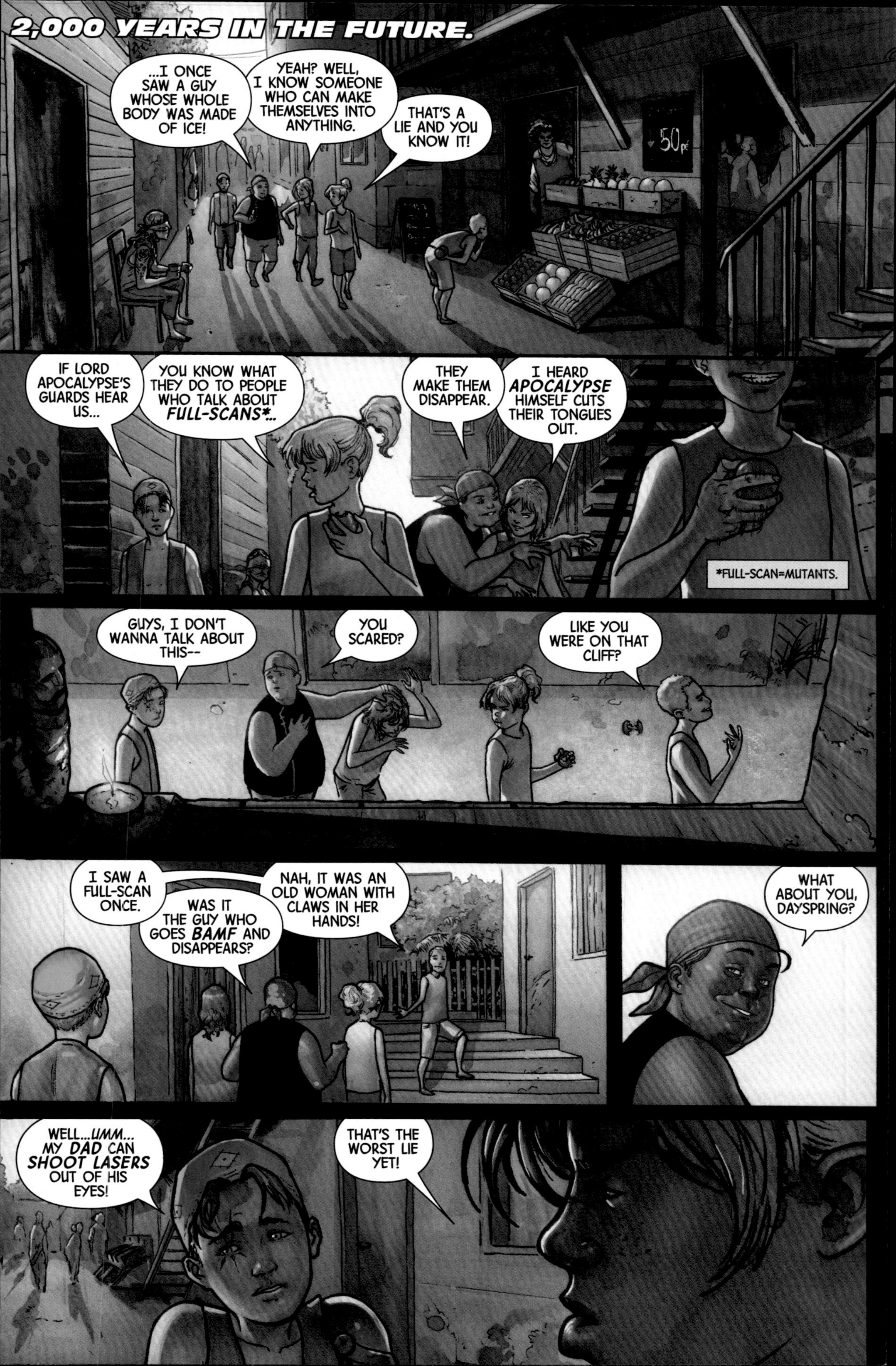
2,000 YEARS IN THE FUTURE.
...I ONCE SAW A GUY WHOSE WHOLE BODY WAS MADE OF ICE!
YEAH? WELL, I KNOW SOMEONE WHO CAN MAKE THEMSELVES INTO ANYTHING.
THAT'S A LIE AND YOU KNOW IT!
50
IF LORD APOCALYPSE'S GUARDS HEAR US...
YOU KNOW WHAT THEY DO TO PEOPLE WHO TALK ABOUT FULL-SCANS*...
THEY MAKE THEM DISAPPEAR.
I HEARD APOCALYPSE HIMSELF CUTS THEIR TONGUES OUT.
*FULL-SCAN=MUTANTS.
GUYS, I DON'T WANNA TALK ABOUT THIS--
YOU SCARED?
LIKE YOU WERE ON THAT CLIFF?
I SAW A FULL-SCAN ONCE.
WAS IT THE GUY WHO GOES BAMF AND DISAPPEARS?
NAH, IT WAS AN OLD WOMAN WITH CLAWS IN HER HANDS!
WHAT ABOUT YOU, DAYSPRING?
WELL...UMM... MY DAD CAN SHOOT LASERS OUT OF HIS EYES!
THAT'S THE WORST LIE YET!

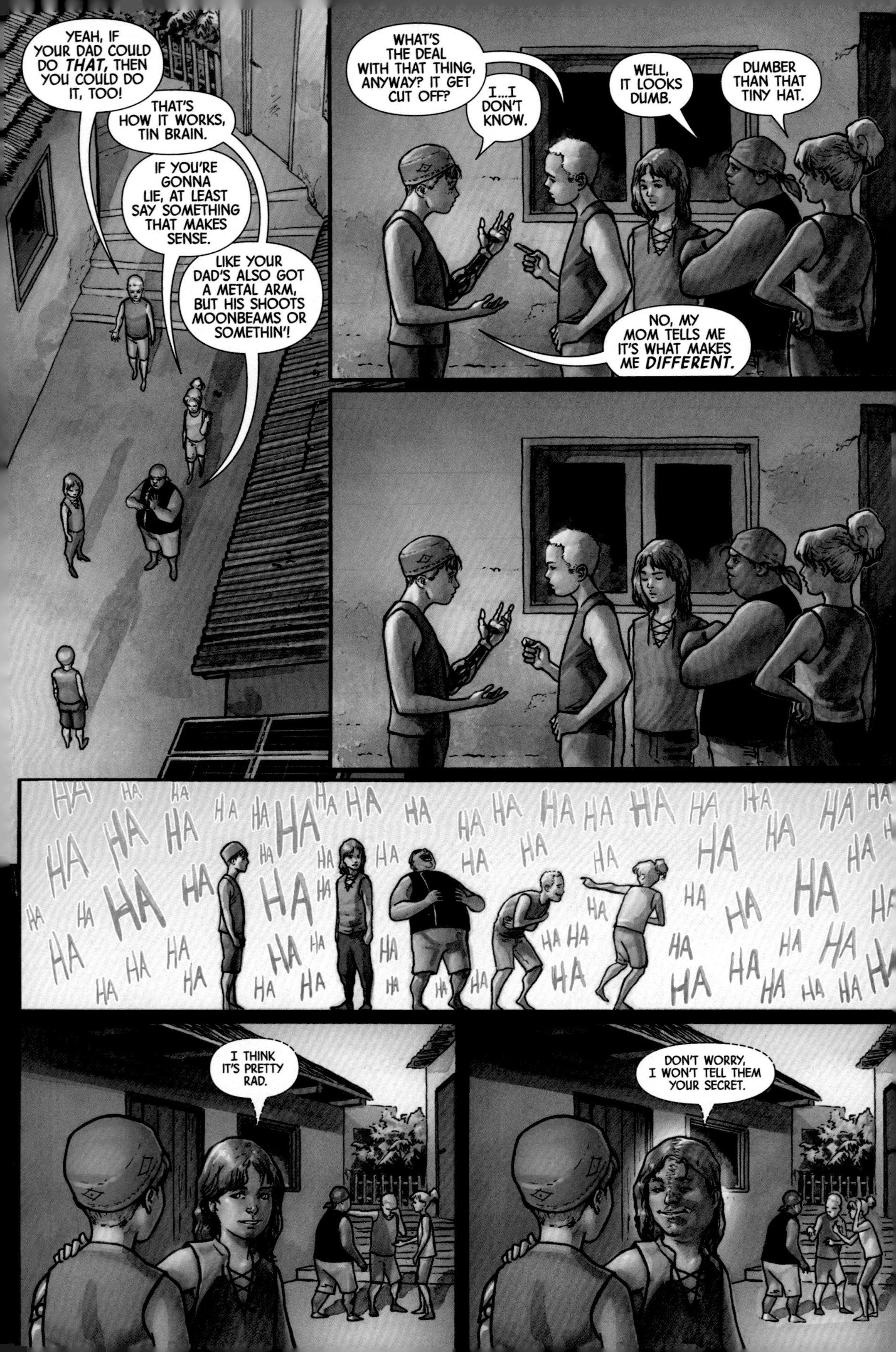
YEAH, IF YOUR DAD COULD DO *THAT*, THEN YOU COULD DO IT, TOO!
THAT'S HOW IT WORKS, TIN BRAIN.
IF YOU'RE GONNA LIE, AT LEAST SAY SOMETHING THAT MAKES SENSE.
LIKE YOUR DAD'S ALSO GOT A METAL ARM, BUT HIS SHOOTS MOONBEAMS OR SOMETHIN'!
WHAT'S THE DEAL WITH THAT THING, ANYWAY? IT GET CUT OFF?
I...I DON'T KNOW.
WELL, IT LOOKS DUMB.
DUMBER THAN THAT TINY HAT.
NO, MY MOM TELLS ME IT'S WHAT MAKES ME *DIFFERENT*.
HA HA HA HA HA HA HA HA HA HA HA HA HA HA HA HA HA HA HA HA HA HA HA HA
I THINK IT'S PRETTY RAD.
DON'T WORRY, I WON'T TELL THEM YOUR SECRET.

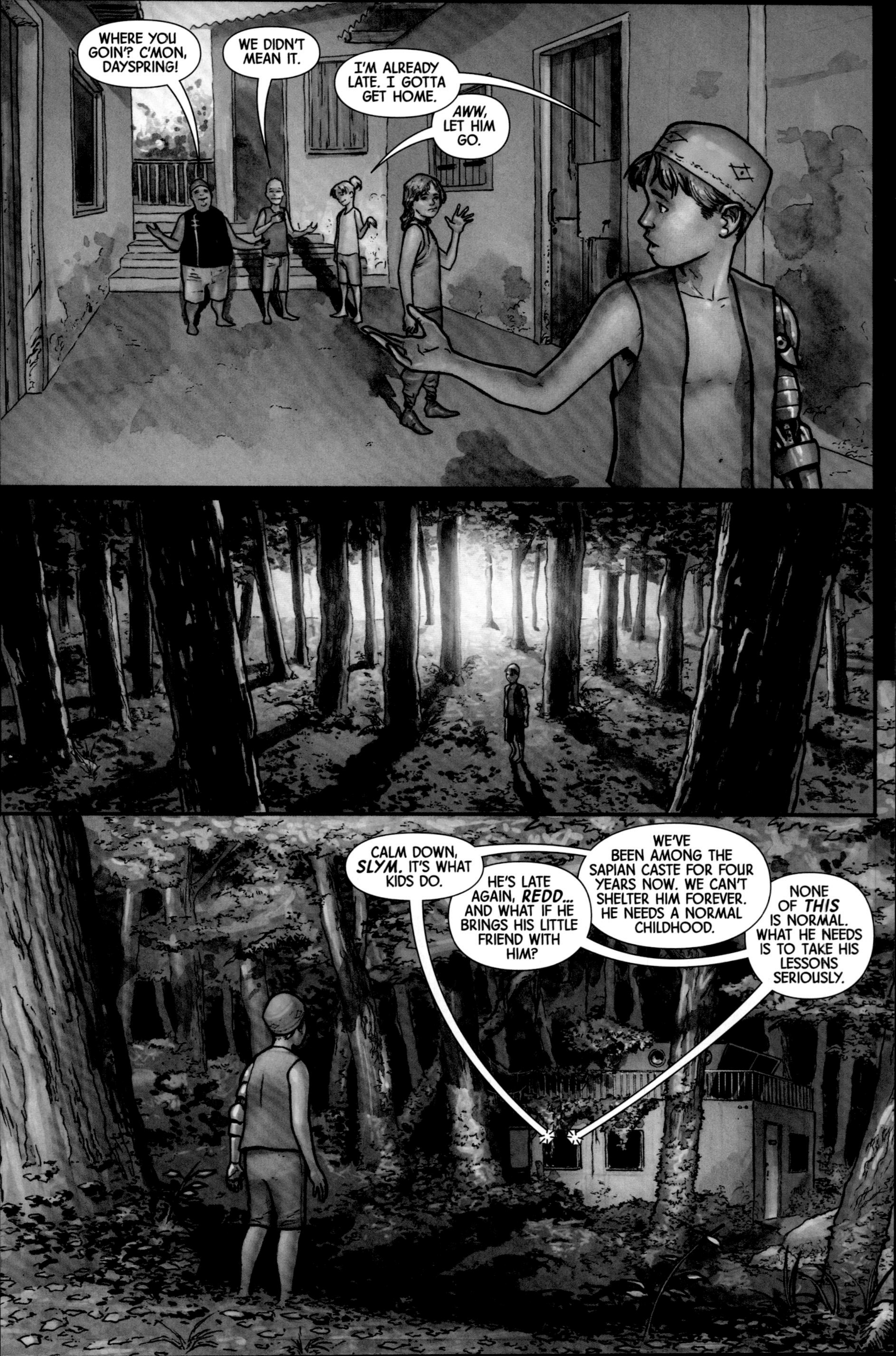
WHERE YOU GOIN'? C'MON, DAYSPRING!
WE DIDN'T MEAN IT.
I'M ALREADY LATE. I GOTTA GET HOME.
AWW, LET HIM GO.
CALM DOWN, SLYM. IT'S WHAT KIDS DO.
HE'S LATE AGAIN, REDD... AND WHAT IF HE BRINGS HIS LITTLE FRIEND WITH HIM?
WE'VE BEEN AMONG THE SAPIAN CASTE FOR FOUR YEARS NOW. WE CAN'T SHELTER HIM FOREVER. HE NEEDS A NORMAL CHILDHOOD.
NONE OF THIS IS NORMAL. WHAT HE NEEDS IS TO TAKE HIS LESSONS SERIOUSLY.

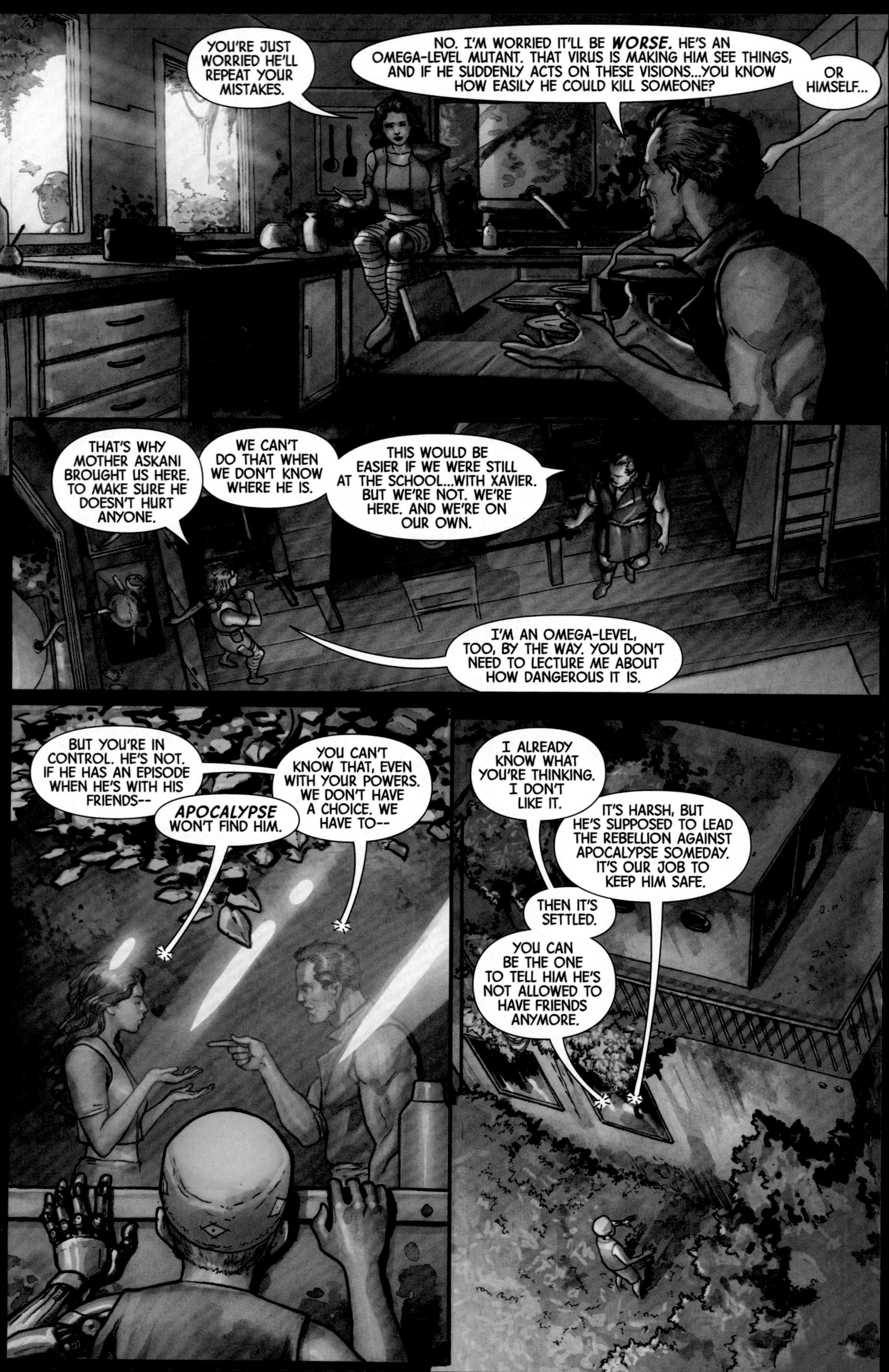
YOU'RE JUST WORRIED HE'LL REPEAT YOUR MISTAKES.
NO. I'M WORRIED IT'LL BE *WORSE.* HE'S AN OMEGA-LEVEL MUTANT. THAT VIRUS IS MAKING HIM SEE THINGS, AND IF HE SUDDENLY ACTS ON THESE VISIONS...YOU KNOW HOW EASILY HE COULD KILL SOMEONE?
OR HIMSELF...
THAT'S WHY MOTHER ASKANI BROUGHT US HERE. TO MAKE SURE HE DOESN'T HURT ANYONE.
WE CAN'T DO THAT WHEN WE DON'T KNOW WHERE HE IS.
THIS WOULD BE EASIER IF WE WERE STILL AT THE SCHOOL...WITH XAVIER. BUT WE'RE NOT. WE'RE HERE. AND WE'RE ON OUR OWN.
I'M AN OMEGA-LEVEL, TOO, BY THE WAY. YOU DON'T NEED TO LECTURE ME ABOUT HOW DANGEROUS IT IS.
BUT YOU'RE IN CONTROL. HE'S NOT. IF HE HAS AN EPISODE WHEN HE'S WITH HIS FRIENDS--
YOU CAN'T KNOW THAT, EVEN WITH YOUR POWERS. WE DON'T HAVE A CHOICE. WE HAVE TO--
APOCALYPSE WON'T FIND HIM.
I ALREADY KNOW WHAT YOU'RE THINKING. I DON'T LIKE IT.
IT'S HARSH, BUT HE'S SUPPOSED TO LEAD THE REBELLION AGAINST APOCALYPSE SOMEDAY. IT'S OUR JOB TO KEEP HIM SAFE.
THEN IT'S SETTLED.
YOU CAN BE THE ONE TO TELL HIM HE'S NOT ALLOWED TO HAVE FRIENDS ANYMORE.

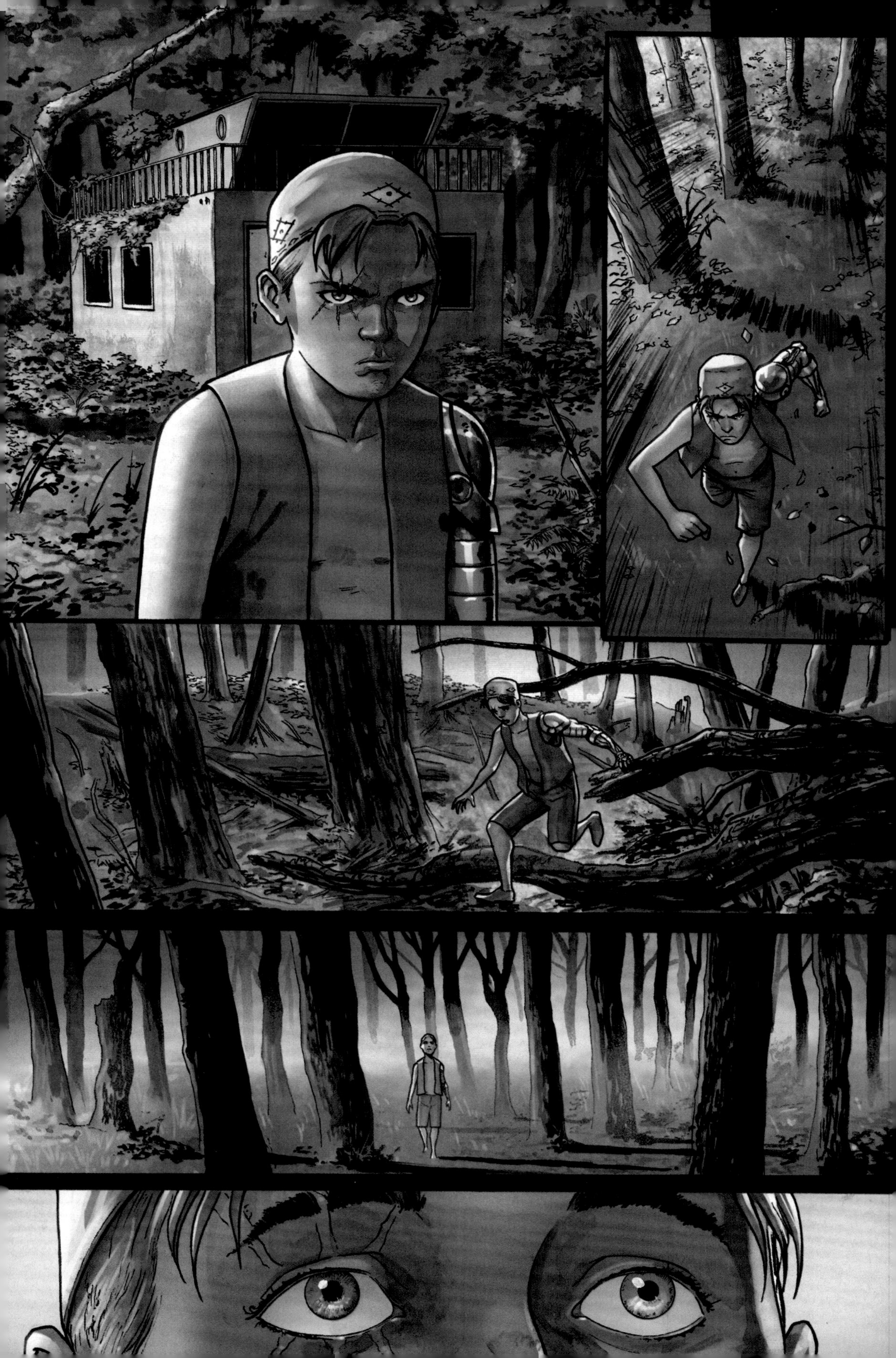

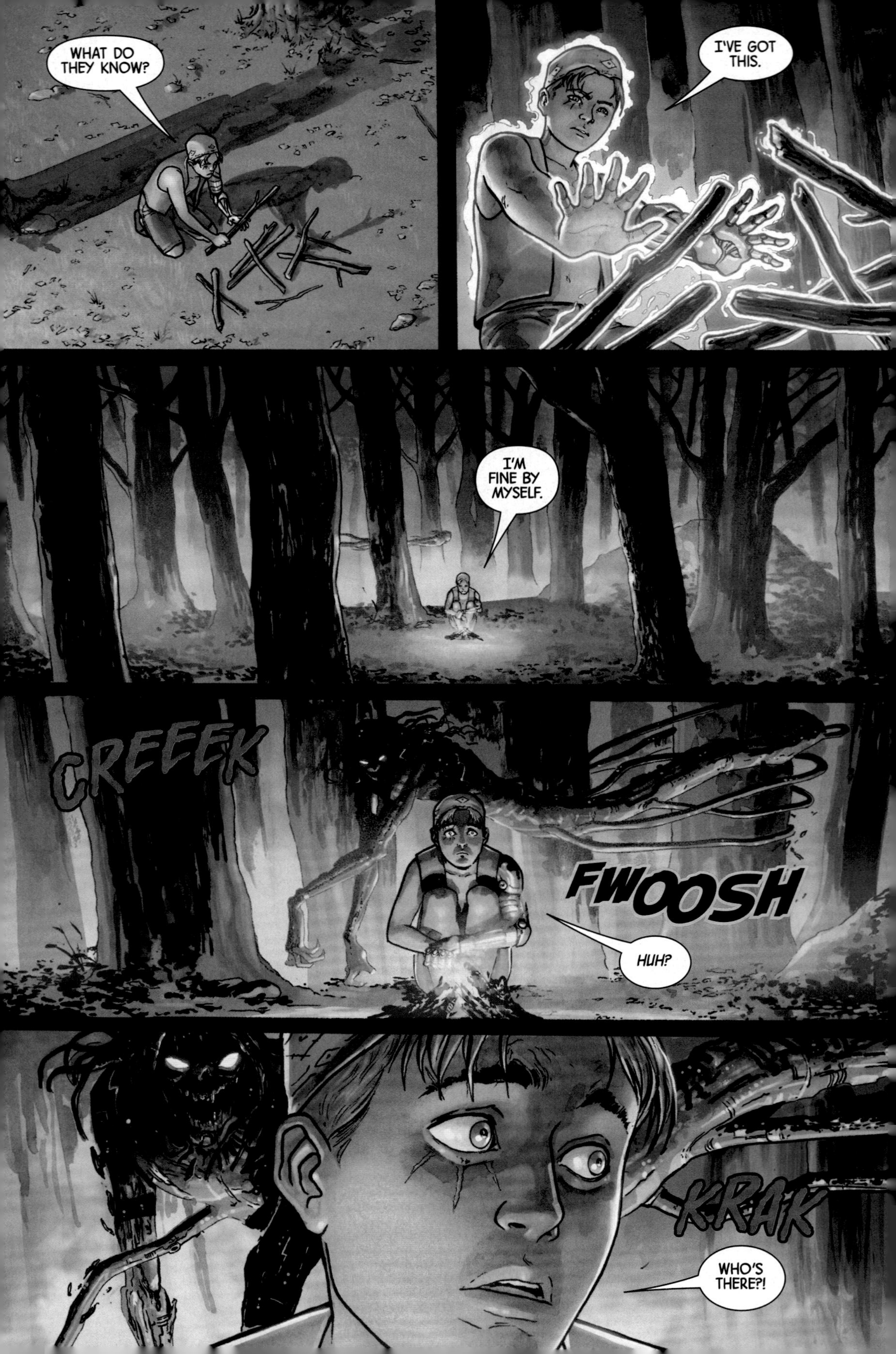
WHAT DO THEY KNOW?
I'VE GOT THIS.
I'M FINE BY MYSELF.
CREEEK
FWOOSH
HUH?
KRAK
WHO'S THERE?!

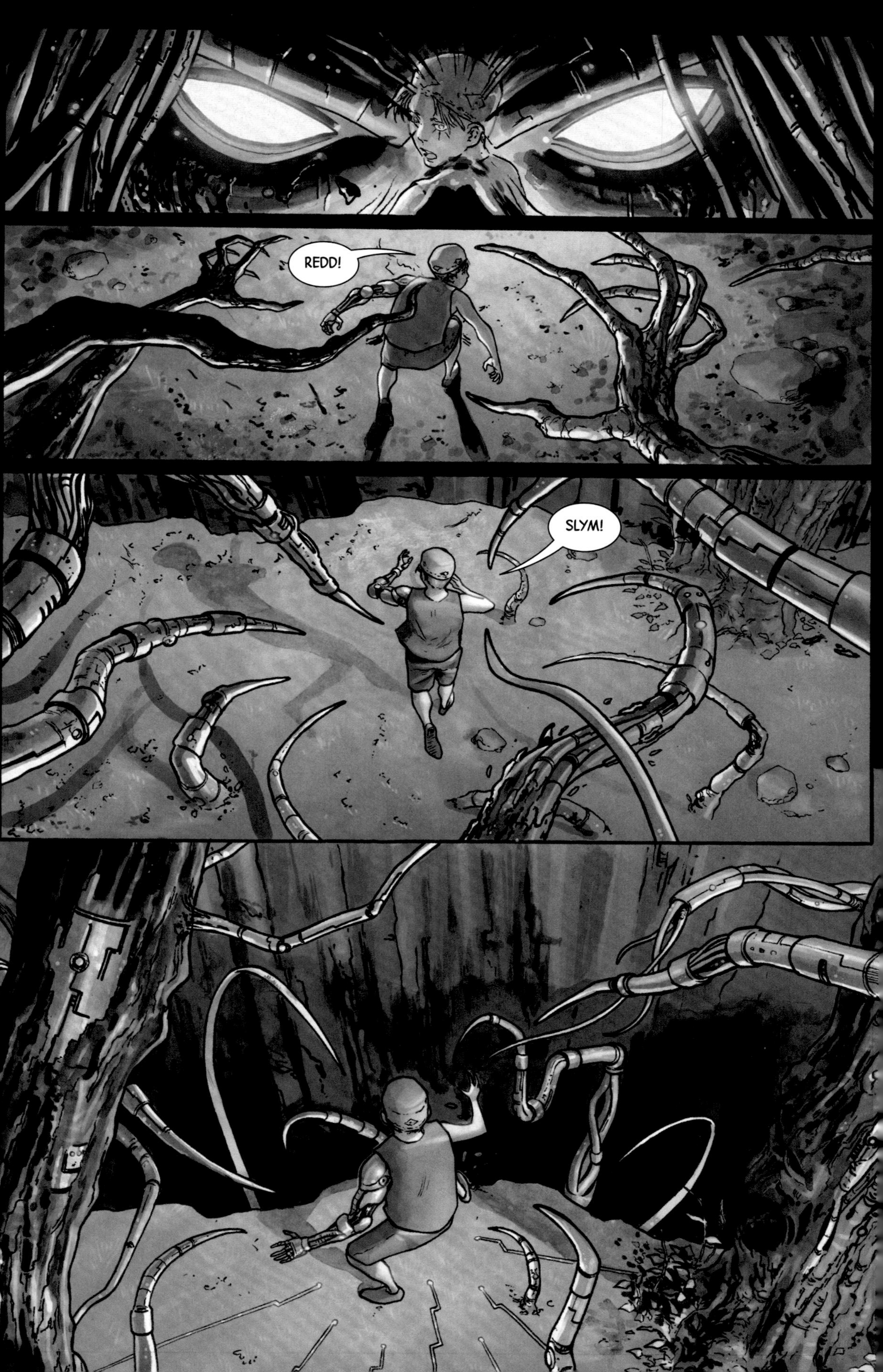
REDD!
SLYM!

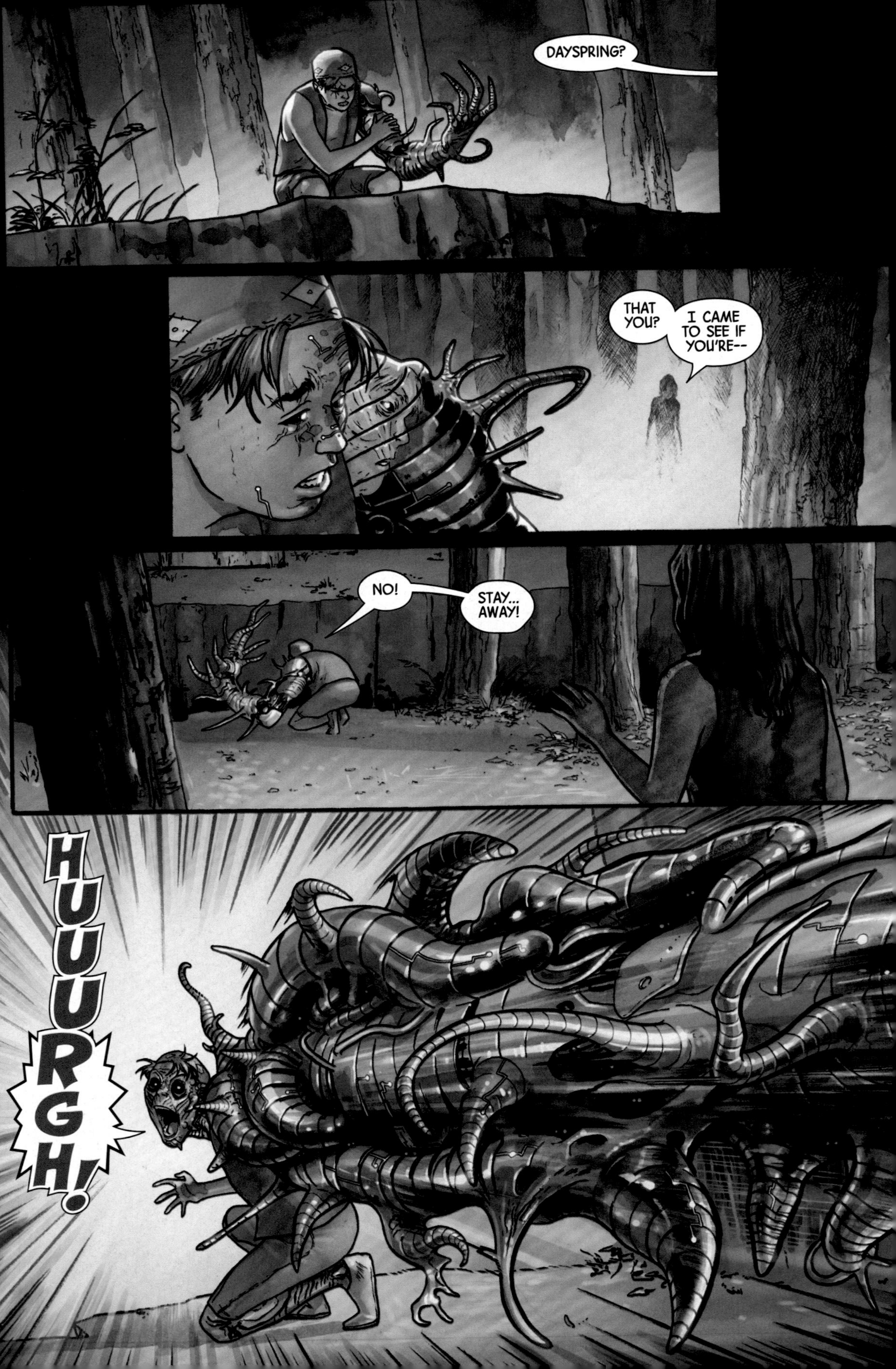
DAYSPRING?
THAT YOU?
I CAME TO SEE IF YOU'RE--
NO!
STAY... AWAY!
HUUUURGH!

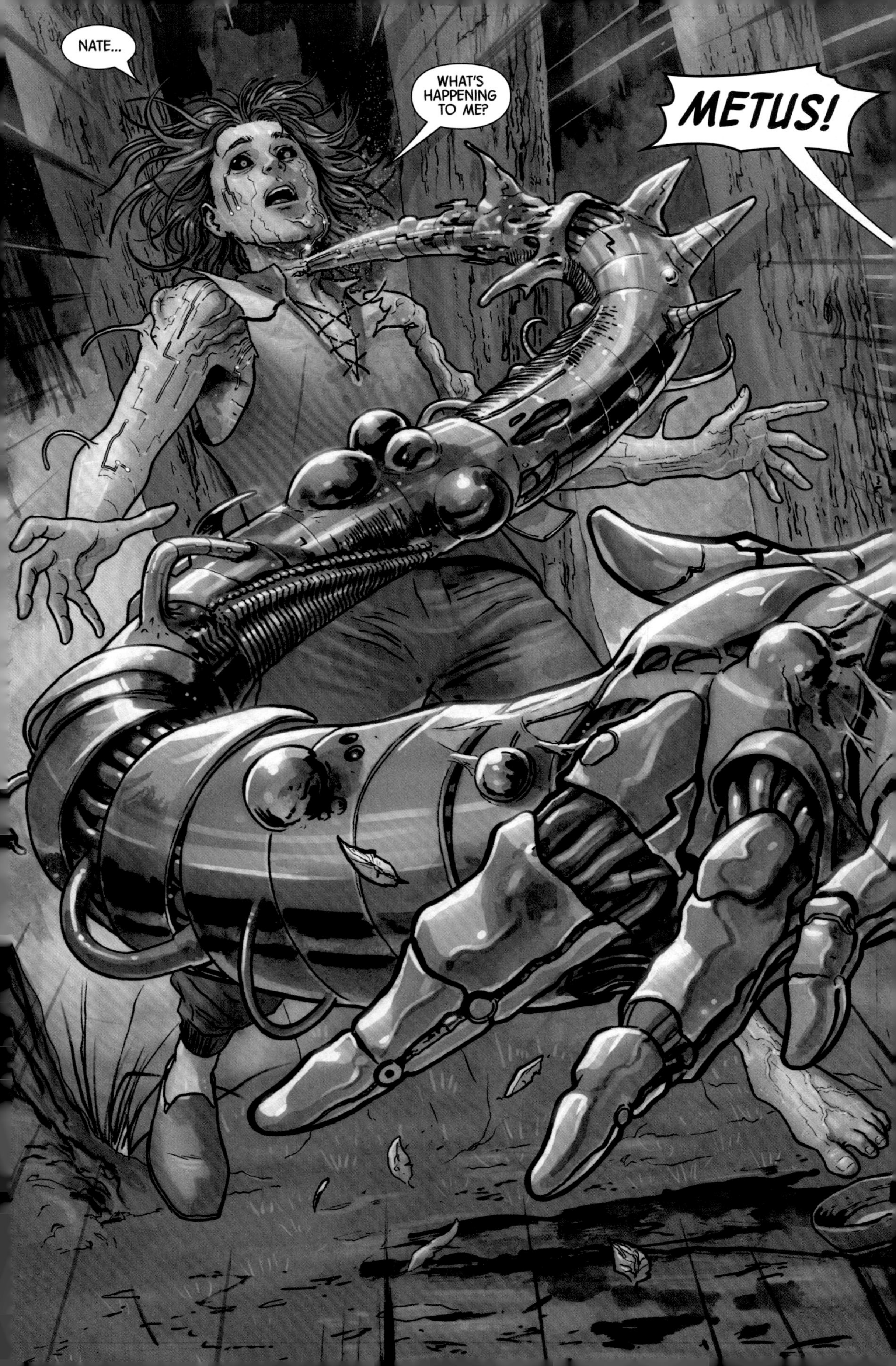
NATE...
WHAT'S HAPPENING TO ME?
METUS!

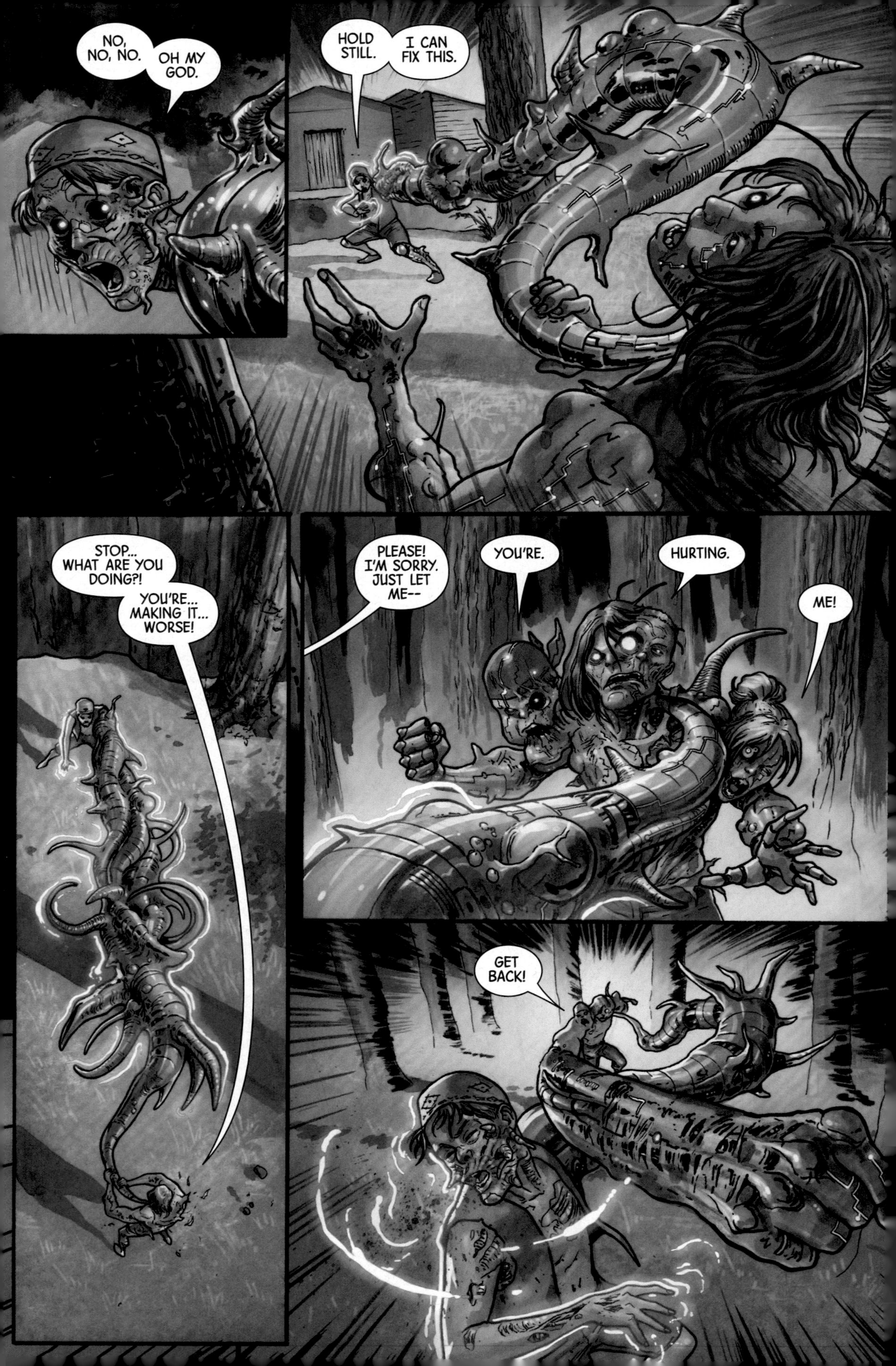
NO, NO, NO.
OH MY GOD.
HOLD STILL.
I CAN FIX THIS.
STOP... WHAT ARE YOU DOING?!
YOU'RE... MAKING IT... WORSE!
PLEASE! I'M SORRY. JUST LET ME--
YOU'RE.
HURTING.
ME!
GET BACK!

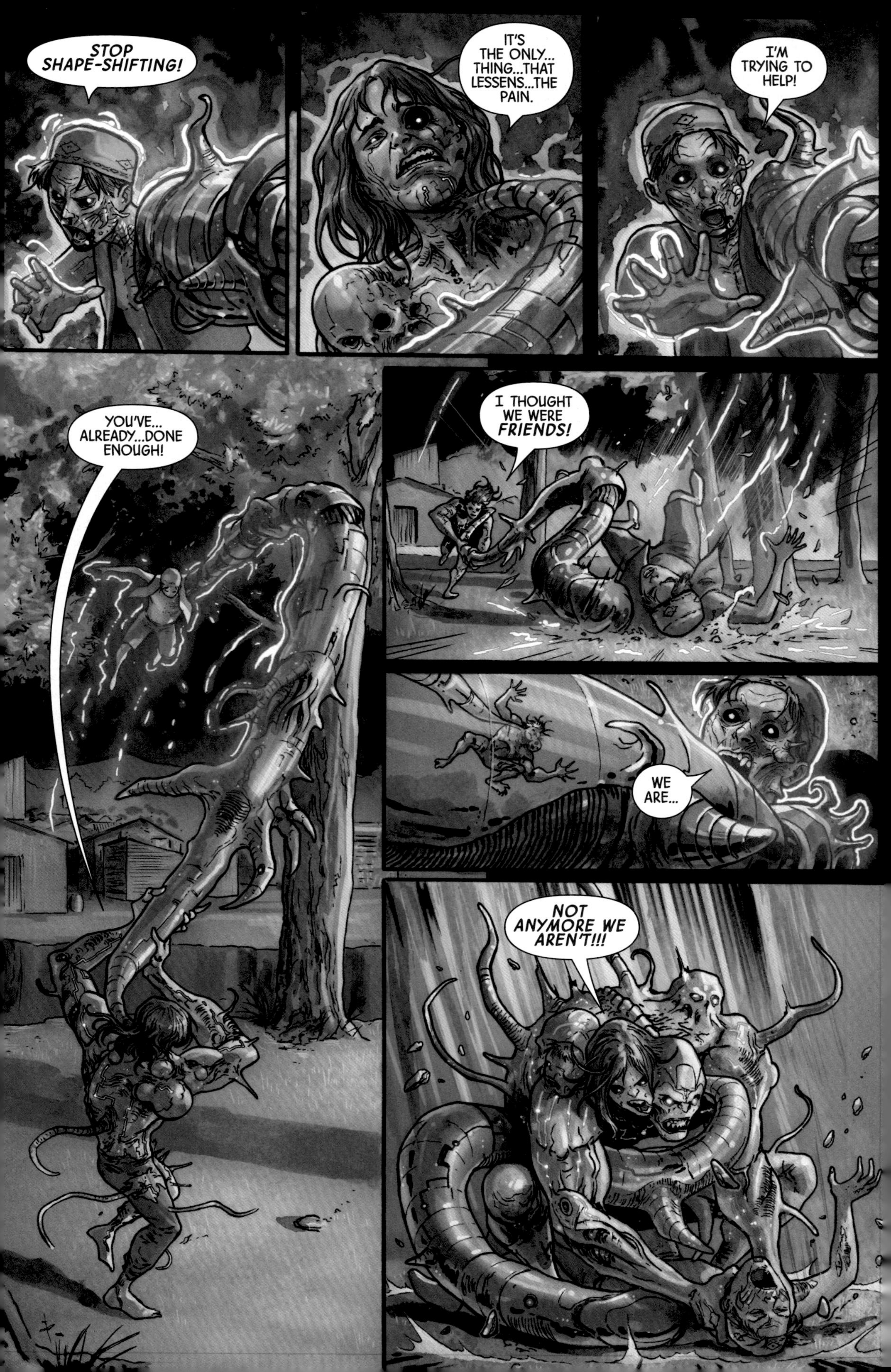
STOP SHAPE-SHIFTING!
IT'S THE ONLY... THING...THAT LESSENS...THE PAIN.
I'M TRYING TO HELP!
YOU'VE... ALREADY...DONE ENOUGH!
I THOUGHT WE WERE FRIENDS!
WE ARE...
NOT ANYMORE WE AREN'T!!!

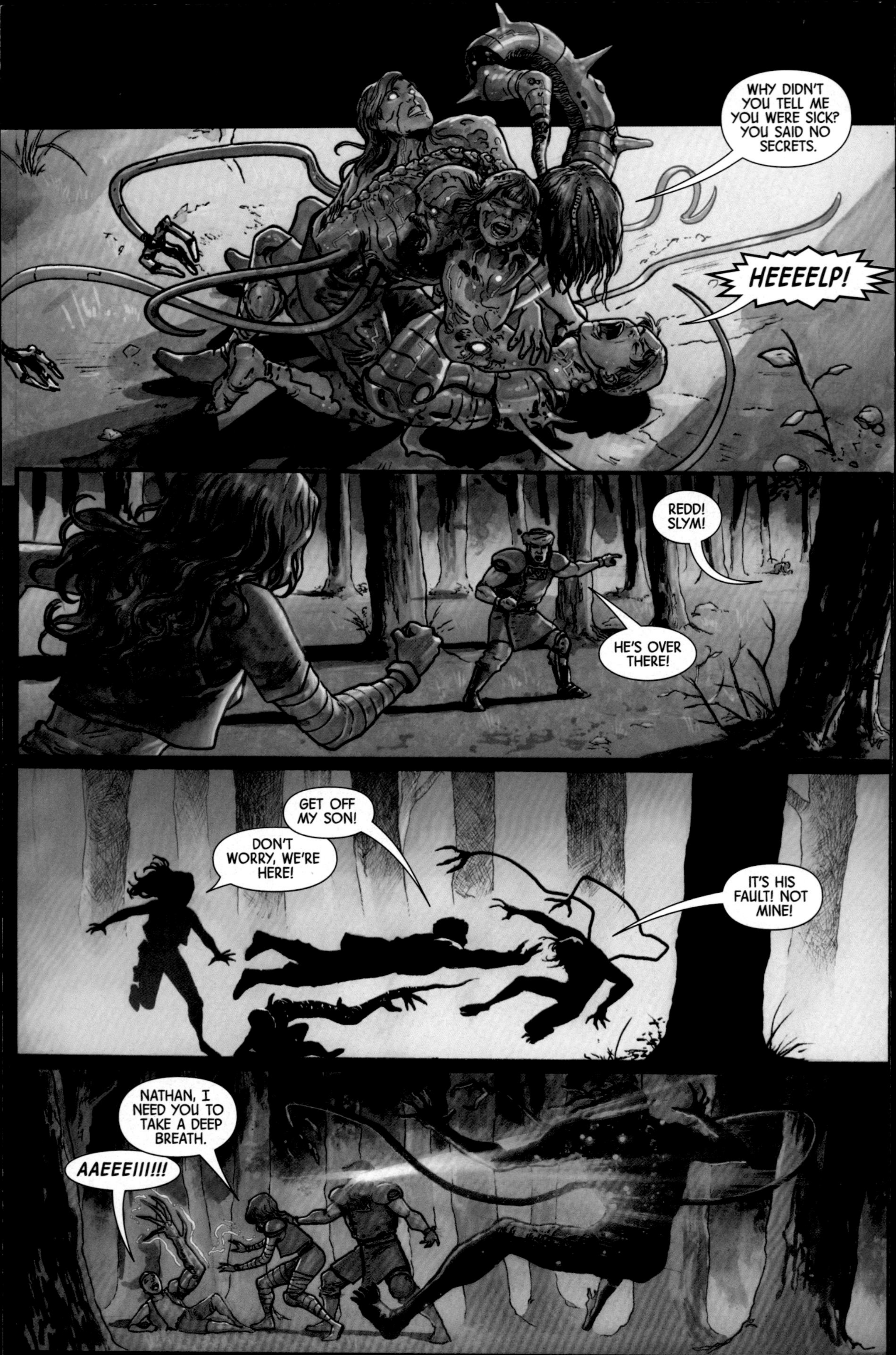
WHY DIDN'T YOU TELL ME YOU WERE SICK? YOU SAID NO SECRETS.
HEEEELP!
REDD! SLYM!
HE'S OVER THERE!
GET OFF MY SON!
DON'T WORRY, WE'RE HERE!
IT'S HIS FAULT! NOT MINE!
NATHAN, I NEED YOU TO TAKE A DEEP BREATH.
AAEEEIIII!!!

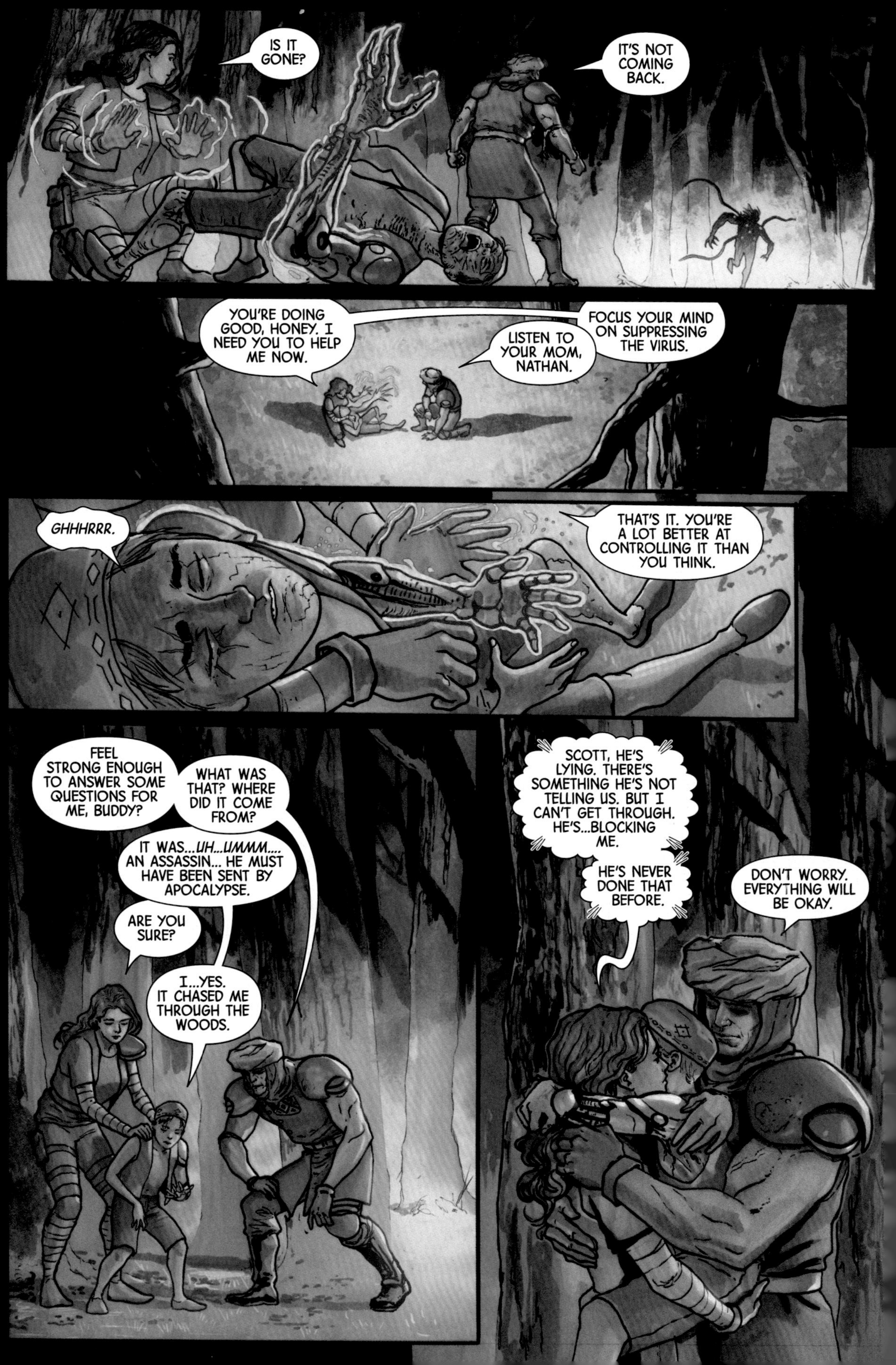
IS IT GONE?
IT'S NOT COMING BACK.
YOU'RE DOING GOOD, HONEY. I NEED YOU TO HELP ME NOW.
FOCUS YOUR MIND ON SUPPRESSING THE VIRUS.
LISTEN TO YOUR MOM, NATHAN.
GHHHRRR.
THAT'S IT. YOU'RE A LOT BETTER AT CONTROLLING IT THAN YOU THINK.
FEEL STRONG ENOUGH TO ANSWER SOME QUESTIONS FOR ME, BUDDY?
WHAT WAS THAT? WHERE DID IT COME FROM?
IT WAS...UH...UMMM.... AN ASSASSIN... HE MUST HAVE BEEN SENT BY APOCALYPSE.
ARE YOU SURE?
I...YES. IT CHASED ME THROUGH THE WOODS.
SCOTT, HE'S LYING. THERE'S SOMETHING HE'S NOT TELLING US. BUT I CAN'T GET THROUGH. HE'S...BLOCKING ME.
HE'S NEVER DONE THAT BEFORE.
DON'T WORRY. EVERYTHING WILL BE OKAY.

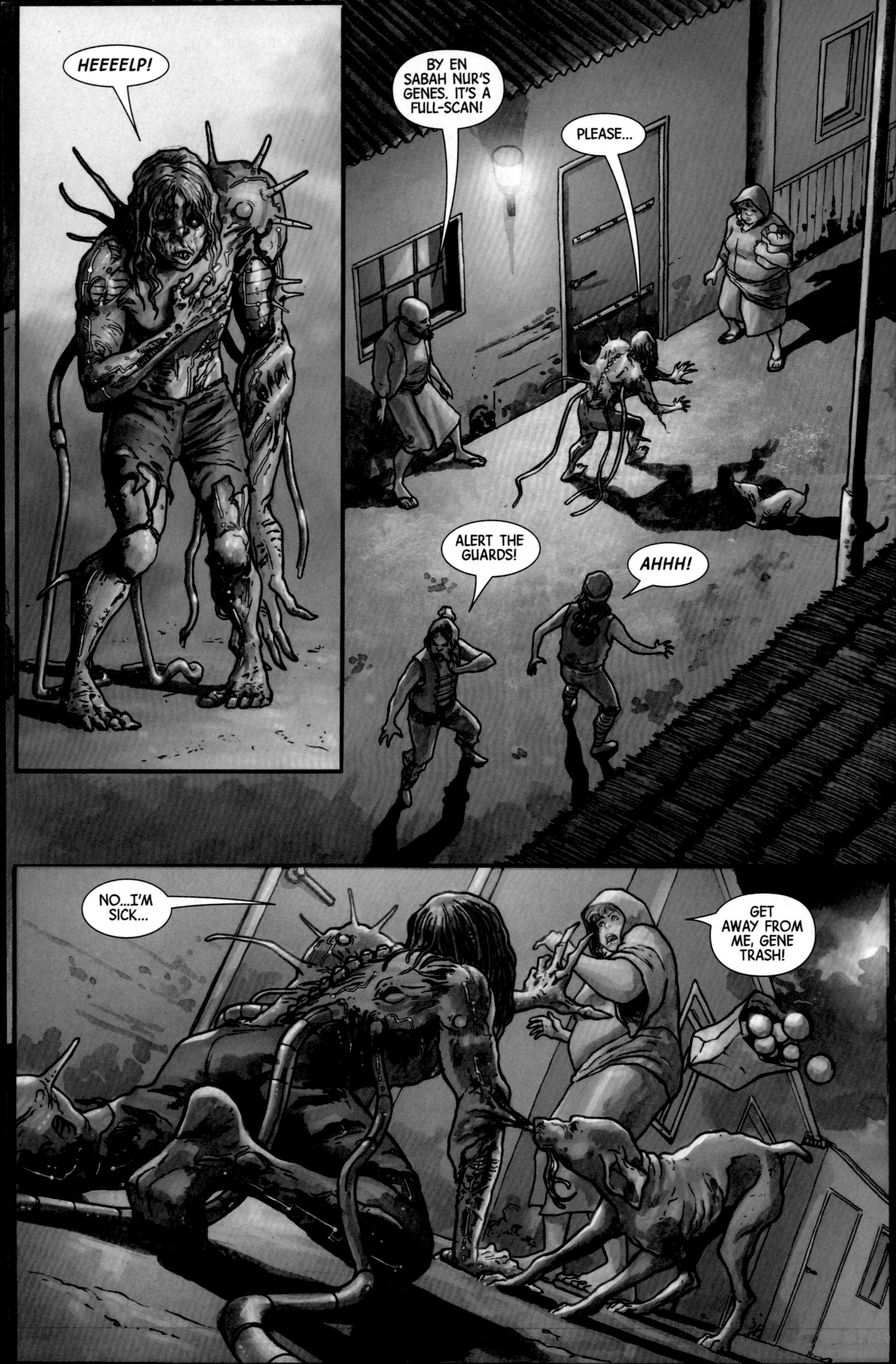
HEEEELP!
BY EN SABAH NUR'S GENES. IT'S A FULL-SCAN!
PLEASE...
ALERT THE GUARDS!
AHHH!
NO...I'M SICK...
GET AWAY FROM ME, GENE TRASH!

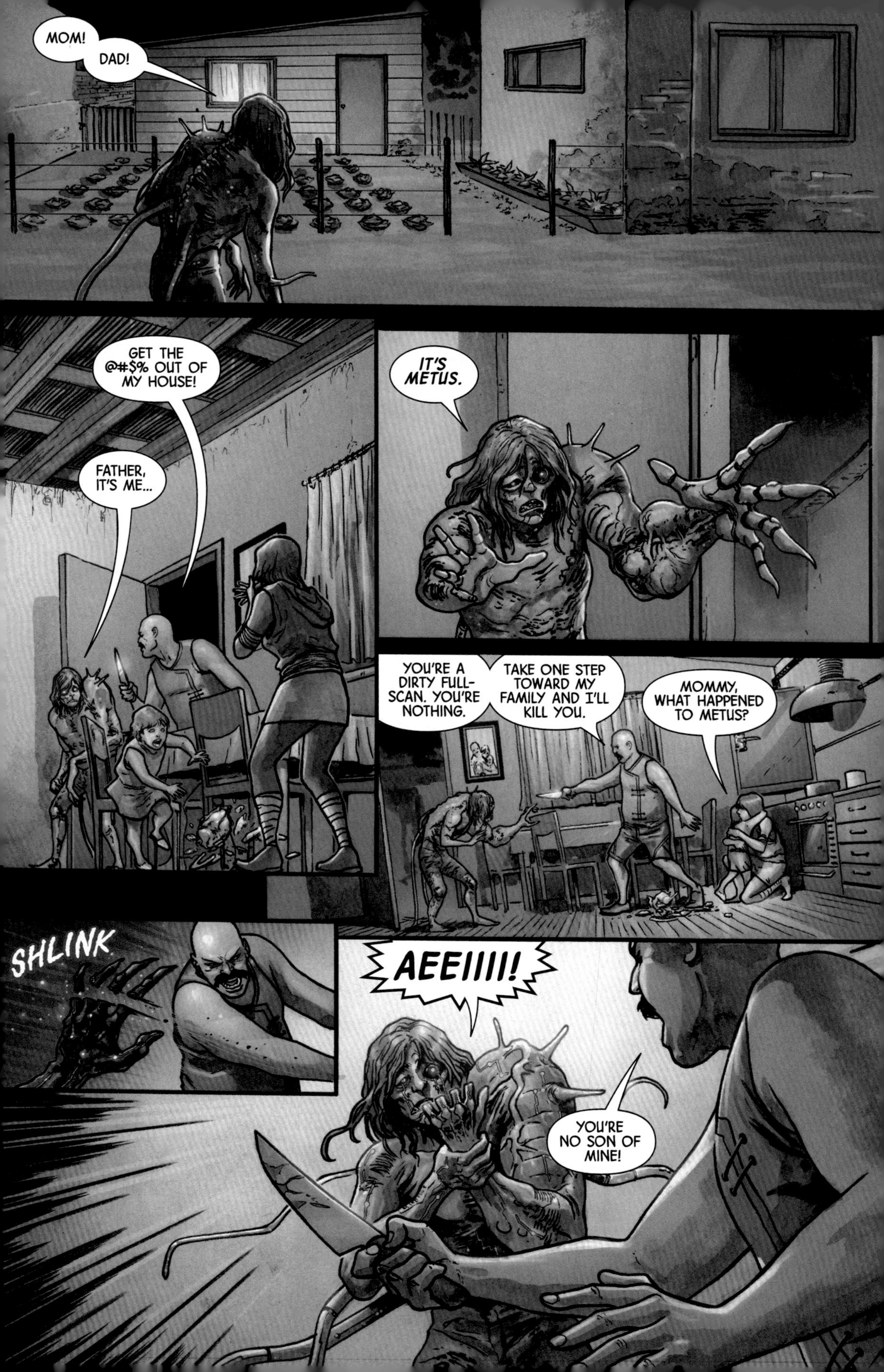
MOM!
DAD!
GET THE @#$% OUT OF MY HOUSE!
FATHER, IT'S ME...
IT'S METUS.
YOU'RE A DIRTY FULL-SCAN. YOU'RE NOTHING.
TAKE ONE STEP TOWARD MY FAMILY AND I'LL KILL YOU.
MOMMY, WHAT HAPPENED TO METUS?
SHLINK
AEEIIIII!
YOU'RE NO SON OF MINE!

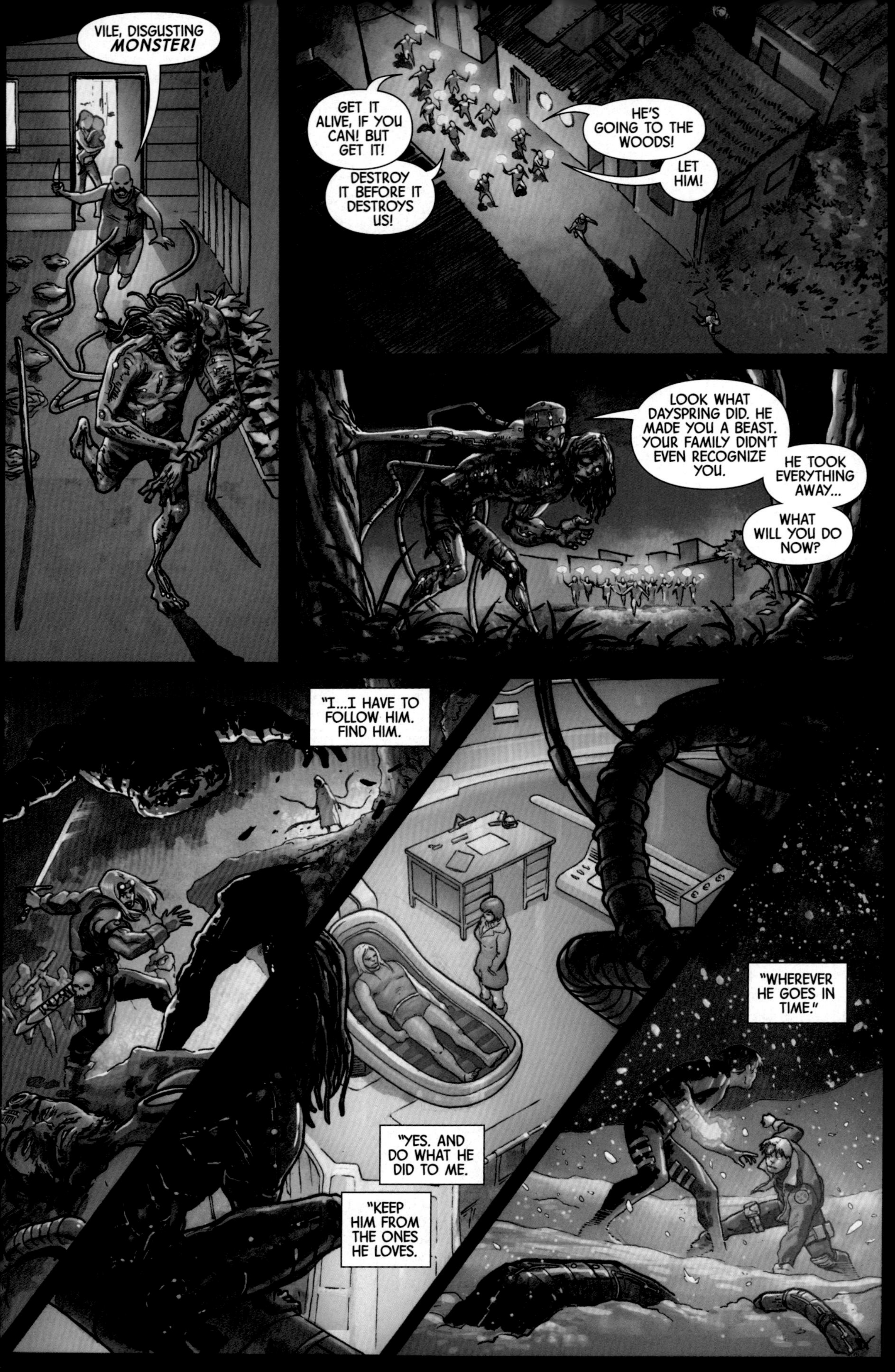

VILE, DISGUSTING MONSTER!
GET IT ALIVE, IF YOU CAN! BUT GET IT!
DESTROY IT BEFORE IT DESTROYS US!
HE'S GOING TO THE WOODS!
LET HIM!
LOOK WHAT DAYSPRING DID. HE MADE YOU A BEAST. YOUR FAMILY DIDN'T EVEN RECOGNIZE YOU.
HE TOOK EVERYTHING AWAY...
WHAT WILL YOU DO NOW?
"I...I HAVE TO FOLLOW HIM. FIND HIM.
"YES. AND DO WHAT HE DID TO ME.
"KEEP HIM FROM THE ONES HE LOVES.
"WHEREVER HE GOES IN TIME."

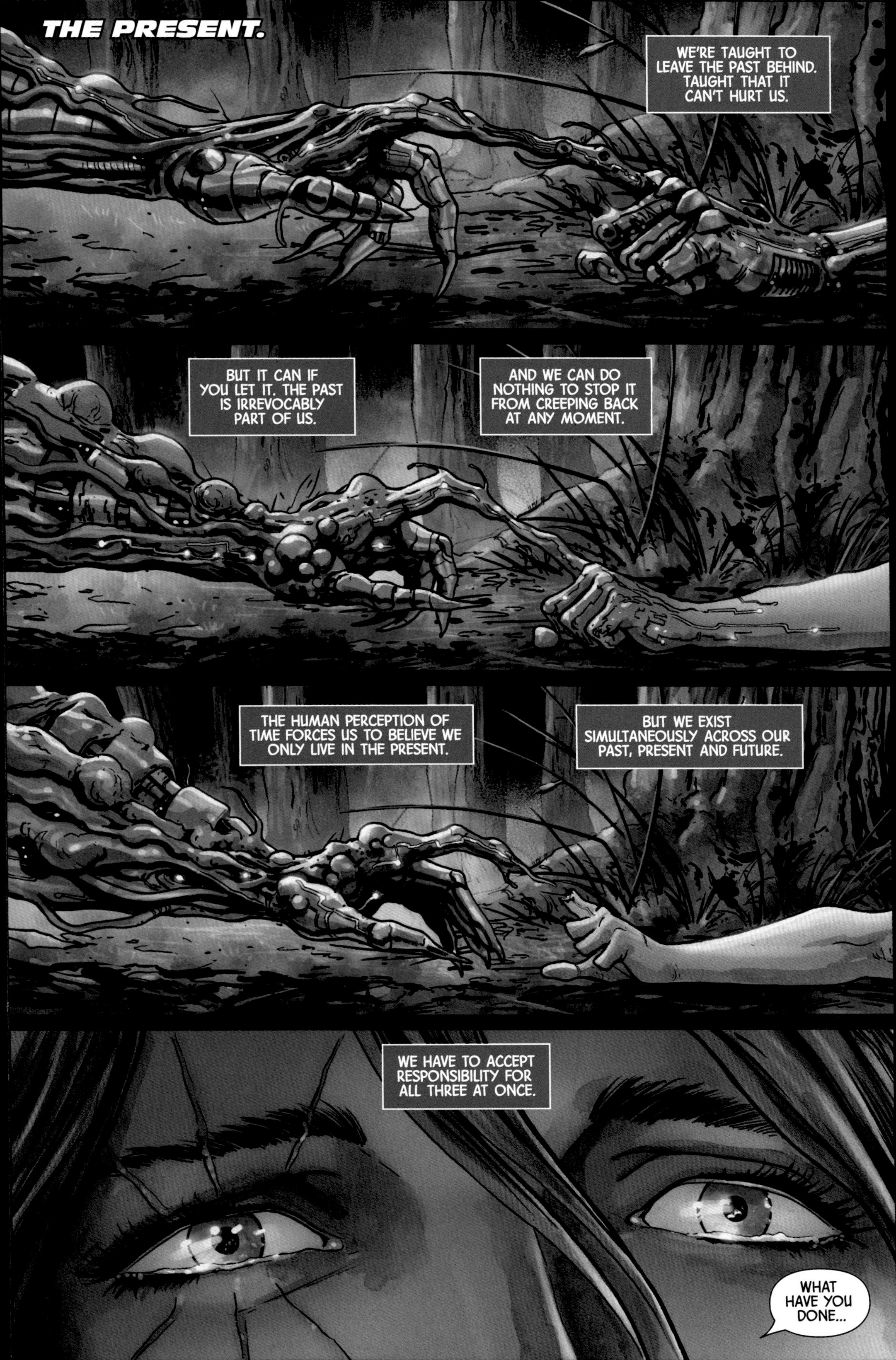
THE PRESENT.
WE'RE TAUGHT TO LEAVE THE PAST BEHIND. TAUGHT THAT IT CAN'T HURT US.
BUT IT CAN IF YOU LET IT. THE PAST IS IRREVOCABLY PART OF US.
AND WE CAN DO NOTHING TO STOP IT FROM CREEPING BACK AT ANY MOMENT.
THE HUMAN PERCEPTION OF TIME FORCES US TO BELIEVE WE ONLY LIVE IN THE PRESENT.
BUT WE EXIST SIMULTANEOUSLY ACROSS OUR PAST, PRESENT AND FUTURE.
WE HAVE TO ACCEPT RESPONSIBILITY FOR ALL THREE AT ONCE.
WHAT HAVE YOU DONE...

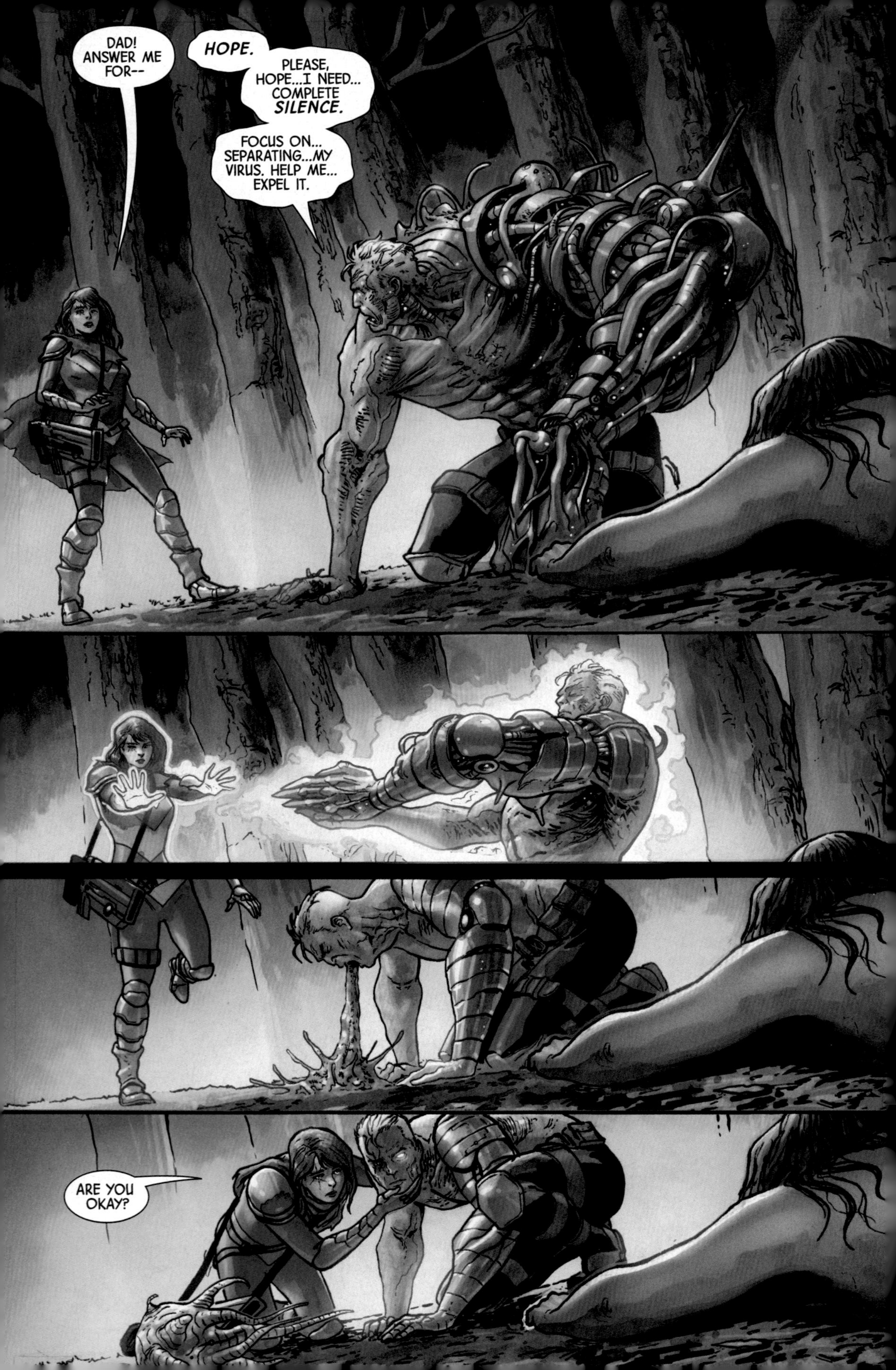
DAD! ANSWER ME FOR--
HOPE.
PLEASE, HOPE...I NEED... COMPLETE SILENCE.
FOCUS ON... SEPARATING...MY VIRUS. HELP ME... EXPEL IT.
ARE YOU OKAY?

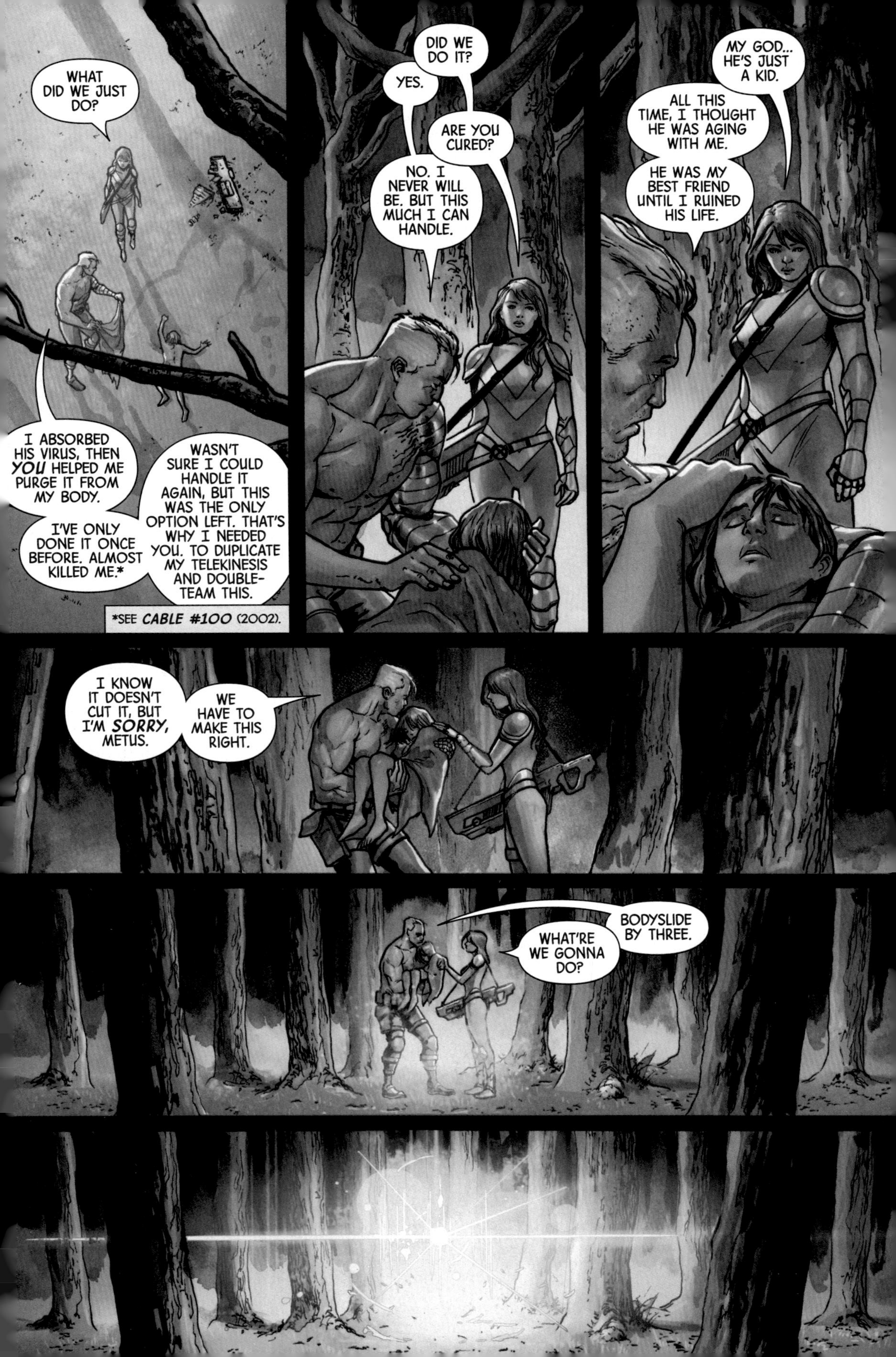
WHAT DID WE JUST DO?
I ABSORBED HIS VIRUS, THEN YOU HELPED ME PURGE IT FROM MY BODY.
I'VE ONLY DONE IT ONCE BEFORE. ALMOST KILLED ME.*
WASN'T SURE I COULD HANDLE IT AGAIN, BUT THIS WAS THE ONLY OPTION LEFT. THAT'S WHY I NEEDED YOU. TO DUPLICATE MY TELEKINESIS AND DOUBLE-TEAM THIS.
*SEE CABLE #100 (2002).
DID WE DO IT?
YES.
ARE YOU CURED?
NO. I NEVER WILL BE. BUT THIS MUCH I CAN HANDLE.
MY GOD... HE'S JUST A KID.
ALL THIS TIME, I THOUGHT HE WAS AGING WITH ME.
HE WAS MY BEST FRIEND UNTIL I RUINED HIS LIFE.
I KNOW IT DOESN'T CUT IT, BUT I'M SORRY, METUS.
WE HAVE TO MAKE THIS RIGHT.
WHAT'RE WE GONNA DO?
BODYSLIDE BY THREE.

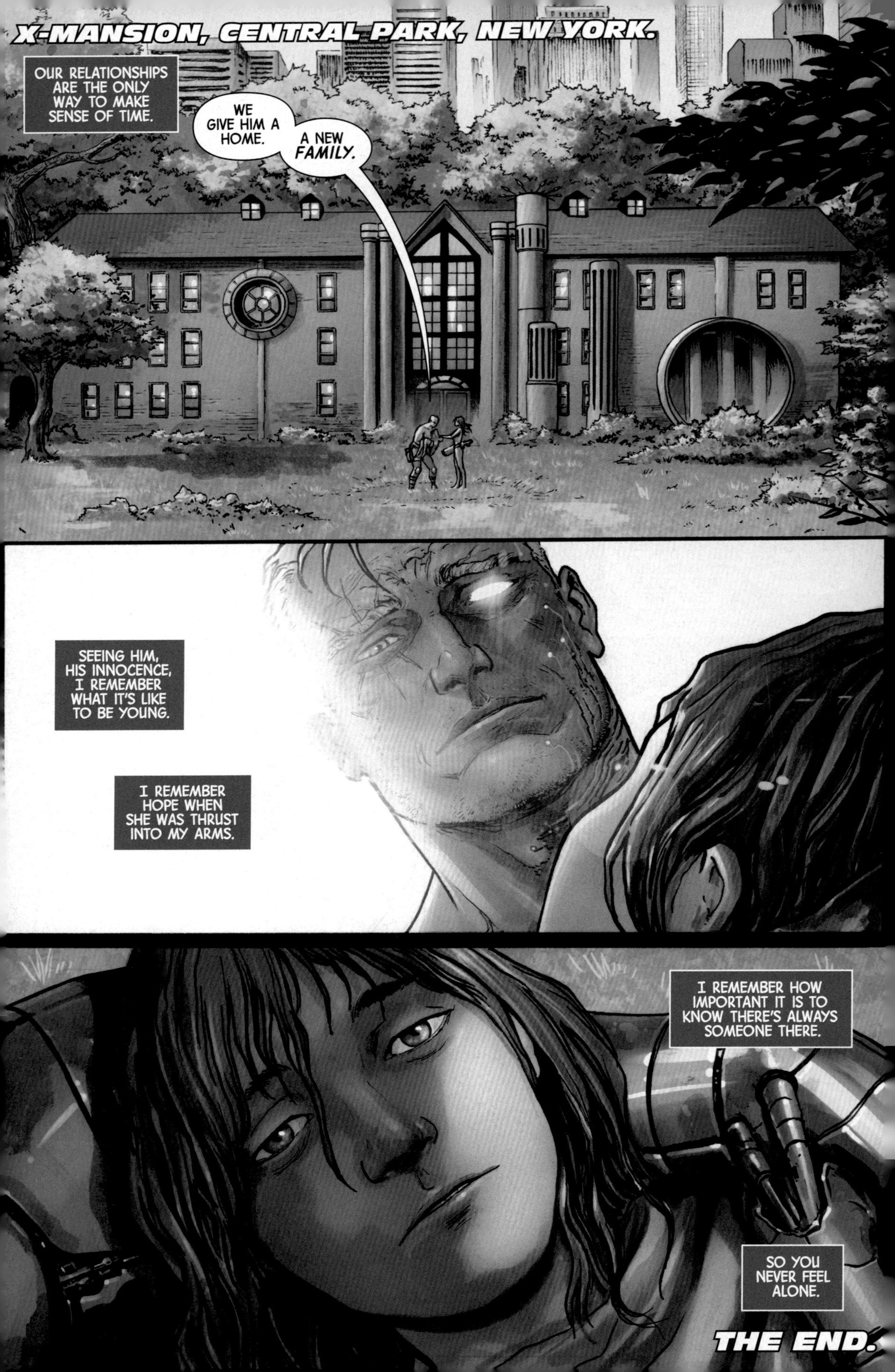
X-MANSION, CENTRAL PARK, NEW YORK.
OUR RELATIONSHIPS ARE THE ONLY WAY TO MAKE SENSE OF TIME.
WE GIVE HIM A HOME.
A NEW FAMILY.
SEEING HIM, HIS INNOCENCE, I REMEMBER WHAT IT'S LIKE TO BE YOUNG.
I REMEMBER HOPE WHEN SHE WAS THRUST INTO MY ARMS.
I REMEMBER HOW IMPORTANT IT IS TO KNOW THERE'S ALWAYS SOMEONE THERE.
SO YOU NEVER FEEL ALONE.
THE END.

#155 NEW MUTANTS VARIANT
BY TYLER KIRKHAM
& ARIF PRIANTO

#155 VARIANT
BY RYAN STEGMAN
& MIKE SPICER

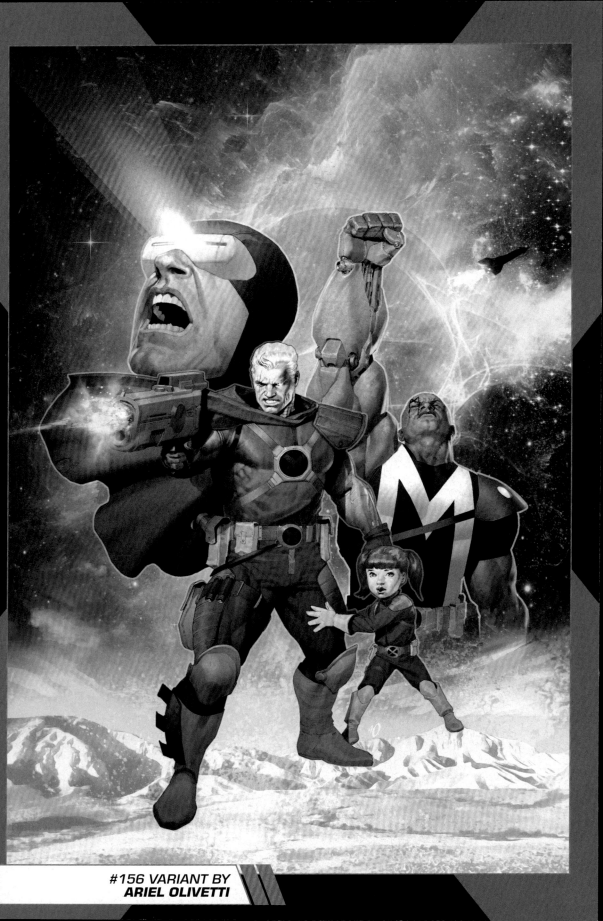

#156 VARIANT BY
ARIEL OLIVETTI

#157 VARIANT BY **CHRIS BURNHAM**
& **NATHAN FAIRBAIRN**

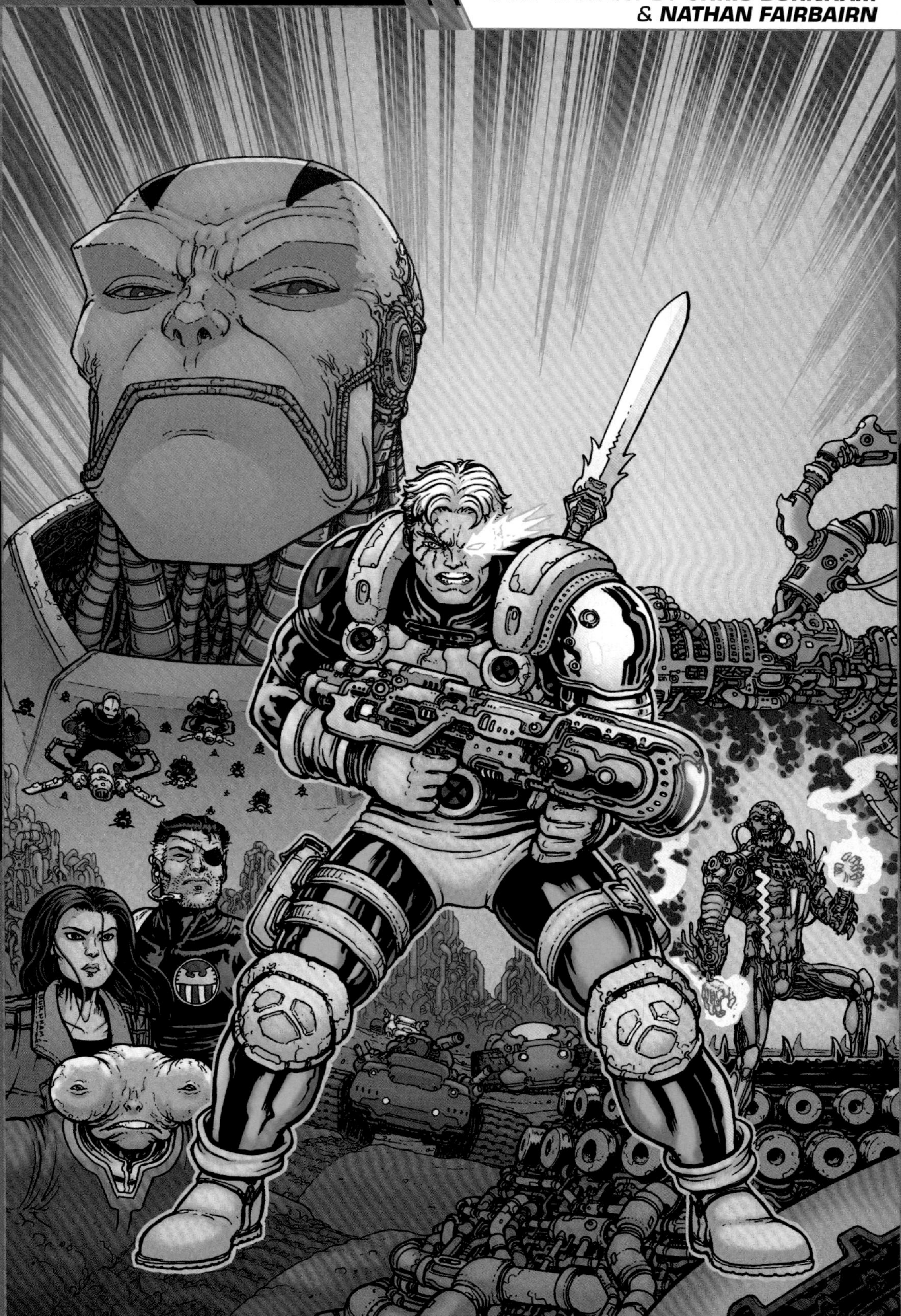

#158 VARIANT
BY **ROB LIEFELD**
& **FEDERICO BLEE**

#159 VARIANT
BY **JAY ANACLETO**
& **RACHELLE ROSENBERG**